COUNTY SOCIAL

VIGNETTES FROM PRINCE EDWARD COUNTY'S CRAFT DRINKMAKERS

NATALIE WOLLENBERG **&** LEIGH NASH

Assembly Press

© Assembly Press, 2024

All rights reserved. No part of this publication may be reproduced or transmitted in any form, by any method, without the prior written consent of the publisher, except by a reviewer, who may use brief excerpts in a review, or, in the case of photocopying in Canada, a licence from Access Copyright.

Edited by Leigh Nash and Natalie Wollenberg
Production assistance by Andrew Faulkner
Cover and interior photos by Natalie Wollenberg
Food styling by Ruth Gangbar
Cover design and typesetting by Greg Tabor

The contributors and publisher assert that the information contained in this book is true and complete to the best of their knowledge. All recommendations are made without guarantee on the part of the contributors and publisher. The contributors and publisher disclaim any liability in connection with the use of this information.

Library and Archives Canada Cataloguing in Publication

Title: County social : vignettes from Prince Edward County's craft drinkmakers / Natalie Wollenberg & Leigh Nash. Names: Wollenberg, Natalie, 1977- author. | Nash, Leigh, 1982- author.

Identifiers: Canadiana (print) 20240344049 | Canadiana (ebook) 20240344057 | ISBN 9781738009800 (softcover) | ISBN 9781738009817 (EPUB) Subjects: LCSH: Microdistilleries—Ontario—Prince Edward. | LCSH: Microdistilleries—Ontario—Prince Edward—Pictorial works.

Classification: LCC TP590.6.C2 W65 2024 | DDC 641.2/509713587—dc23

Printed and bound in Canada

We acknowledge that we work, live, meet, and create on the traditional territory of the Anishnaabeg, Wendat, and Haudenosaunee peoples and adjacent to the Kanien'keha:ka (Mohawk) community of Tyendinaga.

Assembly Press
Prince Edward County, Ontario
assemblypress.ca

INTRODUCTION	1
555 BREWING CO.	2
ADEGA WINE BAR	6
ALL MY FRIENDS BEER CO.	10
BARE BONES FARM AND DISTILLERY	14
RECIPE: BOCADO'S TARTARE DE CARNE	20
BROKEN STONE WINERY	26
CLOSSON CHASE VINEYARDS	32
THE COUNTY CIDER COMPANY	40
DOMAINE DARIUS	46
RECIPE: DRAKE DEVONSHIRE'S BURRATA, HEIRLOOM TOMATO, AND PEACH SALAD	50
DUNE HOPPER BREWING COMPANY	54
GILLINGHAM BREWING COMPANY	60
THE GRANGE OF PRINCE EDWARD	66
RECIPE: THE GRANGE OF PRINCE EDWARD'S TOMATO FRITTERS WITH PESTO AIOLI	70
HINTERLAND WINE COMPANY	76
HUBBS CREEK VINEYARD	80
HUFF ESTATES WINERY	84
KARLO ESTATES WINERY	90
KINSIP HOUSE OF FINE SPIRITS	98
RECIPE: LA CONDESA'S CHEESE-STUFFED MEATBALLS WITH CHIPOTLE CREAM SAUCE	102

LACEY ESTATES WINERY	106
LIGHTHALL VINEYARDS	110
LOCH MÓR CIDER CO.	114
MATRON FINE BEER	118
MERRILL HOUSE	122
MIDTOWN BREWING COMPANY	126
PARSONS BREWING COMPANY	130
PRINCE EDDY'S BREWING CO.	136
ROSEHALL RUN VINEYARDS	140
THE ROYAL HOTEL	146
RECIPE: THE ROYAL HOTEL'S BRAISED PICKEREL CHEEKS	150
SLAKE BREWING	154
STANNERS VINEYARD	158
RECIPE: STELLA'S EATERY'S WINE-BRAISED RABBIT STEW WITH FRIED BANNOCK	164
STOCK & ROW CIDER	170
SUGARBUSH VINEYARDS	174
THREE DOG WINERY	178
TRAIL ESTATE WINERY	184
TRAYNOR FAMILY VINEYARD	188
WAUPOOS ESTATES WINERY	194
WILD LOT FARM DISTILLERY	198
ACKNOWLEDGEMENTS	204

Introduction

We both love a good story, and this book contains a bushel of them. *County Social* is a collection of many of Prince Edward County's notable beveragemakers talking about what they do and why they do it. In these pages you'll find personal histories, entrepreneurial journeys, colour commentary about the highs and lows of brewing, distilling, and fermenting, and you'll get an up-close look at why so many driven and talented people have come to call this special community home. We're also big cookbook fans, and we couldn't help but ask a half-dozen local chefs to provide delicious recipes that pair well with the drinks you'll find around the County.

Each of these winemakers, cidermakers, brewers, and distillers has followed a unique path to get to where they are. Part of that is temperament, part of it is palate, and as a result, the range of beverages produced in the relatively small geographic region of PEC is enormous.

Making the drinks we all enjoy is incredibly hard work. It takes farming and industrial labour and cleaning and chemistry and marketing and sales—not to mention the challenge of working in a cool-climate region with its wild swings in weather. This book offers an unfiltered view of the effort and craft that goes into filling your bottles and cans, and it just might give you a greater appreciation for all of the love, sweat, and artistry that goes into every glass.

County Social is meant to be the literary equivalent of a "tasting flight"—we've tried to include a broad range of approaches, styles, and businesses in this selection of profiles. Our goal is to offer a snapshot of the region's vibrancy rather than document each individual producer's history. We hope you use this book as a starting point for your own beverage adventures.

Cheers,
Natalie Wollenberg & Leigh Nash

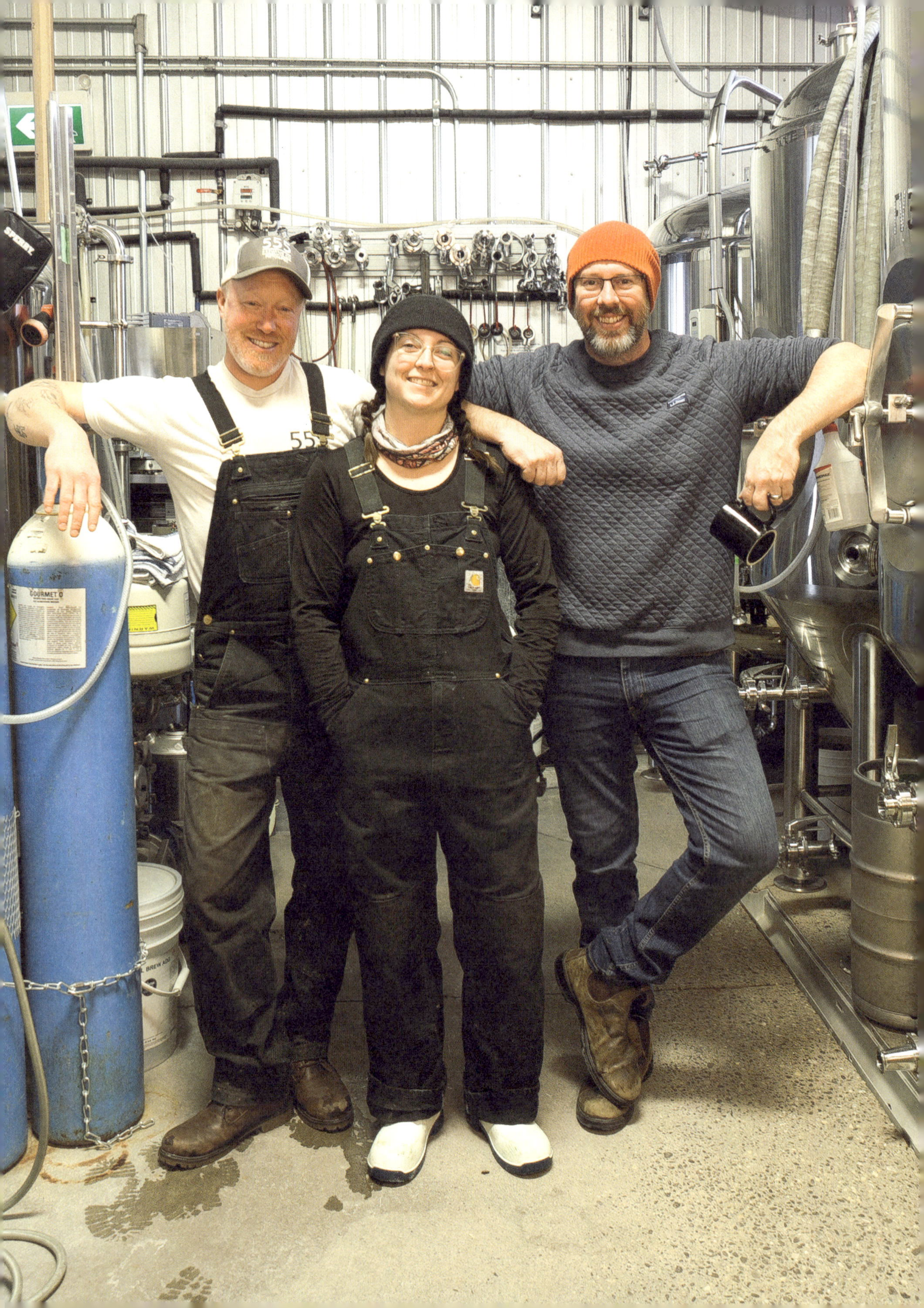
555

555 Brewing Co., Picton

Located in the heart of Picton, 555 is a casual craft brewery featuring wood-fired pizza.

BRETT FRENCH, DANI LEAVITT, DREW WOLLENBERG

Drew: I met my wife and business partner, Nat, in Australia in 2000—we were in a band, and I got into brewing with our drummer, Brent. Brent and I started roping off the kitchen to make beer because we realized we could make our own stubbies. And then we became more interested in learning how to brew, started buying books and new toys like chillers. We got more and more carried away.

There was a supply shop and brewery called Deliverance around the corner from our house. The owner, Roy, taught me how to scale things from home brewing to large-scale brewing, as well as all the processes I'd need to run a brewery.

I thought about opening a brew pub the first time we went down to Margaret River. Margaret River was awesome, but it was expensive—it was the Napa Valley of Australia. Instead, we moved back to Canada in 2014 to be closer to family. My grandparents and parents wanted our kids to know them; we had four generations all living within 15 kilometres of one another.

In 2015, with two partners, we bought a falling-down building, and that's where Nat and I opened the County Canteen as a brew pub with snacks. Everyone was super interested in that project because the gastro-brew pub thing hadn't been done before here; we had to put a big sheet of plywood up at the front to stop people from sticking their heads in. We opened a month later than planned, on June 24. One of our biggest early supporters was Grant Howes—he and Jenifer Dean of The County Cider Company firmly believed that what we were building was a good idea.

A year after we opened the Canteen, we realized we'd run out of space. We could no longer move our fermenters around the main room, and we needed the space that we were brewing beer out of to meet the restaurant's needs. One day, I was walking home past the five-way intersection where Tim Horton's is, and I happened to look over at the building the brewery's in now. It was in complete disrepair. There was still a Money Mart sign above it. Later, I took Nat for a walk, stopped her in front of the building, and said, "This is a beer garden." So we started another renovation and build all over again. 555 opened on March 25, 2017—on our anniversary.

Brett: My first motivation was listening to winemakers talk about flavours, and I realized that beer can be tasted the same way.

The brewer at Barley Days was leaving, so there was a vacant position, and it all kind of fell into place. I read every book on brewing I could get my hands on to learn how everything worked. I talked to every single brewer who would talk to me, plus I had a 90-day crash course with the outgoing brewer. And then they handed me the keys and that was that. The capacity at Barley Days was large, and at the time the County was so different;

we were only busy from the May long weekend to September. It wasn't like it is now, where it never dies. So I started contract brewing for other new breweries. Working with different recipes really helped me expand my brewing portfolio, and it also kept the lights on. You can't sell empty tank space, so better to fill it up one way or another.

At 555, we pretty much stick to brewing clean, traditional styles. Our beers are never finished; we're always talking about how we could tweak something to make it a little bit better, whether that's adjusting our water profile or temperature, using different yeast or hop ratios.

One thing that excites me about beer is that it's four ingredients. Every beer you've ever had—it's those same four ingredients. There's so much room to be creative. Why limit yourself to doing the same thing over and over when you can tweak things a little bit all the time? Beer is three things: art, science, and doing something physical. If you have two of those things, you can make a pretty good beer. But if you can get all three, you can make amazing brews.

Dani: I've been in the service industry since I was 13. My first serving job was at the diner in Cherry Valley, and then I went on to work at Waupoos Estates Winery throughout high school. At Prince Edward Collegiate Institute, where I went to high school, my favourite courses were fashion and woodworking—both were hands-on, production-style learning. After high school, I moved to Toronto to enroll in college for fashion arts.

A few years later, after working for a costume design company and a custom window covering company, I moved back home to Milford to start working off my student debt. I got a job as a sales rep for wine, cider, and craft beer, which got my foot in the door at Barley Days Brewery. I became the assistant brewer there. That's where I met Brett.

As someone who doesn't drink beer, it's funny that I'm even in this industry. I don't love beer itself. What I love is the physical production of beer: moving the beer from fermentation to filtering, carbonation to kegging, canning and labelling. I don't know a ton about the science behind the brewing, but I do know I appreciate the production of it. That's what I enjoyed most about fashion too: taking a pattern from drafting to sewing to wearing. I was never going to be a fashion designer, much like I'm never going to be a brewmaster, but I'm going to keep running a smooth production line to bring other people's ideas to life. Brett and Drew really run the show and I just keep them, and The Fives, well organized.

Drew: One of the best things about beer is how the act of drinking can remind you of another time or place. I remember, back in Australia, when all our brewing stuff was in the garage, I used to put on a Toronto Maple Leafs game—it was nine o'clock in the morning and the Leafs were playing at seven o'clock at night back in Canada. I'd try a beer from my last batch, see what I could improve on. The garage door would be open and people would pop in. It was about camaraderie, shooting the shit, just as much as making the actual product.

It's so easy to work with Dani and Brett. Dani and I can work in silence for hours, and with Brett, it's the opposite, neither of us can shut up—we're very different people with similar interests, one of which is making quality beer.

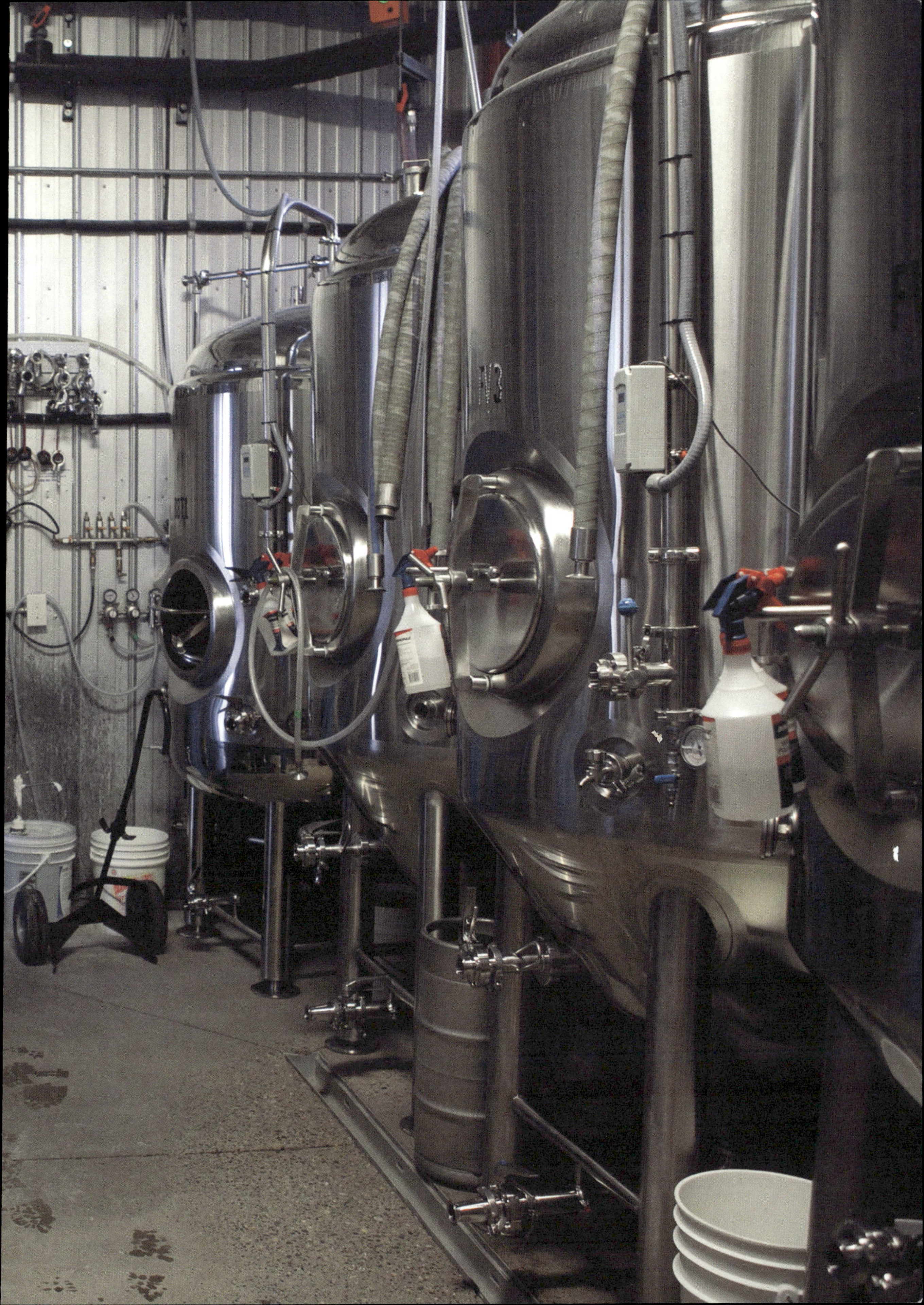

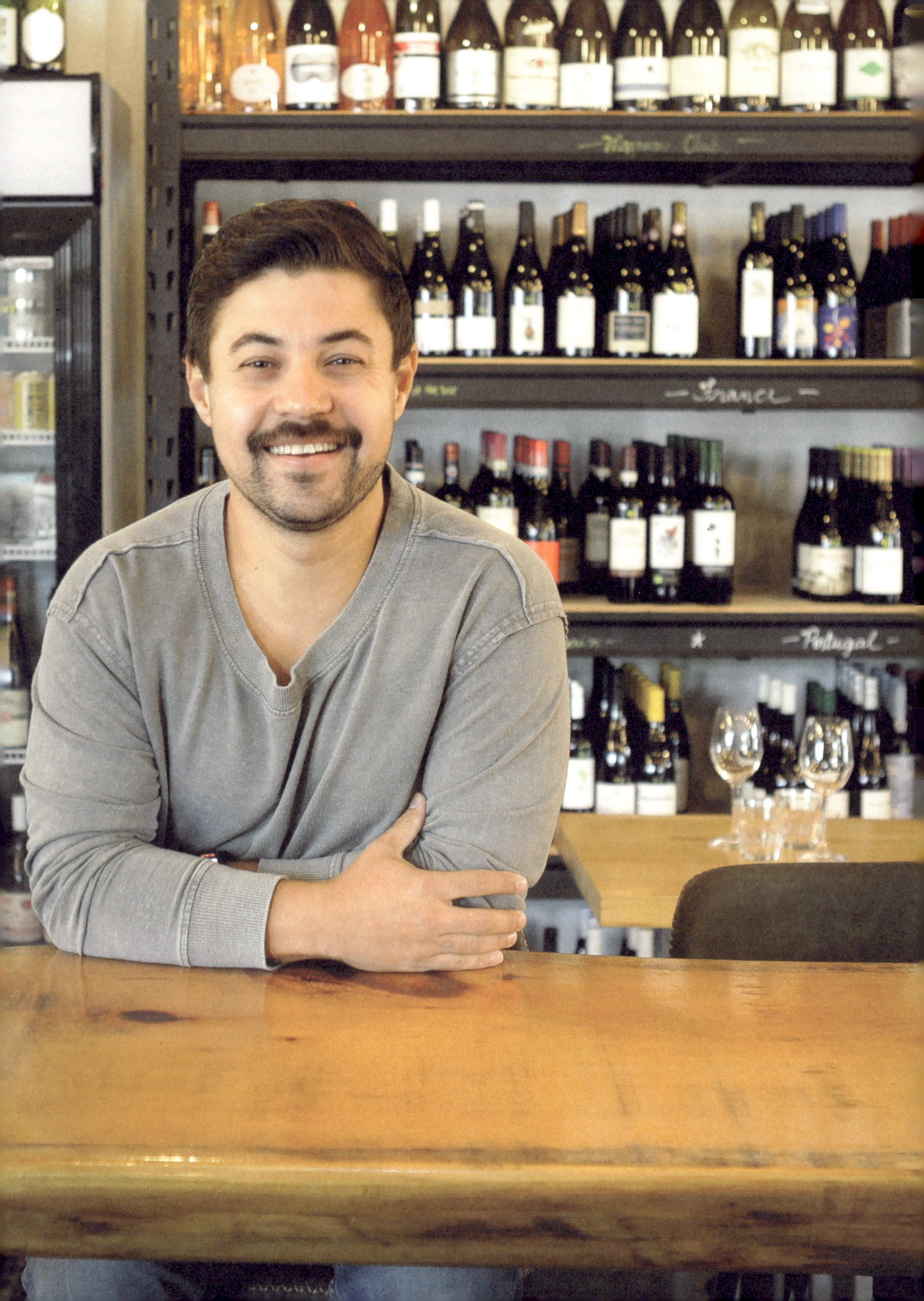
France
Portugal

Adega Wine Bar, Consecon

Adega is a fun and welcoming wine bar offering tapas-style dishes and an impressive selection of wines.

THIERRY ALCÂNTARA-STEWART

I grew up in Brazil. I went to university for accounting and then moved abroad to study in Ireland for a few years. I started working on my first cruise ship in October 2013, and my second day on board, I met AJ. He had a month left on his contract as a singer. And we've been together ever since.

I moved to Canada for college—I went to George Brown for hotel management. I worked for Marriott, I worked for Fairmont, I worked for Hilton, and then I excelled at a wine course, so I did my sommelier accreditation.

In 2019, I was working as the sommelier and manager of Air Canada's premium lounge at Toronto's Pearson airport, and AJ left in July to work on another cruise ship. He flew back to Canada in March 2020, and we were both laid off, so I started applying for jobs literally everywhere—Niagara, BC, the County. I'd always wanted to work in a winery. Stanners Vineyard hired me, and AJ got a job at Flame + Smith. I was also working at a restaurant on the floor and leading wine tours. And during those wine tours, people kept asking if there was a place to hang out near the wineries, like a wine bar or something. At the time, there wasn't; Decanter didn't exist. So I thought that might be an opportunity and I asked a real estate agent to keep an eye out for me. One day, he got in touch, and was like, "Hey, there's a place in Consecon you might be interested in." And I said, "Where the hell is that?"

AJ and I sat down with the owners, and I was like, this is my plan: I want to open a wine bar. They agreed to do the renovations and gave me the space, completely done up to the drywall.

I was lucky enough to meet Brittiny, who used to run the Grist Mill, and she offered me her place to hold pop-ups until our space was ready. And that's how we started. My wine shelf was a little wobbly thing from Ikea that almost fell on us during a party we held for Flame + Smith. I try not to buy anything new; my cutlery is from one of Picton's thrift shops.

When I was getting ready to open, I called several friends in Toronto who had gone through similar start-ups, and my main question was whether I should get a financial partner. I've met with a number of people who were interested in investing in my idea, but everybody was concerned about their return on investment. After each conversation, I was left feeling like it wasn't a good idea for them, nor for me. People do this because they love wine or food. People don't do this because they want to get rich.

We've had to deal with a lot of flack from a lot of people because we are in a community that can be tough if you think differently, if you're gay. But I'm not going to compromise on my beliefs or my integrity. This business is an extension of me—it's an extension of my beliefs.

We are really off the beaten path, but I want to say that 85% of our customer base is locals who visit throughout the year, not just in the summer. Very recently, we were mentioned in a couple of *Toronto Life* articles. Jamie Kennedy was very gracious to say that Adega is one of his favourite spots to hang out; Alex at Fawn Over Market said the same thing. And we got a bit of traction from that.

AJ is able to feed his passion for music from this space. That was another big reason for opening Adega. We've held musical theatre open mic nights, and it's always busy, always packed. People love it. We have a piano player, and he comes in and people bring their sheets of music. You can really see AJ's eyes light up when that happens.

Five years from now, maybe we'll open a second location. You never know. I'm a firm believer in sticking to what you do and doing that to perfection instead of trying to do everything. Do one thing extremely well before you move on to something else. I think I learned that from my dad. I don't want to be mediocre. I want to do something extremely well and be really good at it. And that's what I think we're doing here. Every day is a learning curve. And to this day, sometimes when we finish service and I go home, I look at AJ and think, I can't fucking believe we own a bar.

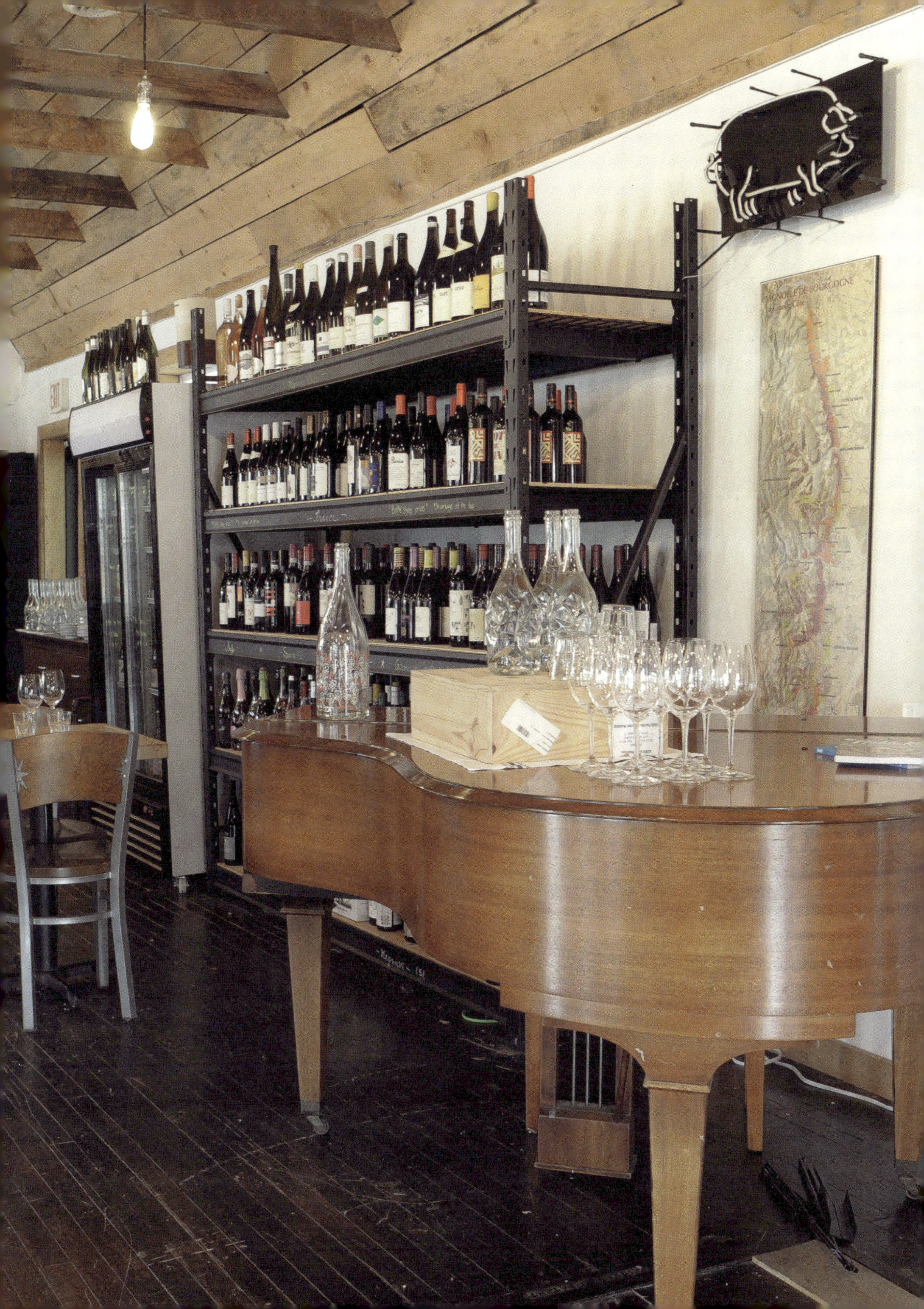

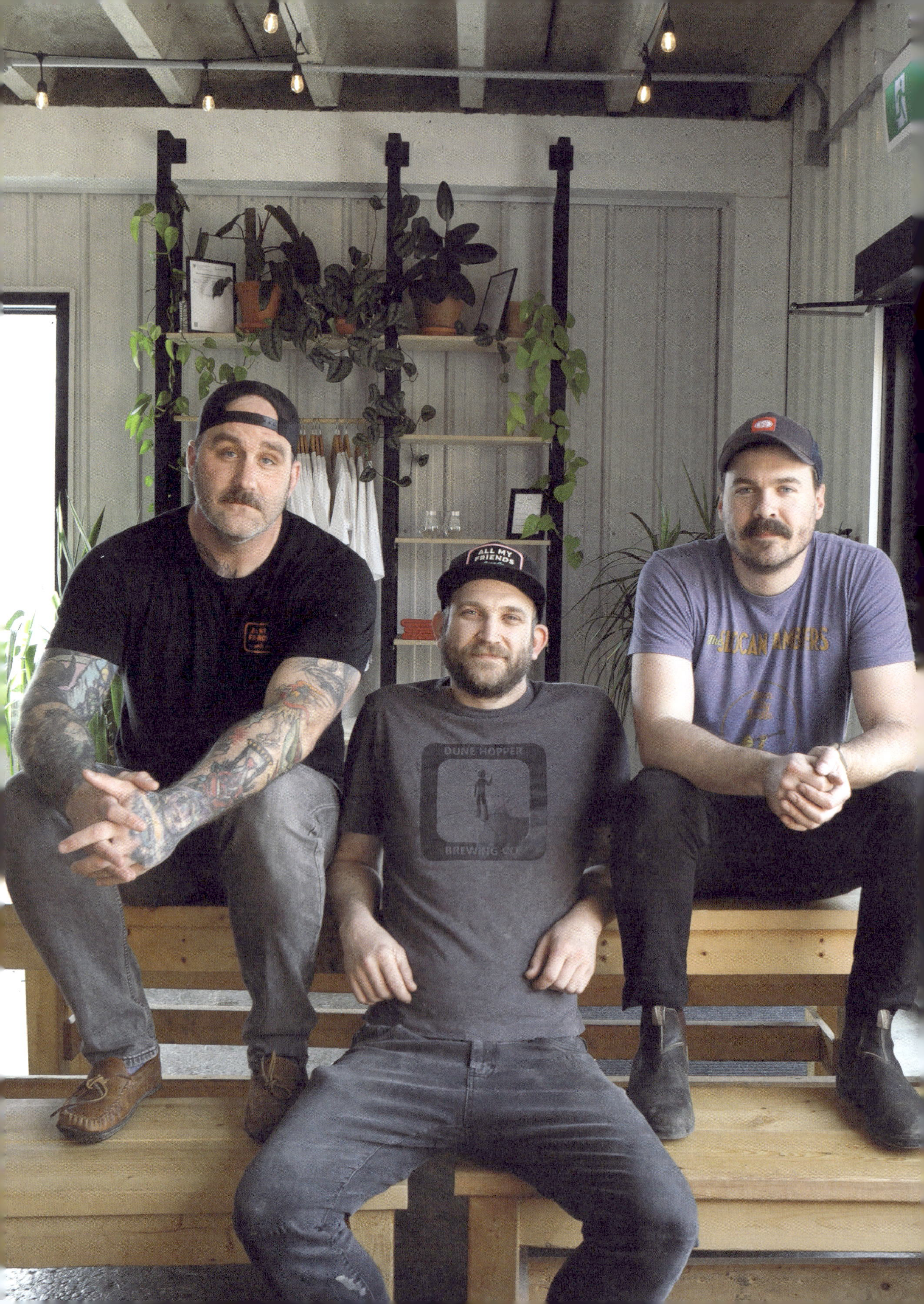
ALL MY FRIENDS
DUNE HOPPER
BREWING CO.
The SLOCAN RAMBLERS

All My Friends Beer Co., Bloomfield

This small-batch brewery is dedicated to unlocking the potential of American-style brewing with a focus on hoppy pale ales, IPAs, and fruit beers.

BILL MCMENOMY, ROB SNOWDON, RYAN TURCOTTE

When we started talking about opening our own brewery, Prince Edward County was the obvious spot. We live nearby in Belleville, but we mostly play down here in the County, and we wanted to focus on something that was a little more niche, so it seemed to make sense to set up shop in a high-traffic spot. We're a focused brewing company with a taste for modern craft beer, especially hazy IPAs. We saw a gap in the industry that we wanted to fill, and we definitely have our own style. Quality is always number one; we set ourselves up on the production side for no excuses on that front. As a brewer, the easy thing to do would be to make the same beer every day. But that's not what our customers want.

All My Friends was born out of four years of conversations. We all met working for a start-up brewery north of the County. We saw the potential there, but it just never came close to what it could have been. So we naively opened our own brewery, thinking we would be getting rid of stress, when really it's extremely stressful all the time. But all three of us are very passionate about making this work and we have very similar visions of how we want it to go.

When we were signing the incorporation papers, our lawyers said, "Okay, now you guys are legally as good as married." All three of us went, "Pardon?" And it's very true. We have to solve similar problems—financial, direction, relationships, all the other smaller stuff. Bill and Ryan talk a lot about sales, and Ryan talks to Rob a lot about his ideas for beer because he's going to be out selling it. And Rob and Bill talk all the time about costs of brews and schedules. We each have our own lane, but we also overlap with each other in certain ways. We complement one another. Together, we are one confident brewery owner.

Our first location fell through because of zoning issues, but our current place is way better. This building was a concrete box—there was nothing in it. It already had three-phase power, a septic system, water. We just had to build bathrooms and an office and then clean it up. We started construction here the November prior to opening, and I think around then we were like, if we're not open by the May long weekend, that's it, we'll pack it up. Everything was in shambles, but we got the brew equipment set and ready so that as soon as we had our licence, we could brew. We knew we could call for help to finish the details, but getting the beer ready to go so it wasn't holding us up was a big step. Rob started brewing in April 2022.

Opening weekend, we posted on an Instagram account we'd just created and put our sign out on the road. It didn't take long, actually. It was the May long weekend and there was a huge windstorm; it went through Uxbridge and took out Second Wedge Brewing Co. And then it headed down this way. We had a packed patio, with all the umbrellas up, and out of nowhere this windstorm came in. It was one giant gust, followed by rain. That really created a bond with our customers; the people who were there still talk about how we all huddled inside and laughed and drank beer.

A lot of people start by fussing over their pilot batches because those are going to be their core brands. In reality, the consumer dictates your core brands. After a year of being open, we have data that we can use to make better decisions about what to produce and how far we can push without overextending our finances. We try to keep our blonde ale and our hazy pale ale as our staples, but what makes us unique is that we've been open for 56 weeks and we've made 34 or 35 different kinds of beer. We didn't start off with that idea, but we noticed that release day for a new beer was huge for sales. We were seeing lineups. People were excited. It's like pushing content out—people want the newest stuff.

It works because we've set ourselves up to be able to pivot with the market. We haven't invested in shipping containers full of printed cans and we're not making big batches; these are 1,200-litre batches. So we can pivot what we're brewing month to month. We can keep innovating and pushing our limits. Mostly, we just love making new beers.

We had a lot of discussions about what to call the brewery. We wanted to express ourselves as an inviting place, as not pretentious. It's who we are: we're a group of friends who bonded over beer. And we've made quite a few more friends since we've opened.

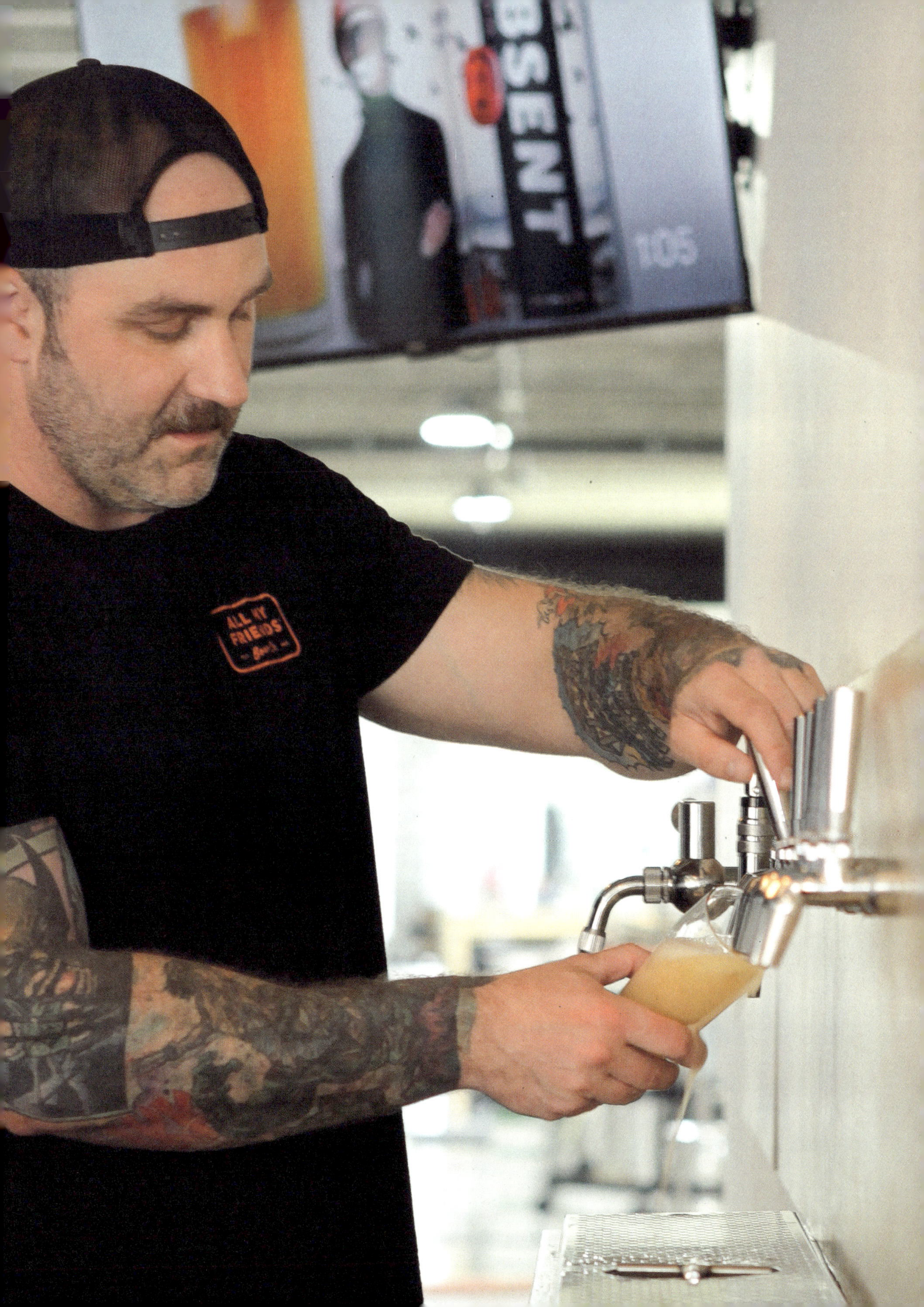
BSENT
1.05
ALL MY FRIENDS

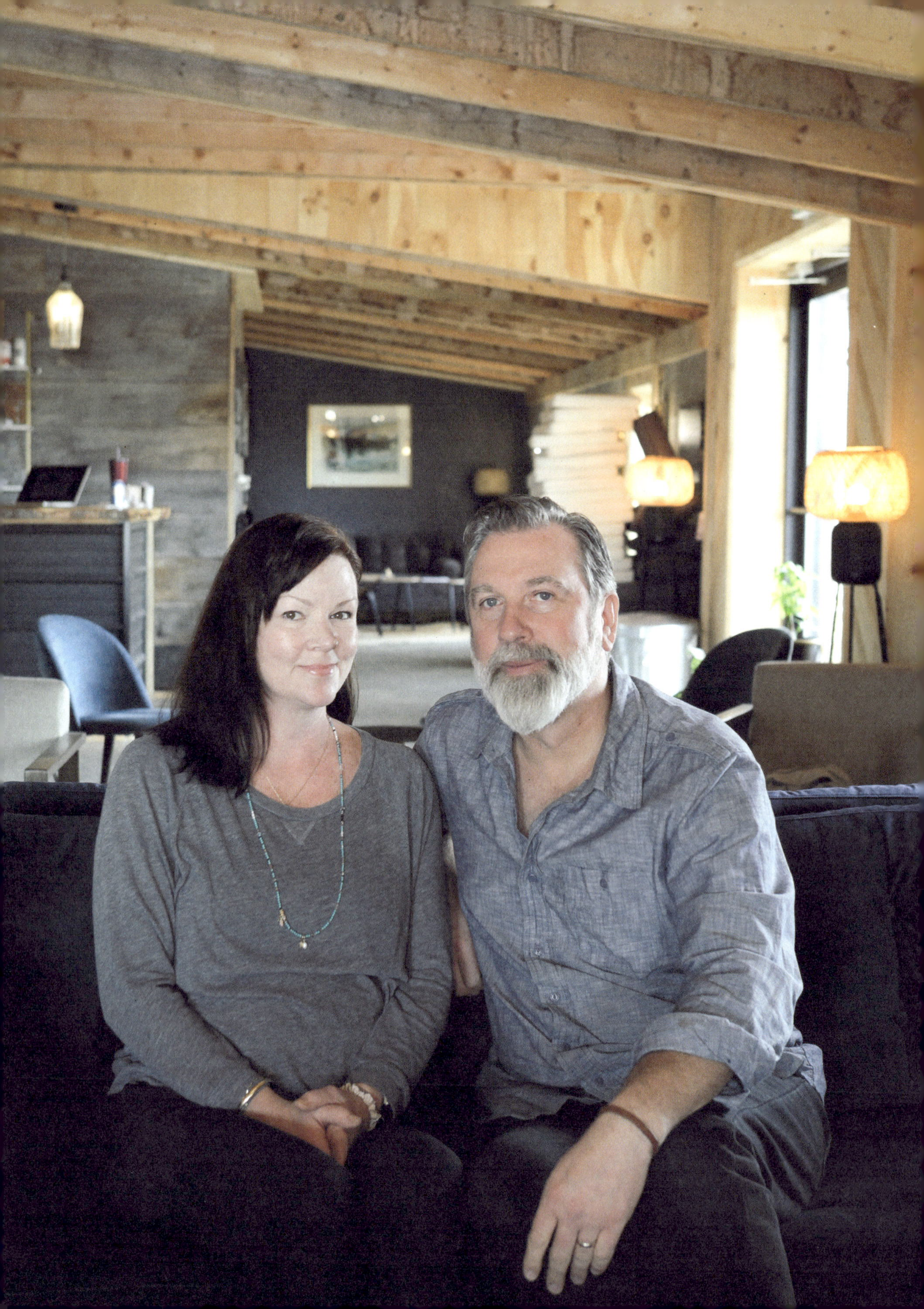

Bare Bones Farm and Distillery, Hillier

Bare Bones is a microdistillery that makes small-batch vodka and gin using ingredients from their farm.

JASON CLARKE, NICOLE CLARKE

We both have backgrounds in hospitality; we met at a Ryerson pub night, and we first worked together at the Arts & Letters Club in Toronto. Jason worked in private club management for 22 years. He was taking club management courses at Cornell University when he noticed they also had a distilling course, and in 2018 it finally worked out that he could go down to learn distilling at Cornell. He'd been thinking about a career change and we felt like we had lots of time to plan.

When the Covid-19 pandemic hit a couple of years later, the timing made sense to make the leap. We were talking about putting our house on the market when Nicole's best friend said, "Oh, we'd love to buy your house." And they did. We didn't even have to list it. Our kids happened to be at the right ages to move out of their schools. I think if we'd waited even a little longer, it might've been more difficult.

Originally, we were going to limp into distilling. Jason would continue to work in club management to give us a steady income as we built the business, until Nicole decided that wasn't going to work: "No, I'm not going to a farm on my own with the girls and you're going to be in the city Monday to Friday and then home on the weekends." She'd watched *Mad Men*. So as we were going through the fifth or sixth iteration of the plan, we decided we'd just leap in and make the move all together.

We took many weekend trips over a couple of years and looked at probably 100 places. Our real estate agent was very patient. We looked at Niagara, and in the end, we felt that Niagara was way too Toronto. We're East Coasters at heart, and that's why we fell in love with the County. It felt like home for some reason. Here, we feel like we're all in it together. Plus, the County sunset is ridiculous. It's one of the best sunsets we've ever seen. It makes us feel like we're back in Cape Breton.

We bought this property in July 2020 and moved in October. I think there were 13 types of flooring in the house and every door handle was different. The building where we built the distillery had dirt floors and feeding stalls for cows. It's just a cinder-block structure, very unassuming, but it's 5,000 square feet. We walked into the building and even though the ceiling was full of raccoon shit, we could see it right away: production here, bottling there, the line working that way to finish the product. And then our retail space and our cocktail lounge—we thought the doors would line up and we'd be able to see the farm right through the opening from the road. We would've loved to have a romantic purple barn like Closson Chase, but when you're dealing with high alcohol volumes, you need non-combustible materials in your building. It would've been beyond us to bring a big timber-frame barn up to code. But it's all worked out.

The windows in the distillery are so deep because we built a new building around the old building in order to keep the cinder blocks inside for insulation. We didn't want the traditional construction of two-by-four stud walls, insulation, and then drywall, so we built the walls on the outside. We hired an architect to help with the floor plan, and we did all the design.

The farm is 80 acres. We try to work the farm into everything we do, including our products and our cocktails. During our first year, we planted 1,204 haskap bushes. Haskap is a superberry from Japan that's high in vitamin C and antioxidants. It looks like an elongated blueberry. We should have planted 600 bushes, not 1,200, but they're still alive.

So we'll produce haskap-flavoured vodka and haskap-flavoured gin. We'll make a vinaigrette. Garlic-infused olive oil—we grow 2,000 heads of garlic a year. Nicole is our beekeeper, and our honey lemon spritz is now made with our honey. We started with three hives, but there was a bad year during which everyone we know lost 75% of their hives, so now we just have one. I think we might ramp it up again. We've got sugar maple trees, and over the last couple of years we've experimented with producing maple syrup. Our smoked maple syrup will be a part of a gin cocktail that we're working on. And then we've partnered with a farmer on 40 acres of cash crop rotation—wheat, soy, corn. The years that we do wheat and corn, we'll take 25% of the crop, and we'll use those grains to make our estate gin and estate vodka. Right now, the grains for our house spirits are all outsourced, but when we produce our estate line, the grain will be from our farm.

We did a soft opening. We didn't tell anyone—we had no social media presence leading up to it by design. There were just way too many other things to focus on and we wanted to keep an easy pace. We're getting a little more presence on social media now; we know we have to embrace it. Our local councillor, Chris Braney, was our first customer. He came over on a side-by-side and knocked on our door, but we weren't ready. It was 12:30 p.m. on a Friday, and he had mud all over his face. We were standing by this apocalyptic temporary sign that Jason had made at midnight the day before we opened; it's only missing that triangle that indicates radioactive or hazardous material. We took a photo in front of that sign with Chris, we made him a cocktail, he bought a bottle of vodka, and left. And then we've been full pretty much every Saturday since.

It's a lot of work. But when you're used to having 215 employees and managing nine restaurants in one property, this is a completely different animal. We've naturally gravitated to different areas and found our niches, with Jason in production and Nicole in front of house. It's nice being our own bosses. One of our greatest successes is working well together; we've got a damn good relationship. And our girls have adjusted really well to our new lifestyle. When their bus driver asked when the brewery was opening up, they replied, "No, it's a distillery." So they know we're making vodka and gin. And that's always been part of the plan: girls, we're opening this business for you to have one day.

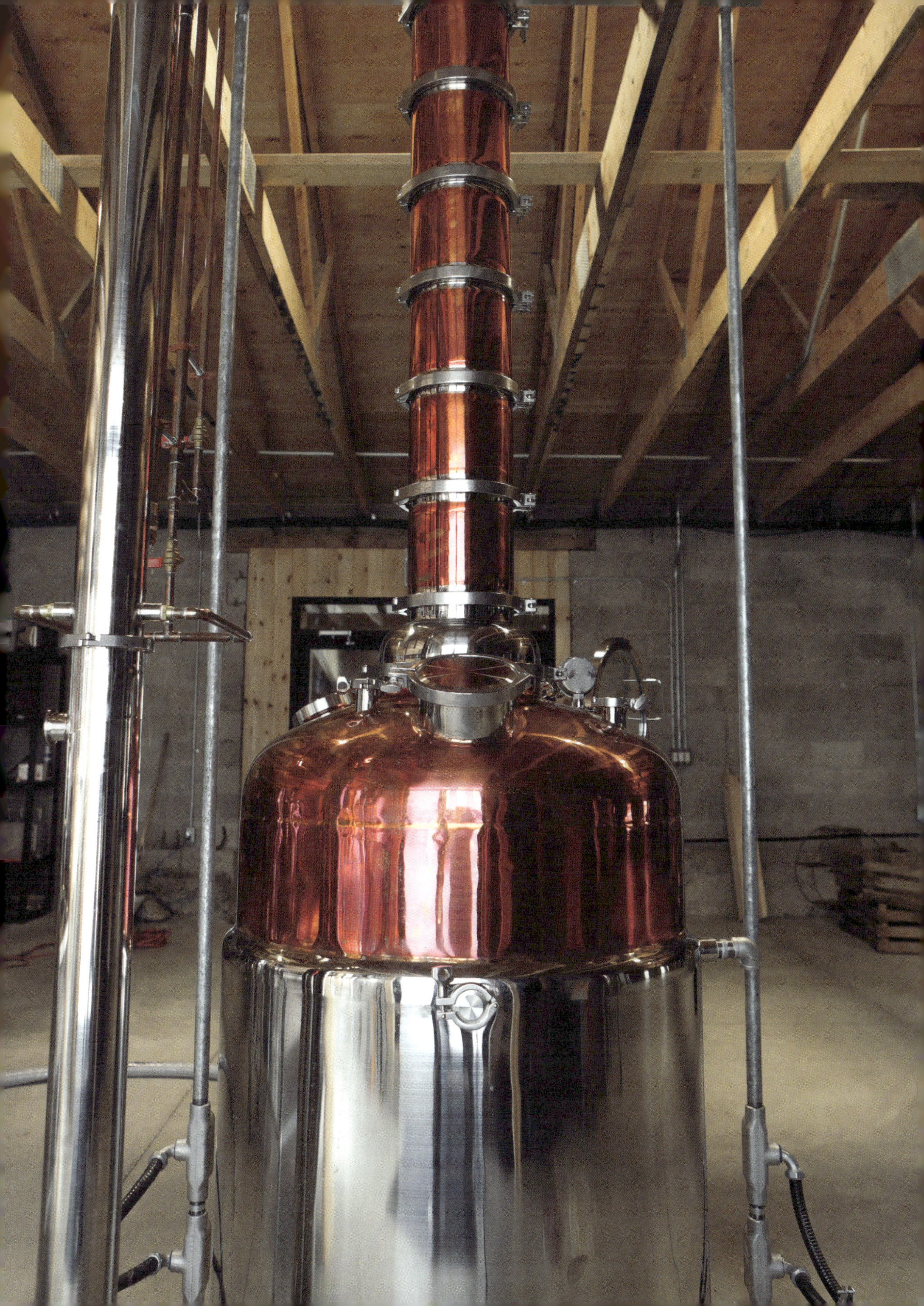

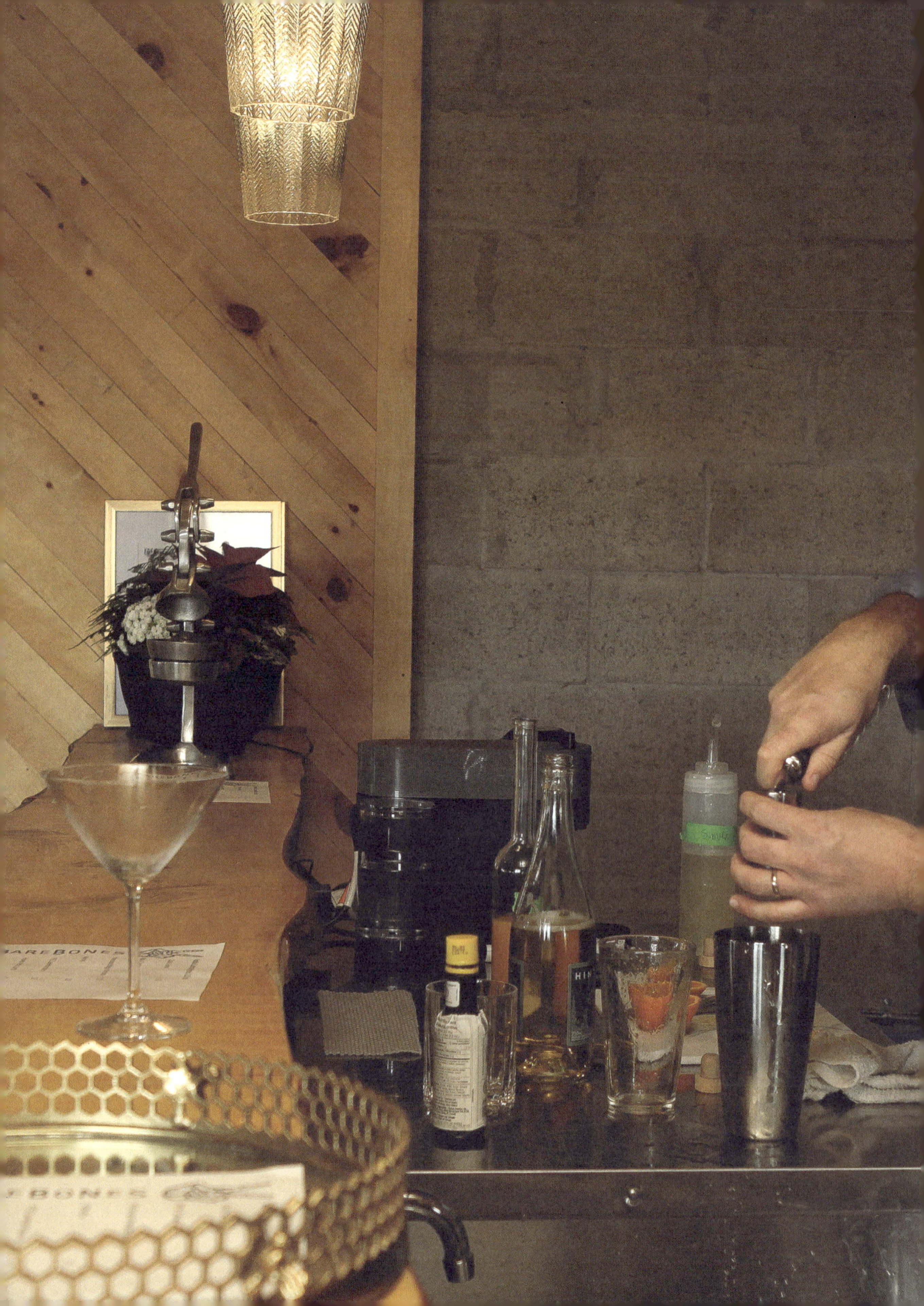

PEC Lavender
Martini
Hinterland
Honey Lemon
Vodka Soda
Crimson Cider
Prince Eddy's

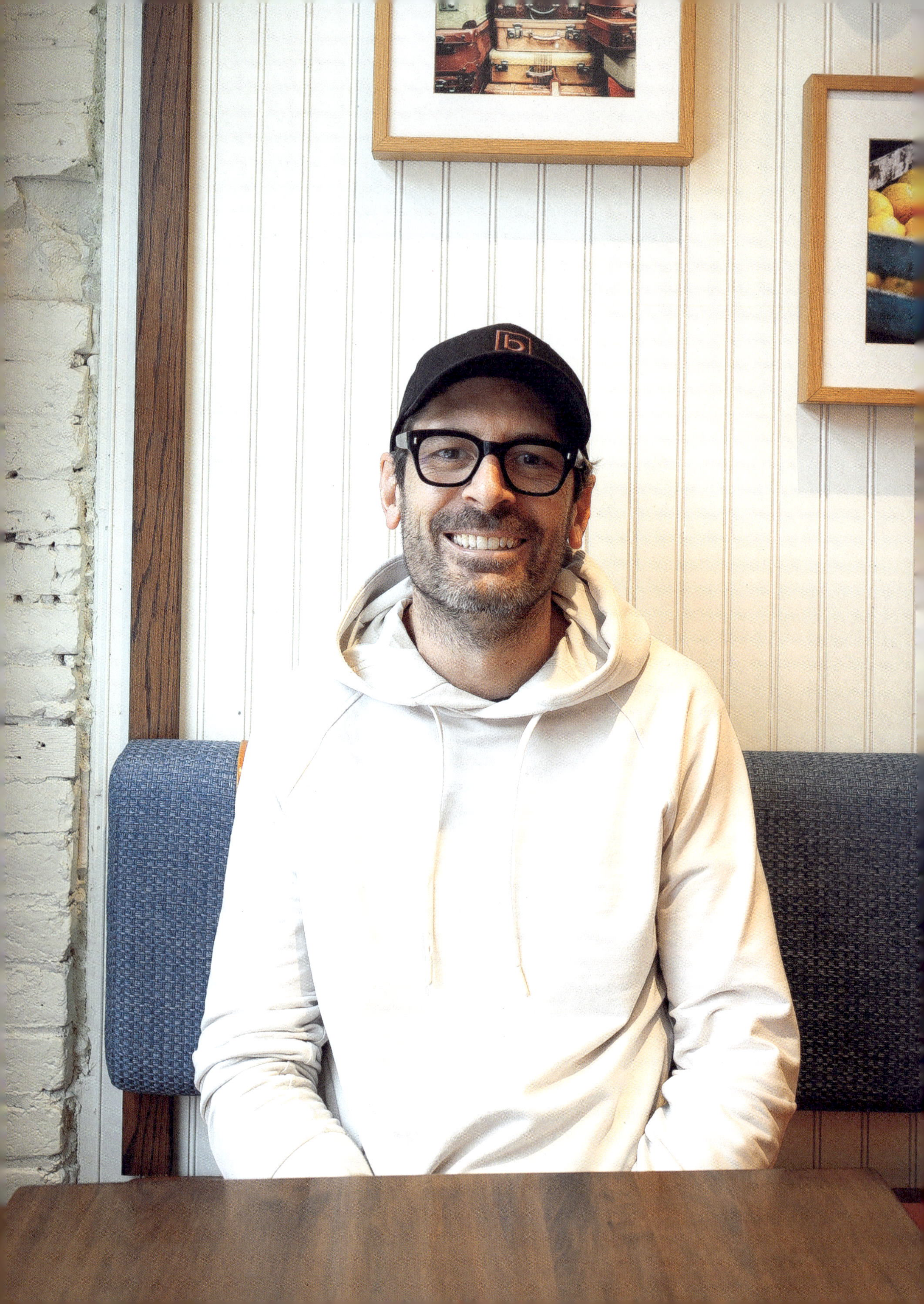

Bocado's Tartare de Carne

with Enright Farms beef, pickled shallots, egg yolk sauce, crispy potato, and Spanish truffle

Serving seasonal and Spanish-inspired food, cocktails, and regional wines, Bocado is a popular restaurant in downtown Picton.

STUART CAMERON, OWNER AND EXECUTIVE CHEF

Seasonal ingredients and outside temperatures have inspired "putting together a bunch of things" for this extraordinary fall/winter tapas dish. This cool-weather version features layers of crisp hash brown potato, salted egg yolk sauce, warming spices, seasoned premium local beef, pickled shallot, and aromatic Spanish black truffle shavings. Make time to prepare all of the components and you'll be rewarded.

Prep time: 30 minutes (plus 24 hours resting time for potatoes and sauce)
Cooking time: 30 minutes
Servings: 4 as an appetizer

Ingredients

Salted egg yolk sauce (or substitute with raw egg yolk)
1 cup kosher salt
1 cup sugar
4 egg yolks
½ tbsp 3% homogenized milk
1 tsp sugar
1 tbsp powdered milk
2 tbsp warm melted butter

Hash brown potato
800 g russet potatoes (about 1.7 lb), peeled
3 tbsp clarified unsalted butter
1 tsp kosher salt
1 pinch ground white pepper

Pickled shallot
½ cup boiling water
⅓ cup red wine vinegar
¼ cup sugar
1 tsp kosher salt
1 cup shallot, thinly sliced and cut into rings

Beef
140 g Enright Farms beef sirloin, finely chopped (5 oz or ⅔ cup)
2 tsp shallot, finely diced
2 tbsp Pyramid Ferments garlic and dill pickles (or other naturally fermented cucumber pickles), finely diced
2 tbsp olive oil
1 tsp Dijon mustard
1 tsp hot sauce
1 tsp lemon zest
1 tsp fresh lemon juice
¼ tsp kosher salt
⅛ tsp freshly ground black pepper
½ tsp parsley, finely chopped
¼ tsp smoked Spanish paprika
black Spanish truffle, to garnish

Method

Salted egg yolk sauce
Mix together salt and sugar on a small tray. Cover egg yolks in salt mixture to cure, covered and refrigerated, for 24 hours. Gently rinse the sugar mixture off the egg yolks; gently pat dry on paper towel. In a blender, combine egg yolks, milk, sugar, and milk powder.

In a thin stream, slowly add warm melted butter into the yolk mixture while blending until fully emulsified. Reserve, refrigerated, until ready to use. (Any excess sauce can be used over steamed vegetables or anywhere you desire a rich sauce.)

Hash brown potato
Peel and grate potatoes; place in the top of a double boiler over boiling water. Cover with lid and stir every 5 minutes, for up to 15–20 minutes, until tender and cooked. Place cooked potato into a large bowl and gently stir in clarified butter, salt, and white pepper.

Line a 10" x 10" tray with plastic wrap. Press potato mixture onto tray, to about 1½" thickness; cover with more plastic wrap. Place another tray on top, topped with a weight (like canned goods) to compress the mixture; refrigerate overnight.

Cut potatoes into four 3" x 3" squares. Preheat deep fryer to 360°F. Add hash brown squares; cook for about 3–4 minutes on each side until deep golden brown and very crispy. Drain and pat dry with paper towel; season with salt to taste.

Pickled shallot
In a small bowl, combine water, vinegar, sugar, and salt, stirring until dissolved. Add the shallots to the warm vinegar mixture and combine; set aside to cool. Store in a sealed container in the refrigerator until time to use. (Can be prepared up to 3 days ahead.)

Beef
In a small mixing bowl, combine beef, shallot, pickles/pickled cucumbers, olive oil, Dijon, hot sauce, lemon zest, lemon juice, salt, pepper, parsley, and paprika. Mix very well with a spoon, adjusting seasoning as desired.

Assembly
Place each hash brown square on individual plates. Cover top of each with a smooth layer of sauce.

Place seasoned beef mixture loosely and evenly over sauced hash brown squares; dust beef with paprika.

Drain shallot rings; arrange on top of each serving. To garnish, use a mandoline to generously shave fresh black Spanish truffles over top of each. Serve immediately.

Chef's Notes
Assemble this dish immediately before serving. Use a very sharp knife to chop best quality beef taken straight from the fridge, just before seasoning, assembling, and garnishing.

Any trimmings from potato squares (and any extra pieces) can be used another time by frying until golden and crisp, topping with any extra sauce, pickled shallot, and a poached egg.

Drink Pairings
Palate cleansing, both these pairings offer lingering aromatics to play off the pickled shallot and paprika: Trail Estate Neon Candy Sauvignon Blanc 2021, Stock & Row Slow & Low Cider.

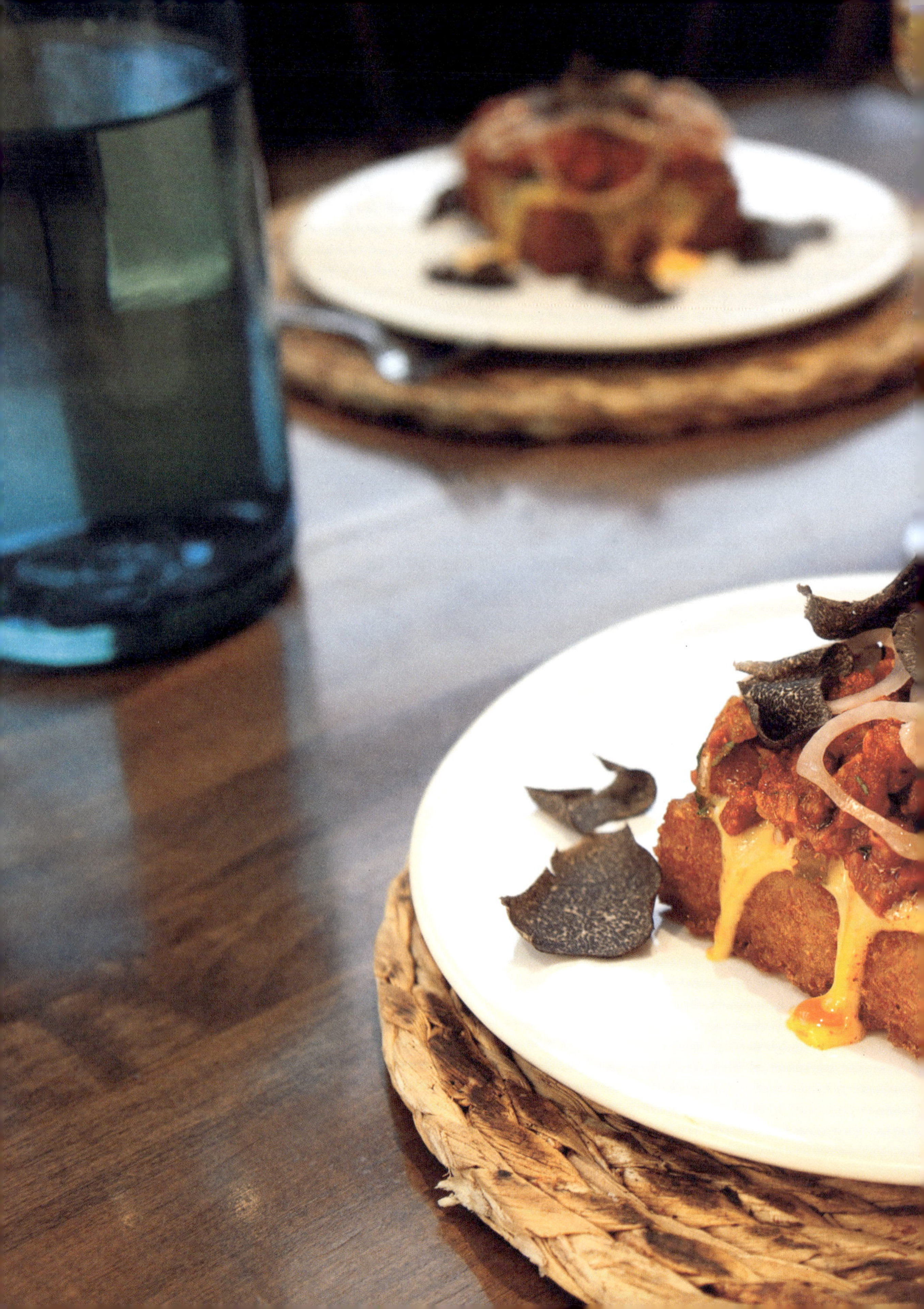

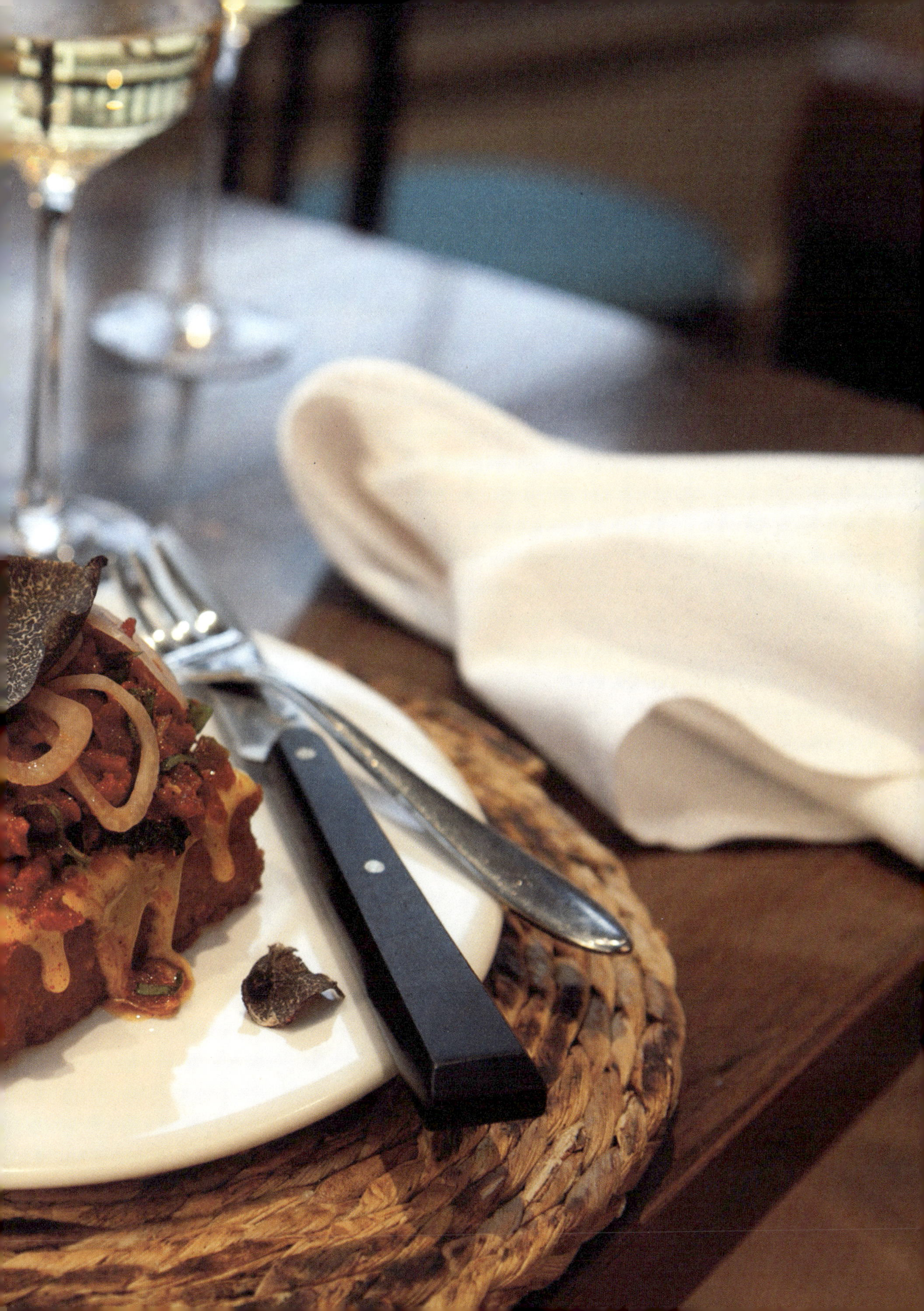

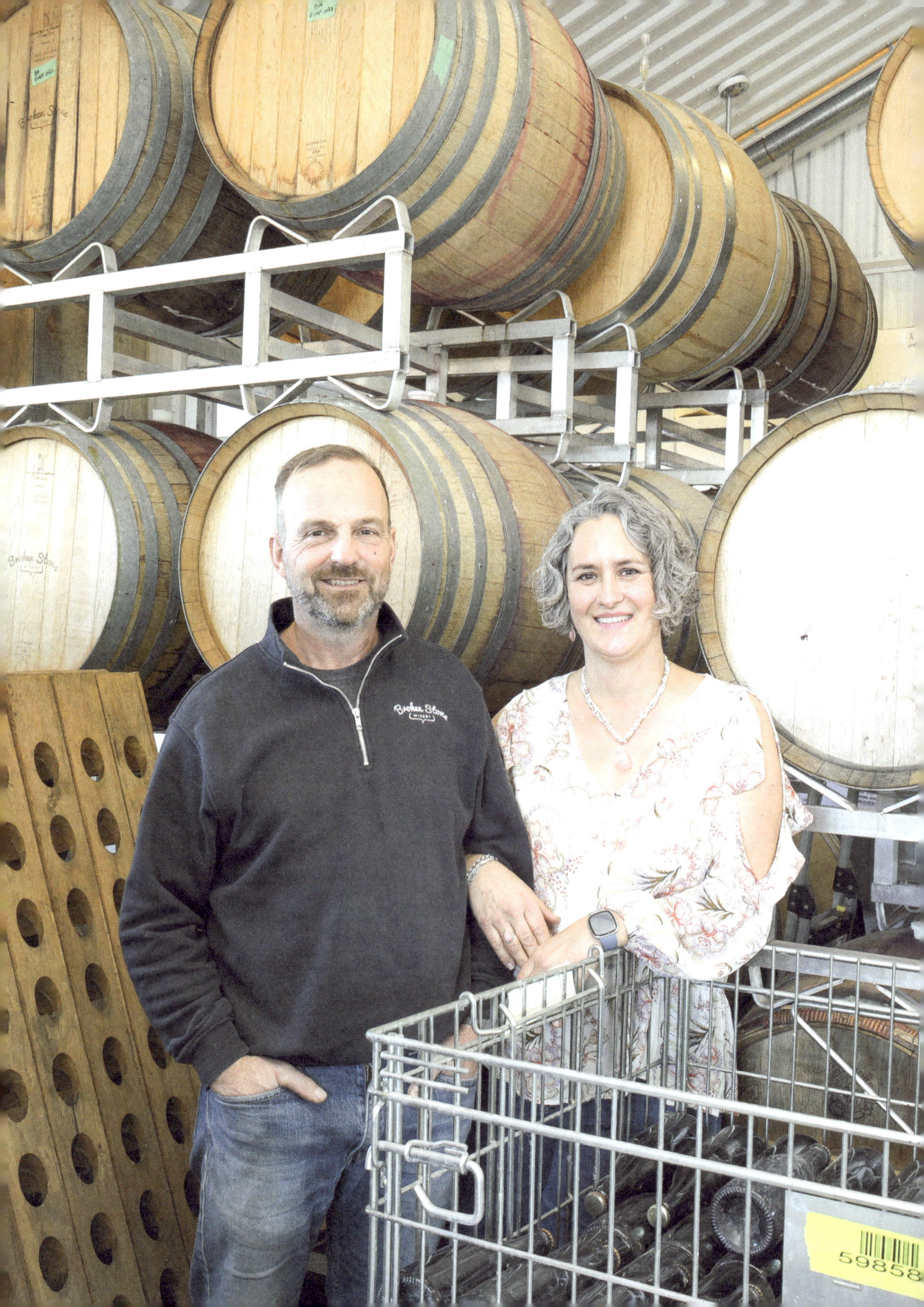
Broken Stone
59858

Broken Stone Winery, Hillier

Broken Stone is a family-run winery featuring an eight-acre vineyard planted with noble varieties that thrive in a cool climate.

MICHELINE KUEPFER, TIM KUEPFER

We started from scratch. When we bought the property in 2009, all it had was an acre and a half of Pinot Noir that had been planted in 2008. They were tiny little seedlings; there wasn't even a trellis system installed. It was just the vines in the ground. In 2008, when we put our first offer on our current property, the sellers declined it. We thought, phew, dodged a bullet there, what would we have done? But then the next year, the property was still for sale, so we went in with the same offer. They said yes. And we said, "Oh shit, now we have to do something."

In the early days, neither of us was very knowledgeable about wine. We drank Ontario wine, though, because there was a Wine Rack right across the street from our Toronto condominium. One Christmas, Tim asked for a book that had to be about one of two things: either a family that buys a sailboat and sails around the world for a year, or a book about a family that sells everything in Toronto and moves to Prince Edward County and buys a vineyard. Micheline found it: the book was Geoff Heinrich's *A Fool and Forty Acres*. It was exactly what Tim had asked for, and that book started our journey to Prince Edward County.

Tim: I volunteered at Sugarbush Vineyards to do some research. I picked grapes with the owners, Sally and Rob Peck, and talked about our plans. Their advice was, "Don't do it, don't buy a vineyard!" Regardless, after I spent one morning picking their grapes, I said, "Okay, I've got this, my knees are sore, I'm done." I didn't even last the whole day.

That first spring, once we bought our land, I had to learn how to run a vineyard. So I bought a wheelbarrow, shovel, chainsaw, hoe, and rake. We already had a Subaru, a trailer hitch, and a trailer. One day, I was hoeing in the field and thinking, wow, this is really rocky, hard soil. And then I looked out at the vineyard, at this acre and a bit, and I realized, oh my God, this is a lot of land to hoe by hand.

We needed a tractor, and Black Prince Winery happened to be selling an old one. So I borrowed $9,500 from Micheline's mom, bought the tractor, and drove it over here. It's still running today; we included it in the family photo hanging in our tasting room.

I kept talking to Rob. I'd go to Sugarbush for a wine tasting, lean on the bar, and ask, "So, Rob, what are you doing in your vineyard this week?" Then I'd run over here and do the same thing. It turned out to be a very successful strategy for vineyard management. Rob had been doing it for eight, nine years at that point. I learned a lot at those impromptu wine tastings.

In the very early days, our family camped in a tent during our weekend stays. One of those weekends, a neighbour showed up with his loader tractor, carrying an outhouse. He dropped it off and said, "Hey, Tim, if you're going to have those girls here, you're going to need somewhere nice for them to go to the washroom." Our neighbours were always looking out for us, popping up whenever we needed help. We learned that it's just the County way: You see someone in need and you lend them a hand.

Fall rolled around, and I was over at Sugarbush again. Rob asked, "So do you have your vines tied down yet?" I said, "Tied down? What do you mean?" And he said, "Well, in the winter you're going to need to tie down the vines and bury them." I said, "Bury my vines. Are you kidding me?!" That seemed like a lot of work, but it had be done, so I did it—I was out there doing it myself, getting the vines ready for winter.

When the next season came along I didn't know how to use the grape hoe to unbury the vines. So I dug them up by hand, the whole field, an acre and a half of vines. Not the most efficient, very time-consuming and back-breaking.

For our first harvest, we hosted a harvest party. We had family and friends help us pick our 2010 Pinot Noir.

Again, over at Sugarbush, Rob asked, "So, Tim, what are you going to do with all those grapes?" I said, "I don't know, I'm going to sell them or something. Do you want to buy 'em?" He said, "Tell you what, Tim. I'll make your wine for you this year."

Wonderful! Because I didn't have any equipment or any space to make wine.

When the wine was ready, we returned and bottled it by hand. We loaded all the wine into our minivan, drove it back to Toronto, and stacked it in our furnace room. It was like 110 cases of wine. We soon learned that the furnace room is a good place to store wine when the air conditioner is running and a bad place to store wine when the furnace is running. By the end of the winter, because it was so warm all the time, the wine had started to fizz. We had to unbottle it, filter it again, and then rebottle it. We sure have learned a lot since that first harvest.

The name Broken Stone comes from the land. It reminds us that everything comes from the land—the vines, the grapes, the wine—the whole cycle starts with the land. Driving out here, looking at land and seeing the Hillier clay loam with the gravel in it, we became excited. We thought, that's the soil we want. That gravel, the clay, it drains well for the grapes. It's rich in minerality. But when you go to farm it, it can be difficult. There's a lot of rocks. We wanted our winery to be approachable, down to earth. And we also knew that once you start trying to build a winery, it's a lot of cash flow out and a lot of time to get anything back—you soon become stone broke.

Micheline: Tim and our youngest moved here full-time in 2019 for her to start Grade 9 at Prince Edward Collegiate Institute. I moved here with our middle daughter once the Covid-19 pandemic started. It was May 2020. The move was a little earlier than we had originally planned—I was planning to stay in Toronto until our middle daughter finished high school, which was going to be in June 2020. But because everything was remote anyway, we all came here and enjoyed isolating on this beautiful property.

With a vineyard, you can't sit back. You have to keep moving forward once the momentum starts. We kept our Toronto jobs for as long as we could to finance our dream. We made wine for three years, and then we opened our tasting room doors in 2013. We

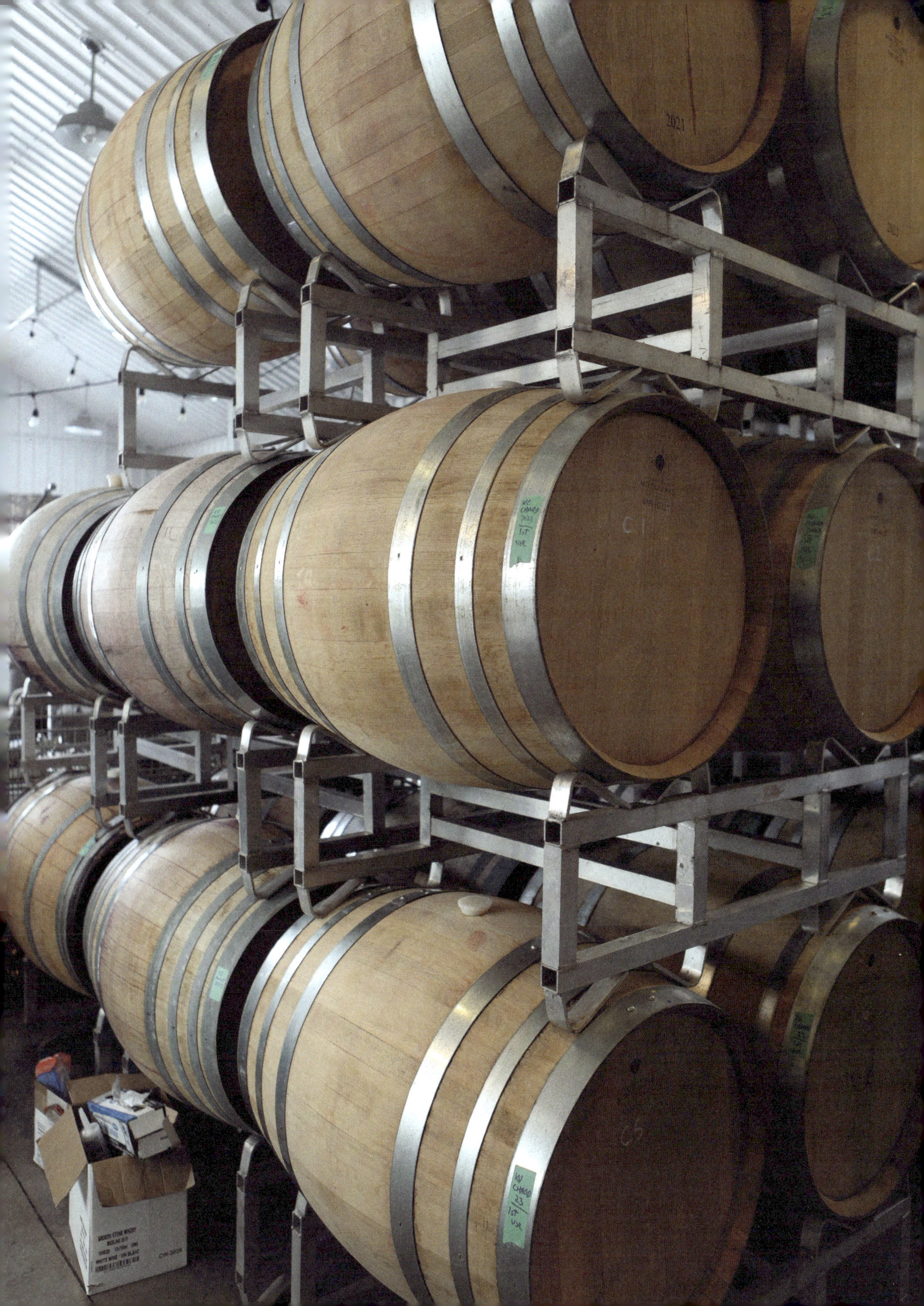

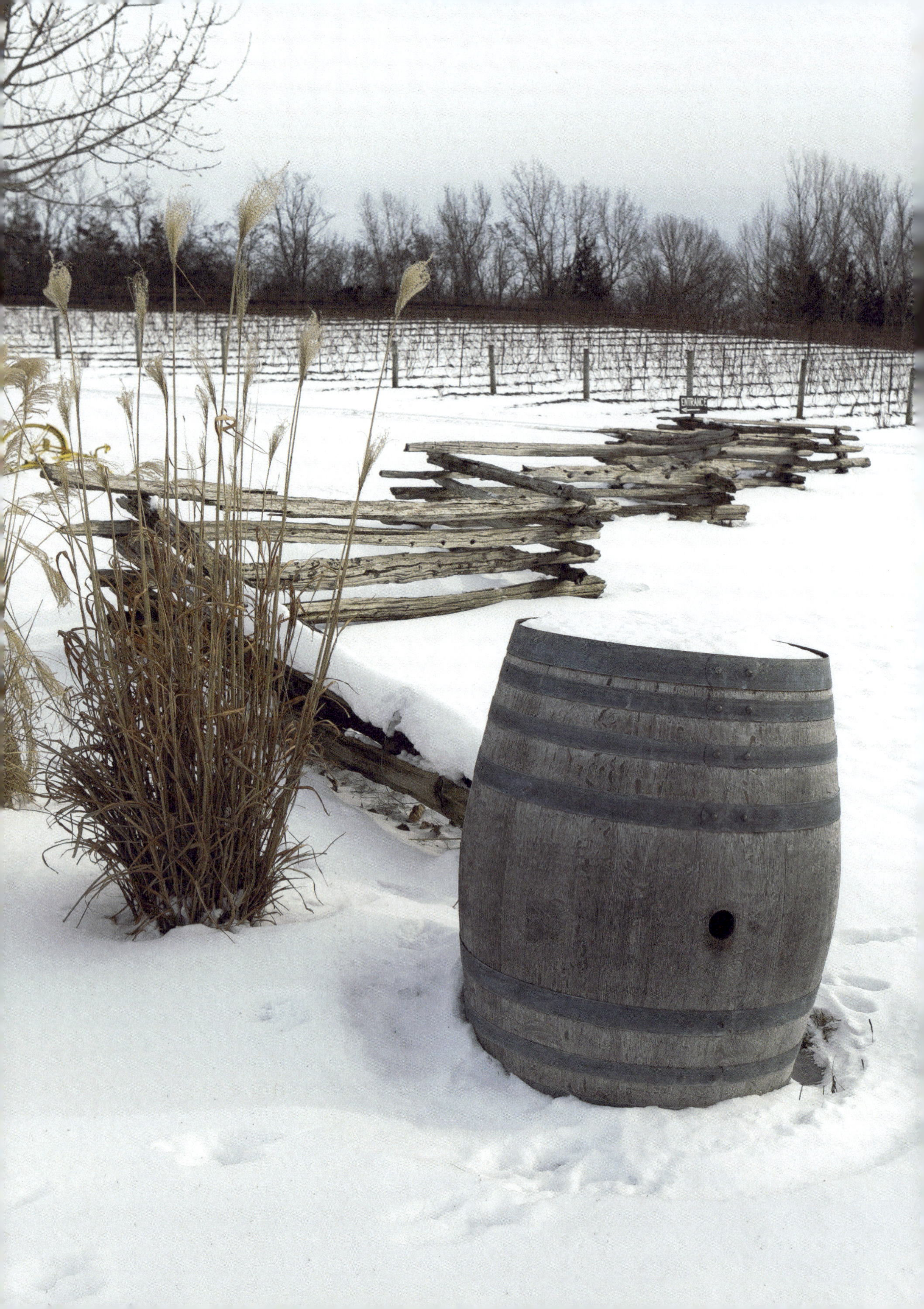
ENTRANCE

offered people Pinot Noir, Pinot Noir, or Pinot Noir. A vertical flight—you could really taste the influence of the different growing seasons.

Our strategy is to be a 100% County-grown winery. We can't supply all the grapes we need from our own land, so we took over managing the By Chadsey's Cairns vineyard in 2019—an extra 15 acres.

Our original plan with managing Chadsey's depended on rapidly growing our restaurant sales. But as our new wines came to market, the pandemic hit. Early on in the pandemic, restaurants weren't taking on new wines; they were struggling to survive. Because of that, the sales haven't materialized fast enough to keep supporting so many local vines under management. So at the end of each year, we're short on cash. Sometimes we think about quitting. This past year, we thought we might have to scale back and give up managing the Chadsey's vineyard. But they would tear out the vines, which would be a shame. After several months of rest in the winter, we thought, we can tighten our belts for another year, we can grow our sales, we can still do this. We will succeed.

You need a lot of working capital to grow a winery. At the end of harvest, you're going to have to store at least one full year of wine until you can sell it. Then, if you make premium traditional sparkling or barrel-aged wine, that's another year's worth of production to hold in inventory. So if you're a 3,000-case winery, that's 72,000 bottles. At $5–$10 a bottle to produce, that's a lot of working capital tied up in inventory. It's a lot of cash out while you're growing. And if you stumble even just a little bit, the expenses increase.

With our own resources, it's been a struggle to grow to the next level. We've put everything we have into the business. We've had a few setbacks, but a lot of success—we've produced some award-wining wines. In 2022, our Chardonnay won a Platinum medal and Best in Show at the WineAlign National Wine Awards of Canada. In the summer, our winery's park-like setting is bustling with people enjoying wine, pizza, and live music. We've learned so much over the years and we've grown a little bit every year since we've started.

We're proud that we took the risk. Moving from that initial thought of, hey, let's buy this piece of land, let's see where it goes, to building a successful winery from the ground up has been a fantastic journey.

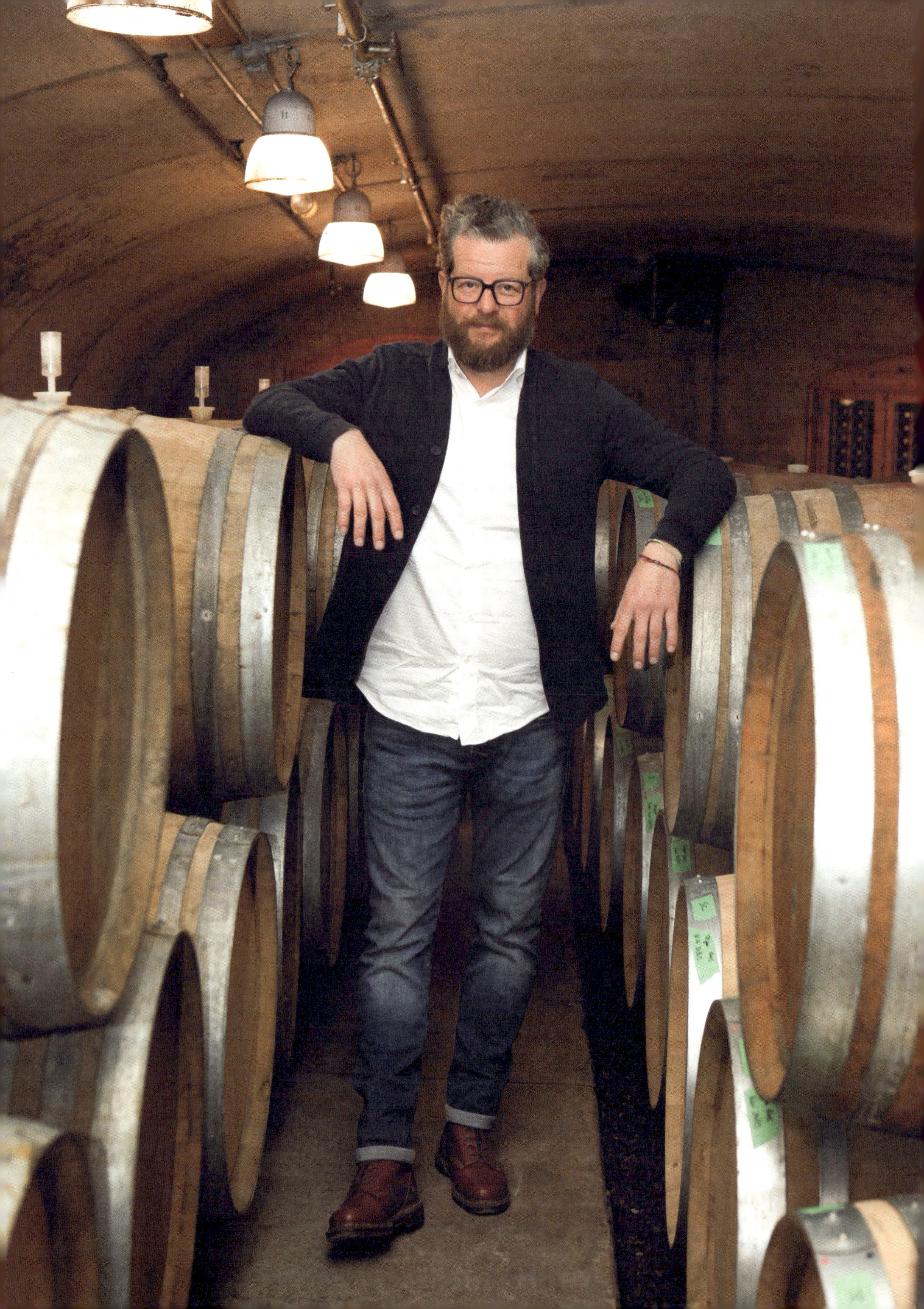

Closson Chase Vineyards, Hillier

Housed in an iconic purple barn, Closson Chase produces award-winning Chardonnay and Pinot Noir and is one of the oldest wineries in the County.

FRANCIS BERTRAND, KEITH TYERS

Francis: My love for wine goes back to Algeria. Every three months, we had to travel because of visa issues, which was typical at the time. So we spent a lot of time in Spain and France. But I remember what it means for everyone around the room if there's a bottle of wine on the table. Parents getting dressed up, festivities, joy. There's something about the dining table and wine—it's romantic.

Music that you know well, songs you can sing to this day—like Belinda Carlisle's "Heaven is a Place on Earth" from 1987—when it plays, you're connected to a sense of time and place, memory. Wine's the same. It connects, it registers, there's emotion associated with it. It's the same with a song, the same with a piece of artwork on a wall. Wine presents a story just like a play or a book. Like movies have characters and structure, wine plays a role; it has an identity as a whole. It's unique. I'll remember the taste and feel and understand how a wine developed through the years. It's the same as if I meet someone again 10 years later—you're you, but I know the differences. It's the same as wine through vintages. You want to know more about the person or the wine. That's how I've always seen it. I just want to know more about the story.

I started selling County wines in 2009 in the Art Gallery of Ontario when I worked at a restaurant called Frank. We'd come here every summer to rent the same house from friends of ours. I just loved it. But I could never bridge being in the world of wine and food, and being in the County. It didn't seem possible back then. Until I made it possible. I chose my life. I chose home. I chose what I wanted and I chose where I work.

I met Keith because I fell in love with Closson Chase wines in 2013. When I had my wine list in Toronto, depending on where I worked, I sought out Closson Chase wine. And then I called up Keith because I just wanted to do wine. I didn't know if it was financially possible, but I wanted to try. And I only wanted to work for Closson Chase. I love being in the wine room, working with the tasting staff and Keith. I'd almost always rather be wearing my Blundstones and walking around and sharing our wines with guests.

Keith: ADHD is a good thing in the wine business because there's just so much multitasking. I'm a winemaker. I'm a purchaser. I'm a researcher. I'm a cleaner. I'm a vineyard worker. I can drive a tractor. I drive a forklift. I wash tanks. I pull hoses. I don't want to do those things anymore after 20 years, but somebody has to do them. It's still a very physical job. But the lifestyle is amazing.

We looked at moving to Niagara first, but I'd read about the County planting grapes in a wine magazine, I believe it was *Wine Tidings*. When I saw that Mike Peddlesden had planted grapevines and that Ed Neuser had opened at Waupoos (though Ed planted

CLOSSON CHASE VINEYARDS

Est. 1998

hybrids), and when I saw that the focus was on Pinot and Chard—I'm going to piss people off here—I understood that Pinot Noir and Chardonnay make some of the best and most memorable wines in the entire world.

My wife and I went to the same high school in Odessa, so we already knew the area. We drove around one day in mid-August and ended up on Closson Road at what's now the Keint-he–Closson vineyard; it was Ken Burford's back then. And then on our second trip down to look at houses, I learned that Deborah Paskus was planting grapes (Chardonnay) on Closson Road—which ended up being the vineyard and winery right beside our house. And I said to Cassandra, my wife, that if Deborah Paskus was here, this was for real.

I thought, well, eventually they're going to need somebody to do hospitality. Closson Chase was literally the 4.2 acres behind the purple barn and a little bit of first-year planting to the right of the purple barn. The whole front east field at The Grange was still wide open; back then, Bob Granger was driving a tractor and pulling a cultivator to prepare it for planting. In 2003, I walked down the road and had a conversation with Deborah. I started working here part-time, tying up grapevines, doing hard labour for, I think, eight bucks an hour. And then Deborah looked at me and said, "Okay, now we're going to teach you the other side of the business." I left Closson Chase in 2010 to do consulting, because I wanted to branch out and continue learning, but in 2012 I came back and took over retail and sales. And then in 2015, Deborah decided to retire, and so the owners looked at me and asked if I wanted the opportunity.

In 2015, we lost everything, and then 2016 was the driest, hottest year in 65 years. I'd been growing grapes here for 13 years by that point. I remember talking to the fourth-generation farmer down the road, and he was like, "Oh yeah, my dad hasn't seen it this dry since he was a kid back in the '60s." And then in 2017 we got four feet of rain, had the wettest July ever, and the wine from that year was exceptional. I'd been told as a Pinot Noir maker that, if you're lucky, you only get to make two great vintages in your life—I couldn't have my first great vintage three years into making wine. So I was like, fuck, this one's great, but also, fuck no, I've only got one left.

These vineyards are going to outlive all of us. I do think I'm a steward of the land because at some point I won't be here, which is why I'm really trying to get us into regenerative farming, or as close as we can be in our current climate.

I know wine consumption is falling but people still want to know where their food comes from. I think everybody's come to understand that wine is a picture of something. It's a time capsule. It tells you everything that went on that summer and it tells you everything that occurred in a defined area.

Most people don't understand that you're drinking my palate. So what I've tasted has influenced the wines I make. I can never make Burgundy because I'm in Prince Edward County and not France. I'm trying to replicate the balance, elegance, and a sense of place. What you're tasting are wines that I want to enjoy.

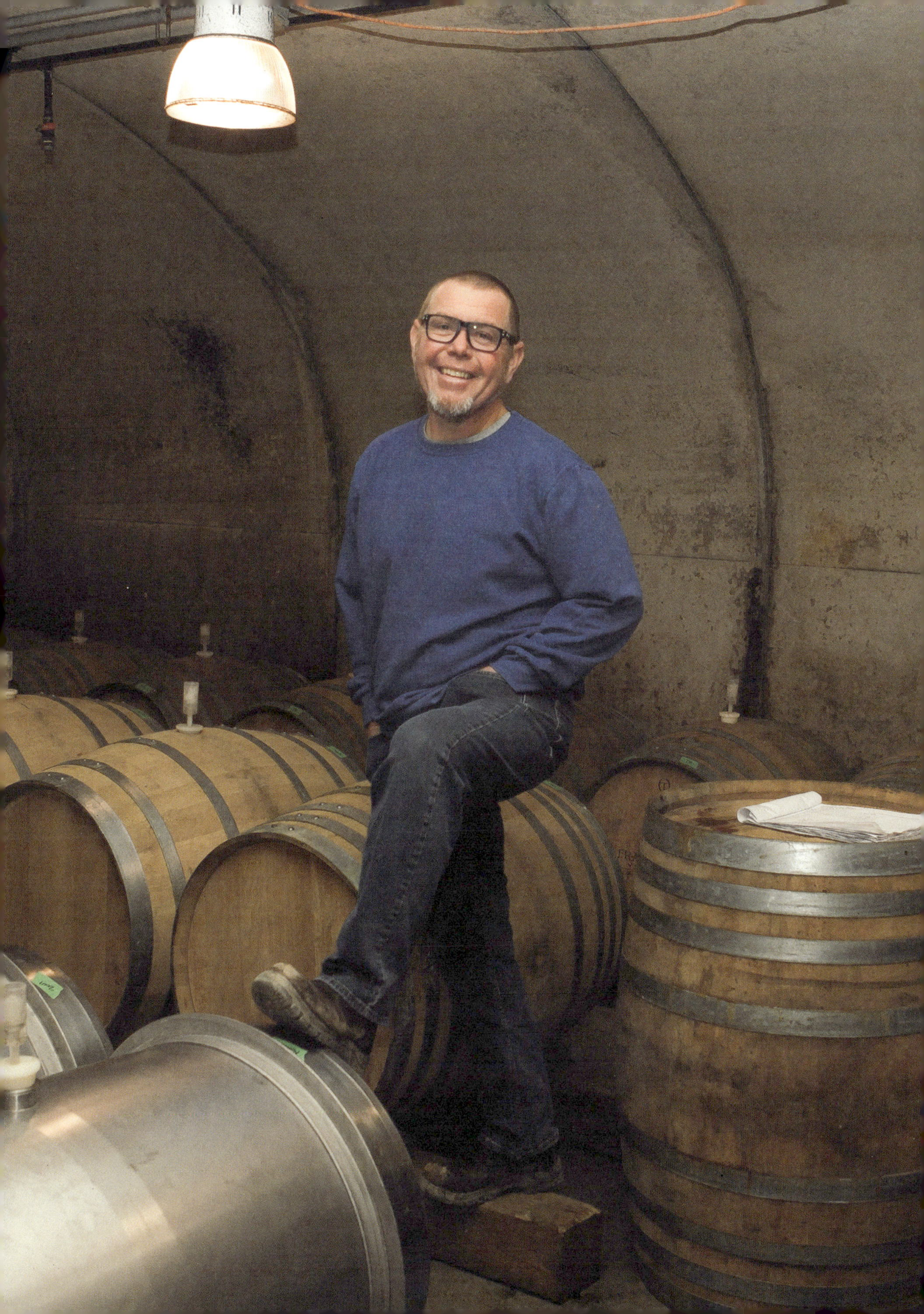

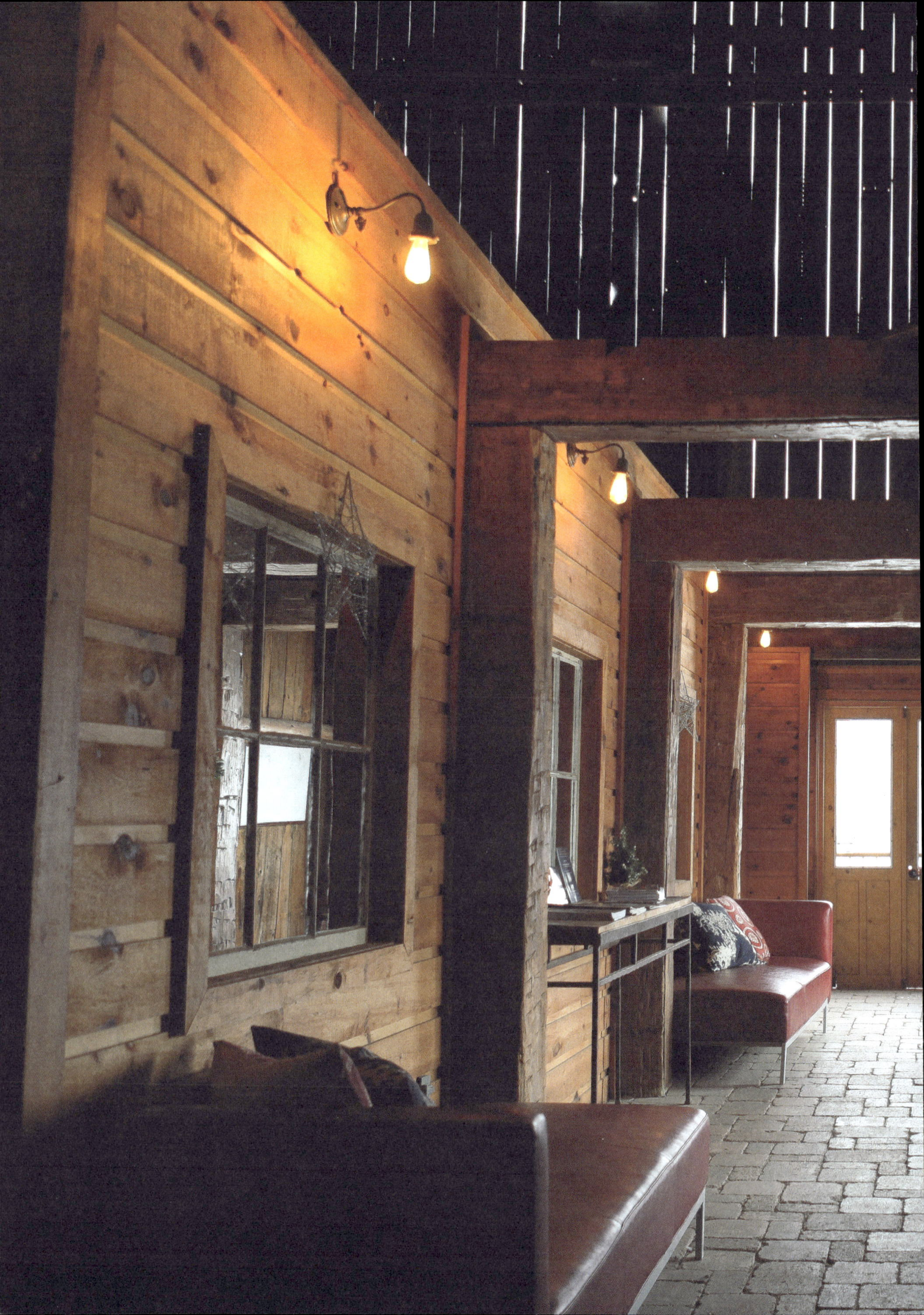

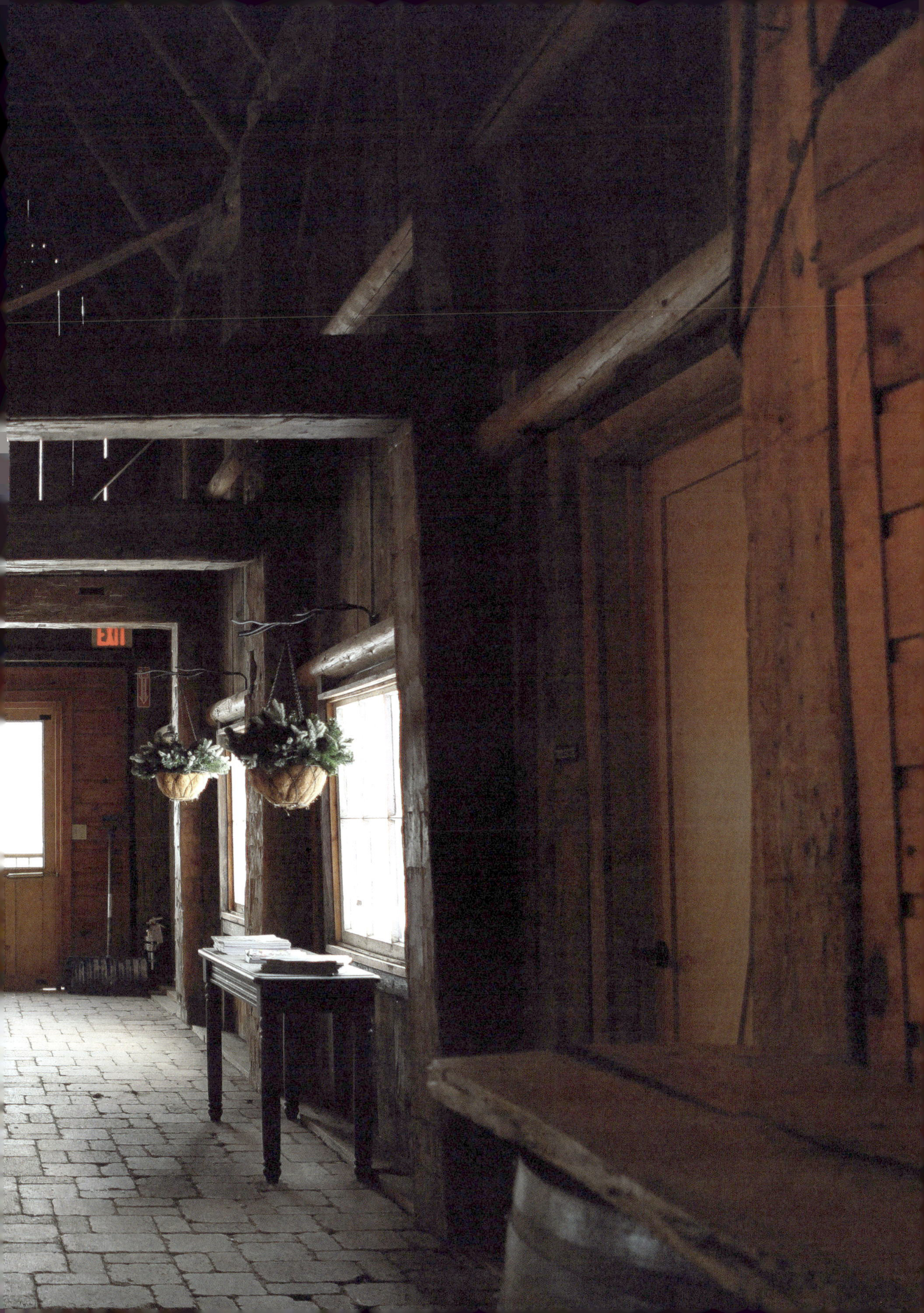
EXIT

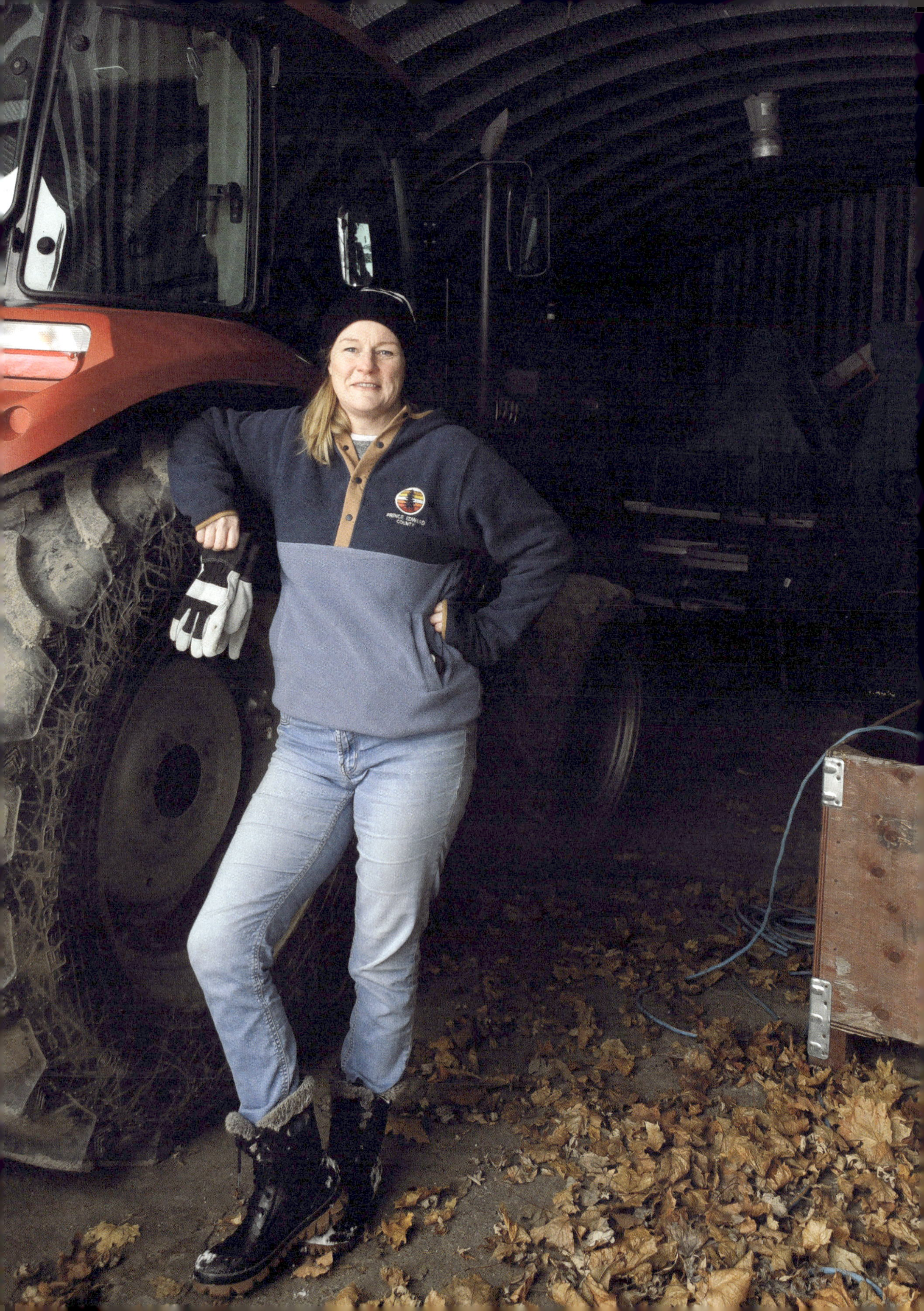
PRINCE EDWARD
COUNTY

The County Cider Company, Waupoos

Since 1995, County Cider has produced hard ciders from over 16 varieties of heirloom and cider-specific apples.

DANNIELLE DAVIDSON

My mom comes from a United Empire Loyalist family—my mom's father, my grandfather, was born in the Hudgin Log House down in South Marysburgh. I worked here for Grant Howes from 1997 to 2001, first as general help and then as the retail manager. Jen Dean, Grant's partner, took over as tasting room manager when I left in 2001. I came back to County Cider because in my graduating year of college, I had to do a placement in a laboratory. I ran into Jen at the grocery store, and I knew she had done a wine science program and was doing testing for other wineries. So I asked her if I could do my two-week placement with her. Those two weeks have lasted 15 years. I just kept coming back every day until Grant was like, "What are you doing here?" I told him I had nothing else to do. So I just never left. He put me on payroll.

Growing up, I thought I wanted to be a lawyer. I took a law class and I realized that, no, I just like to argue. I wasn't one of those people who knew what they wanted to do. I like when things make sense. That's why I like science too. There's a lot of personal human stuff in business, but it comes down to numbers and there's a right and a wrong. Viable and nonviable. I spend a lot of time figuring out what the cost of making our goods is and what's realistic.

Grant and Jen sent me to the Cornell cidermaking course. They will put money into their staff and will invest in you as long as you promise to never leave. I did three different pommelier courses with Peter Mitchell from England. One was a sensory analysis course for people who wanted to pursue a cider professional certification; I'm now certified. The other class he did was lab work. The lab work you need for cidermaking includes things like pH, TA, microbiology, cell counts and visualization, protein analysis, protein removal, haze removal. It's a lot like winemaking—balancing, finding out how much titratable acidity your product has, adjusting your acid, testing for tannins and the concentration of tannins in a product. Back then, we used the old-fashioned method, with reagents and chromatography; now you can get everything through a spectrophotometer. You put a drop in and it gives you a report. But we learned how to do it like I assume they did it in the 1700s, with titrations, pipetting, differential staining.

In 2011, we sat out on the patio and Grant said I had to be the cidermaker. So Jen wrote it up like a contract. I took the job; it was a salaried position. I can't remember what I was paid, but it seemed like a lot to me because back then I was making $5.95 an hour serving tables. That was my first-ever salaried position. I feel like I did a lot of my growing up here. Grant would see something in you—he always saw something in me. I thought he was crazy when he would tell me that I could be the cidermaker, run the production. I don't

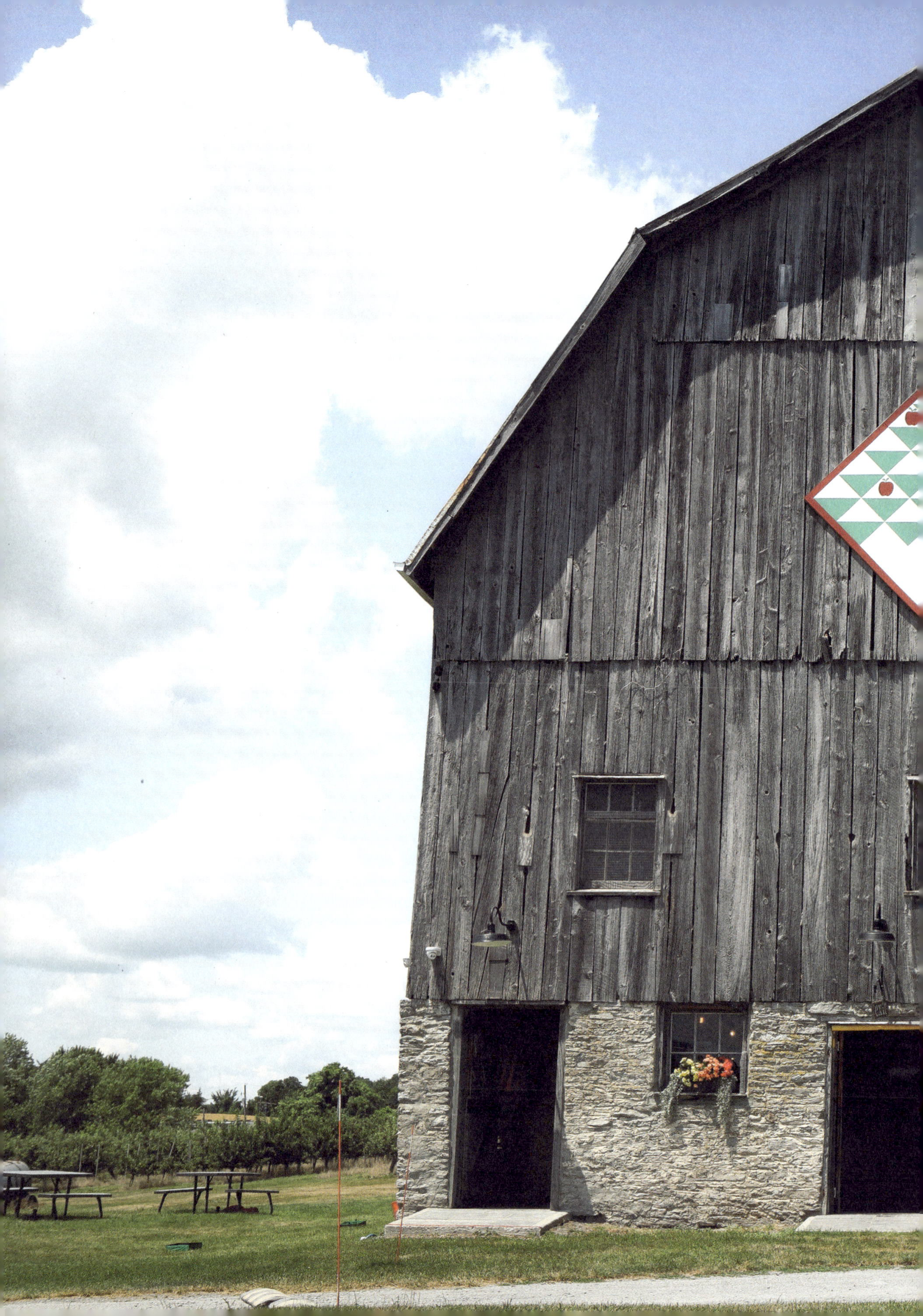

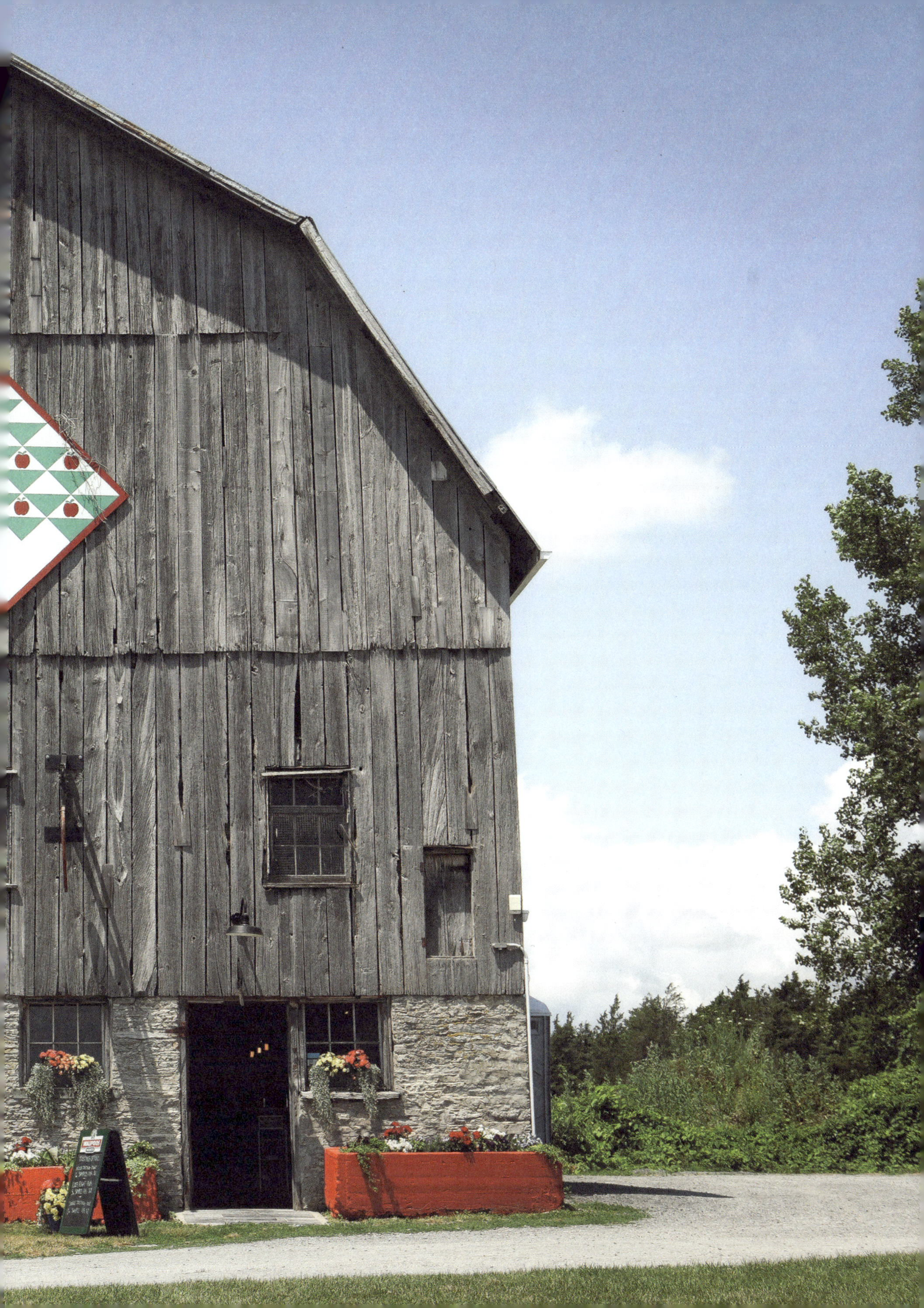

know if he actually did see something in me or if he forced it into me. I'm thankful for him, even though he pushed me hard and we butted heads a lot.

Losing Grant was like losing a second father. We very much had a parent–child relationship. When I got married, Grant bought my wedding dress. So his death was really hard on all of us. He went so suddenly and there was so much left to do. We were working on so many projects and it felt like the company was just starting to take off. We were finally getting to where he wanted to be. He wanted to make the Tortured Path. We were growing—we did 4,000 tree grafts in one summer. We planted those in 2016 and Grant never really got to see the fruit of it all. We felt very rudderless, Jen and I both. I said, "Let's stop." And she said, "People rely on us to pay their bills, to pay their mortgages. People have careers. We don't have that luxury. Let's work one day at a time. Tomorrow, you go and make ice cider. I'll go do this." And that's what we did. I was convinced we couldn't go on.

I'm proud of the trees—the trees I've grown and planted and hand grafted, bud grafted. There are trees I literally created. Grant showed me how to do that.

People have a personal relationship with our brand. The brand exists outside us, and we've built the brand up to a point that it will outlive us all. People are loyal to us and the memory they have of this place and our quality. It's about making cider out of the apples that we grow, that we've pruned, that we've trained. Having someone in Ottawa who knows nothing about us and thinks that this is the best cider they've ever had. That's what it's all about.

Cider is much more like making wine than making beer. You're following the terroir. The soil conditions, the sun conditions, the heat units that year, the weather patterns—those are going to affect your product. When you're making beer, you're buying grain from all over. It doesn't have a place that it's necessarily from; it doesn't have a terroir. That's a big difference.

This is Grant's recipe for making cider:

> These ciders, the truly magnificent ones, were all made by people who grow their own apples, tend their orchards, pick, select, blend, and make their ciders where they live. It is a commitment bordering on religious zeal. Greatness can only be achieved by knowing the characteristics and nuances of the underlying apple varieties, how these apples are affected by yearly changes in weather patterns, and, if you are very lucky, perhaps 30 years of trying to get it right.

Grant was chasing this—I think that's a recipe he was chasing. This dragon, I really see it now. He was trying to find this ultimate cider, make this ultimate cider, which is the Tortured Path. He chased the dragon to get this perfect cider. Every time I go down to Grant's gravesite, someone has left something—they'll leave a bottle, they'll leave an apple. I don't know who they are. Jen doesn't necessarily know. There's a legacy there, and whoever these people are, they're carrying it on.

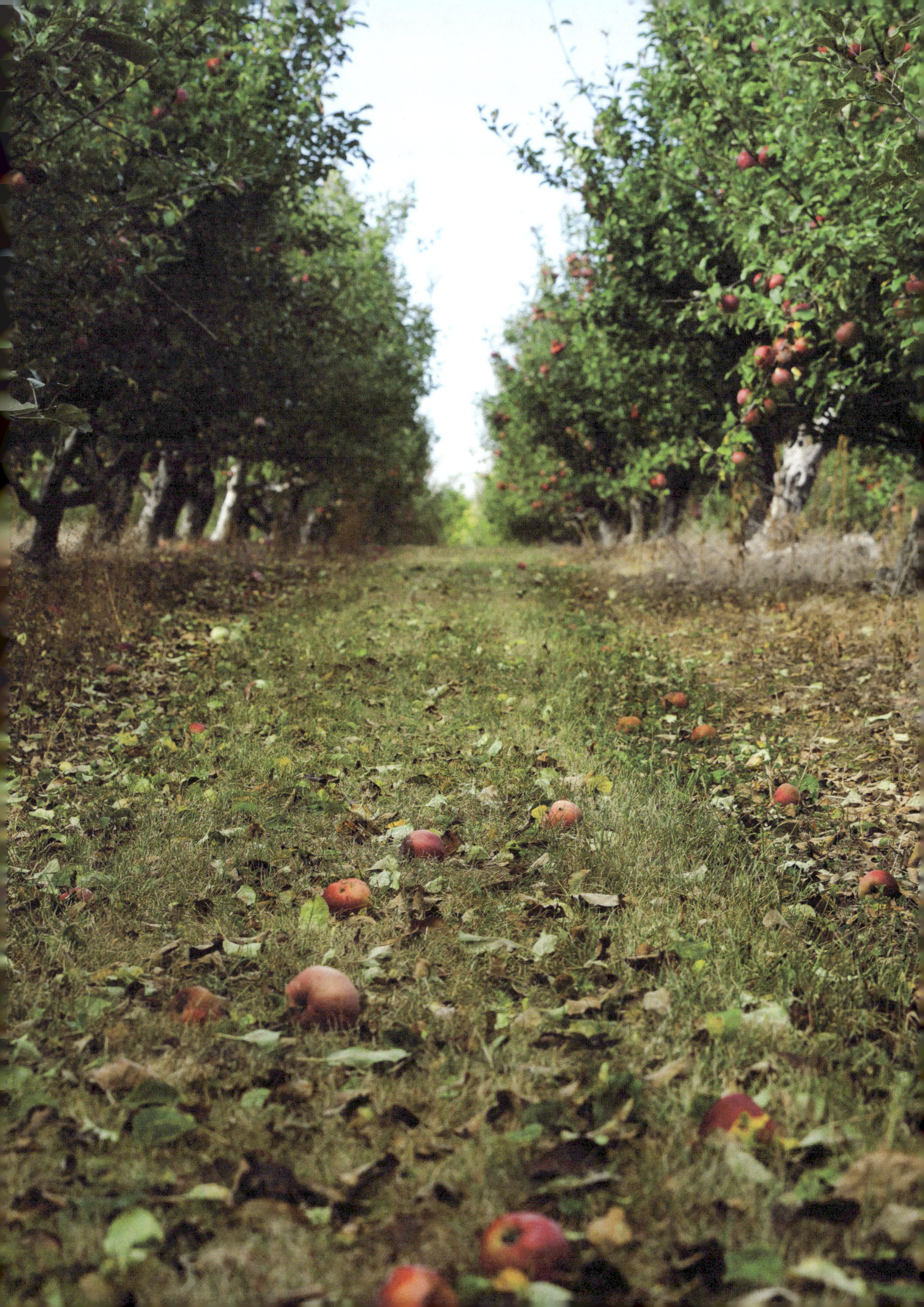

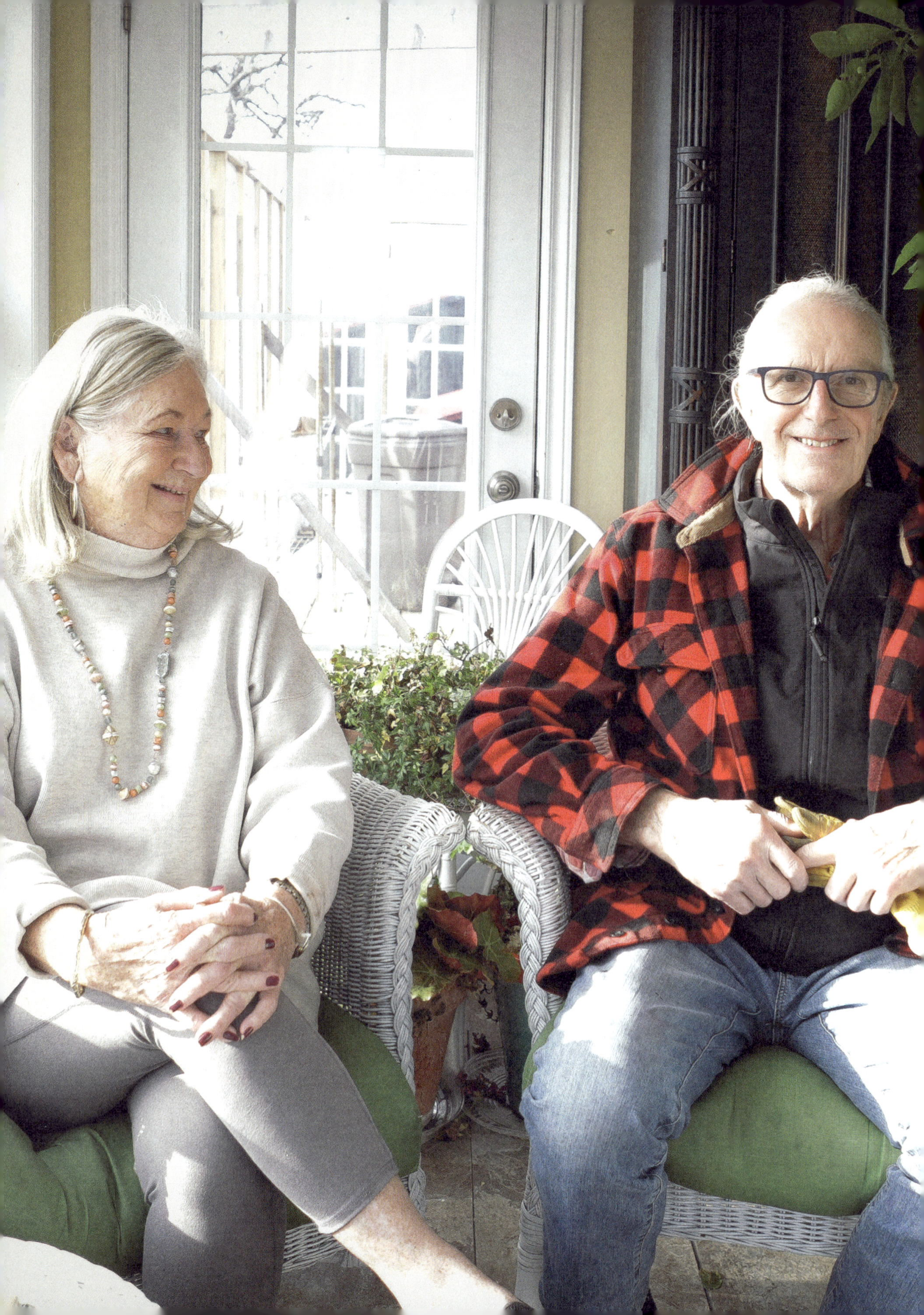

Domaine Darius, Bloomfield

A small-batch winery that respects the terroir and uses gentle winemaking techniques, with a focus on Pinot Noir, Gewürztraminer, Chardonnay, Marquette, and Frontenac Blanc.

DAVE GILLINGHAM, JONI GILLINGHAM

Joni: David said to me one day that we should buy a piece of land in Prince Edward County and we could grow an acre of grapes just for ourselves. I said, "Well, David, do you really want to do that?" He said we could put a little house on the property, and we could come up and have our own place and still hang out with Richard and Sherry Karlo, who were close friends. So I agreed to the one acre of grapes. I loved the County but didn't have any desire to live here. But weekends sounded okay. When we bought the land, Richard and Sherry walked it with us. We tramped up through the forest. There was old rusted tractor equipment everywhere, and the grass was so long that you'd walk on something and God knows if you'd get your leg back out. The courtyard you see today was full of old tin and garbage, and it was just horrible down there. It looks a lot better now.

We had no place to live, so we bought a 10-by-20-foot carport and we put it under the tree out there. David put a plastic floor on it and we bought a blow-up double bed. We kept two plastic containers on either side of the bed to house our clothes, to keep the mould and mice out. Neighbours across the street from us in Pickering threw out a vanity, and we gathered that up and put it in our truck. Then we found an Ikea table with a broken leg, so we gathered that up too and we started to decorate our plastic house. Sherry lent me a little fridge and David hooked it up to a solar panel for electricity. That's how we lived up here; we'd come every weekend and we'd live in the plastic house. We planted the grapes, took care of them, had a little veggie garden. I think it was four degrees the last time we slept in the plastic house; it was so cold that we bought an electric blanket, and of course we had no plugs. David hooked it up to a car battery, which got electricity from the solar panel, to keep us warm. I remember thinking, "Am I going to get electrocuted in this bed?"

Dave: We learned about Prince Edward County from Dan Sullivan right after we moved back from China, and of course we knew Richard and Sherry. This was going to be a cottage, an escape from the city, a bit of property to grow a few grapes. I've been making wine since 1978. Back in the day, I would rely heavily on other members of the Pickering Wine Guild for advice and criticism, to help me figure out what was going on here, what the problem was with this wine, what I should do.

I guess maybe in the back of my mind, I thought we would have a winery someday, a small winery. I've always had a chip on my shoulder about the Ontario government and the way wineries are run in Canada. My vision was that if I could plant an acre and I could sell 10 cases of wine a year, it'd be a bit of fun. In Europe, you can have a row of grapes and you can sell your own wine made from it. But in Ontario, you have to plant a minimum of five acres, and you have to have this license and that license, you have to have all this stuff. But vision aside, one thing led to another, and that's basically how we got here.

We planted one acre in the front and one acre in the back, way too much for personal consumption, and I didn't want to sell the grapes. It's not much fun if you don't carry through the whole process, in my opinion. We planted the first acre in 2008 and we planted the second acre in 2009. We didn't plant anything in 2010; that was basically the decision point of going for a winery. In 2011, we planted a total of five acres. We opened in 2014.

We started with mostly Pinot Noir and Chardonnay. I also planted Gewürztraminer because it's my favourite white wine. I have a couple of hybrids: Marquette, Petite Pearl, and Frontenac Blanc. If I just made Pinot or Chardonnay, I'd drive myself crazy, so I make 14 or 15 variations of the different wines.

Joni: Our son, Andrew, designed our labels, and it took some time for him to get them done. When they were ready, David and I looked at them, and David said, "I don't know if this is what I want, Andrew." Andrew replied, "Well, Dad, this is what you're getting."

I told Andrew that I didn't really like them. His response: "I don't have time. This is what you're getting. They're beautiful. You'll fall in love with them." I said, "Do you do this to your clients, Andrew?" And he said, "The client isn't always right." I hate to eat crow, but we get so many people, especially people in the art world, saying how amazing our labels are. People shoot pictures of those labels constantly. I remember Battista saying to Dave, "I don't know about those labels," and Dave said, "Well, Andrew won't make any more. I need labels to put on the bottles, so that's it."

All our sales come directly from the winery; we are as small as we can be and we like it that way. Dave and I are very blessed because we have no financial backers and we have no partners. Darius belongs to us, and we get to do what we want to do. For us, it was about building a place. It was was my dream to build the gardens so people could come and relax. I'm proud of the whole thing, because of how well two people could build something like this by themselves.

DOMAINE DARIUS | DAVID'S
CUVeE
DOMAINE DARIUS
CHARDONNAY
DOMAINE DARIUS
PINOT

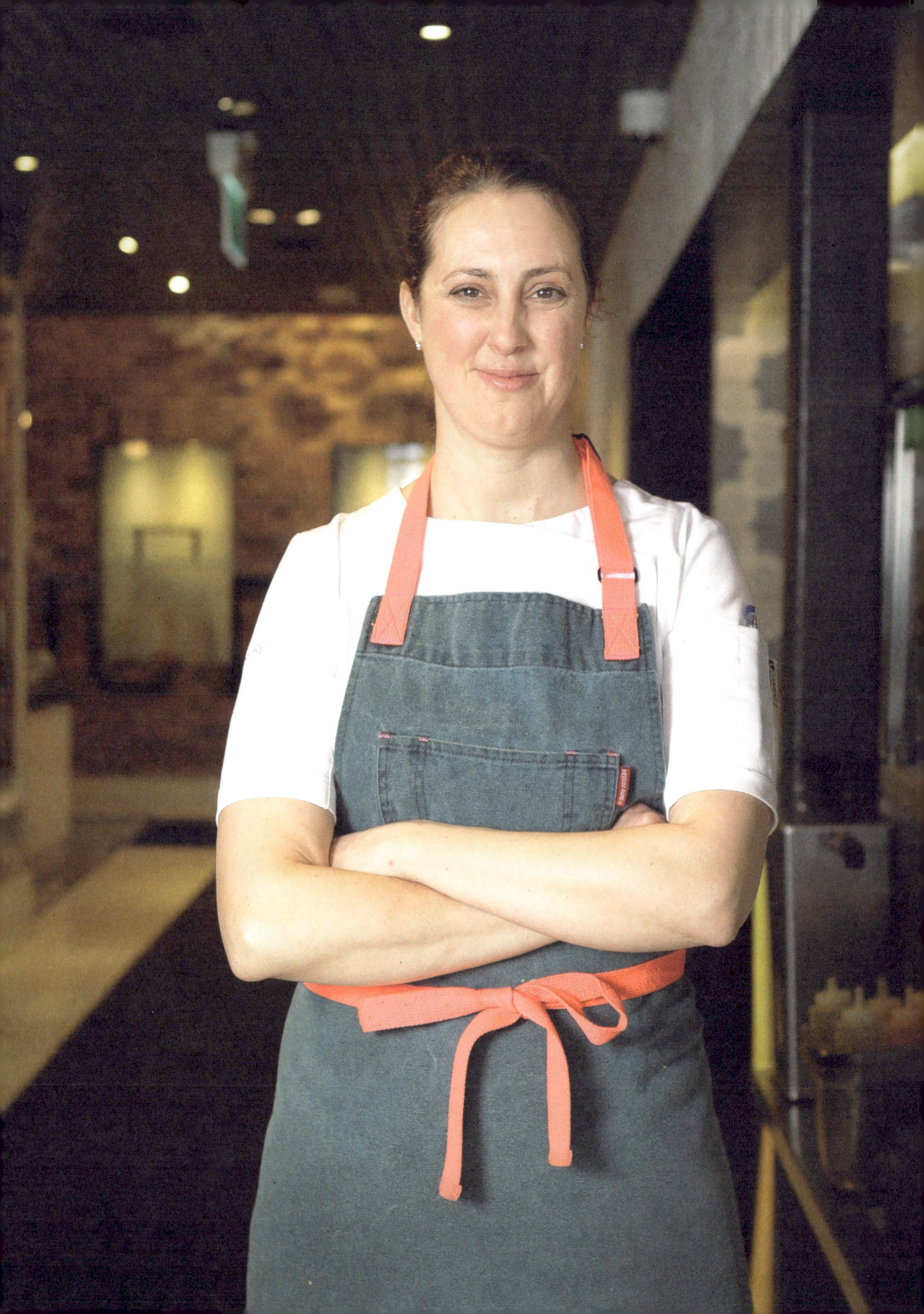

Drake Devonshire's Burrata, Heirloom Tomato, and Peach Salad with Sourdough Toast

The younger sibling of the famous Toronto hotel, the Drake Devonshire is a lakeside hotel, restaurant, bar, and event space in Wellington.

AMANDA RAY, EXECUTIVE CHEF

This summer-ripened recipe comes together with access to so many great County tomato growers, accented with amazing local burrata cheese and some outstanding sourdough from bakery friends. Seasonally inspired, other versions have included a fresh salsa verde with crispy kale, torched snow peas, pickled kohlrabi, and puffed sorghum for spring. Walking the fields with farmers who are continuously passionate is an invigorating part of the County's culinary community. The unique and unexpected pairing of peaches and truffles, which I showcase here, comes from my adventures in France.

Prep time: 15 minutes
Cooking time: 10 minutes
Servings: 4

Ingredients

Salad
2 200 g balls premium-brand burrata cheese
3 firm, ripe peaches
4 slices sourdough bread, 1¼–1½" thick
3 tbsp extra virgin olive oil, divided
3 assorted local heirloom tomatoes (various shapes, colours, and sizes, about 1 lb)
pinch Maldon sea salt
¼ bunch each Italian parsley, tarragon, and basil (about 1 cup total)
4 leaves frisée lettuce (or other baby lettuce), torn
½ cup truffle balsamic vinaigrette
edible flower petals and microgreen sprouts, to garnish (optional)

Truffle balsamic vinaigrette
½ cup plus 1 tbsp balsamic vinegar
¼ cup sherry vinegar
3 tbsp shallot, finely diced
1 tbsp plus 1 tsp truffle paste
2 tsp truffle oil

1¾ cups extra virgin olive oil
2 tsp kosher salt
1 tsp freshly ground black pepper

Method

Vinaigrette
In a medium bowl, whisk together the balsamic and sherry vinegars, shallot, and truffle paste. Gradually whisk in the truffle and olive oils until well blended and slightly thickened; season with salt and pepper. Vinaigrette can be made ahead and refrigerated for up to 3 weeks. Makes about 2½ cups.

Salad
Bring burrata to room temperature for 1 hour. Drain liquid just before using; set on a paper towel to remove excess moisture.

Cut peaches in half and discard pits; cut each half into 4 pieces. Drizzle lightly with 1 tbsp olive oil. Preheat grill to medium-high heat. Grill peaches for 1–2 minutes on each side, until lightly charred (or quickly sear in a hot frying pan). Set aside.

Add the remaining 2 tbsp olive oil to a large frying pan over medium heat; fry bread slices on both sides until toasted and light golden. Set aside.

Cut tomatoes into various shapes and sizes, like slices, wedges, and chunks. Wash and dry herbs, removing stems; toss together in a small bowl with the frisée.

Assembly
Place one slice of toast in the centre of 4 serving plates. Gently slice or tear burrata balls into halves; place one half on the centre of each toast.

Arrange tomatoes around each plated burrata; season with Maldon sea salt. Divide peaches between each plate. Drizzle each plate evenly with truffle balsamic vinaigrette; reserve the remainder for another use.

Top each burrata with a cascade of the frisée and herb mixture, and garnish with edible flowers and microgreen sprouts. Serve immediately.

Chef's Notes
It's important not to season the tomatoes with salt until just before serving so that the tomatoes don't purge their juices.

Drink Pairings
Fruit notes balance with the peaches here and the bright freshness cleans your palate for the decadent cheese: Morandin Pinot Gris 2022, Matron Bobo Farmhouse Ale.

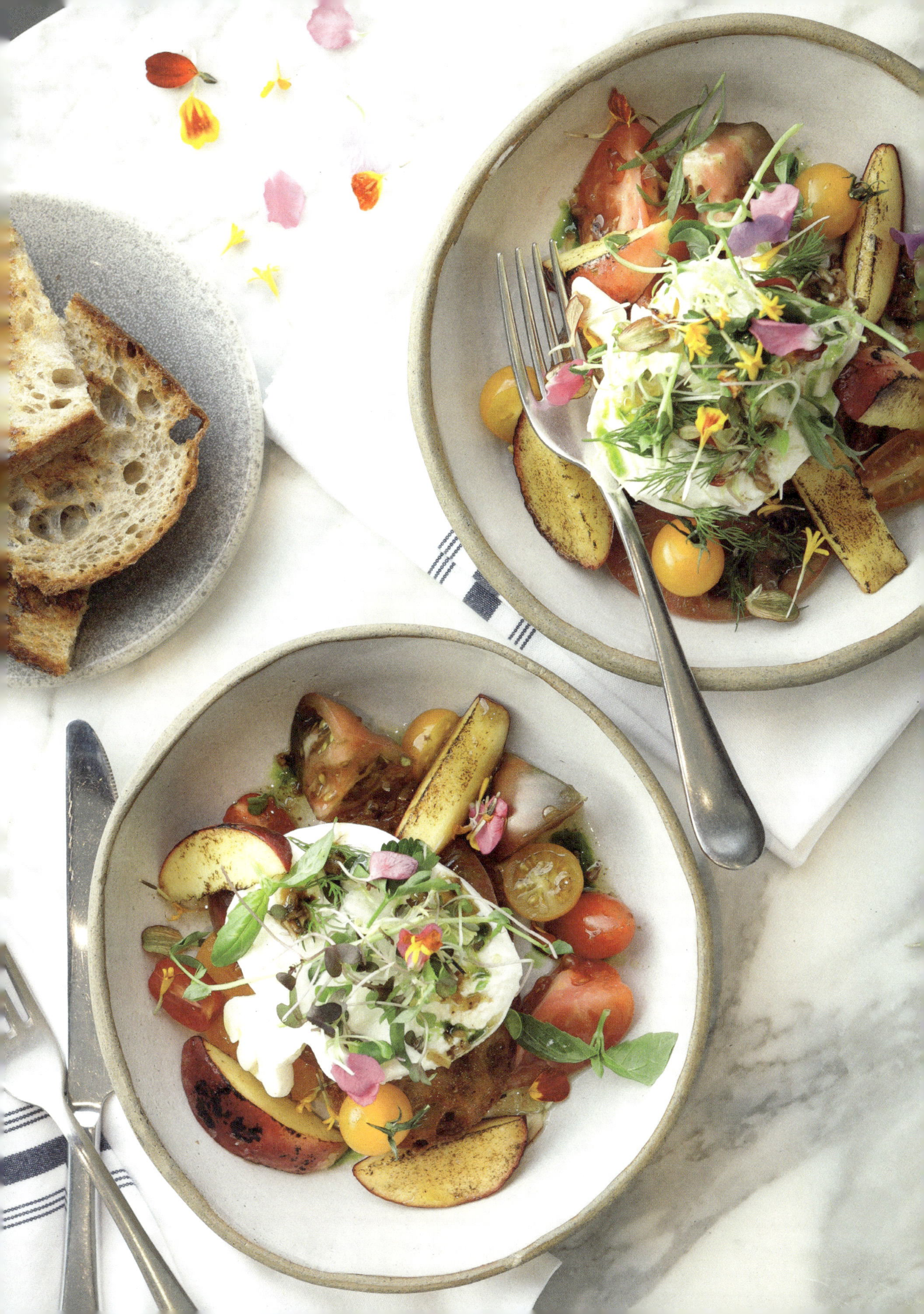

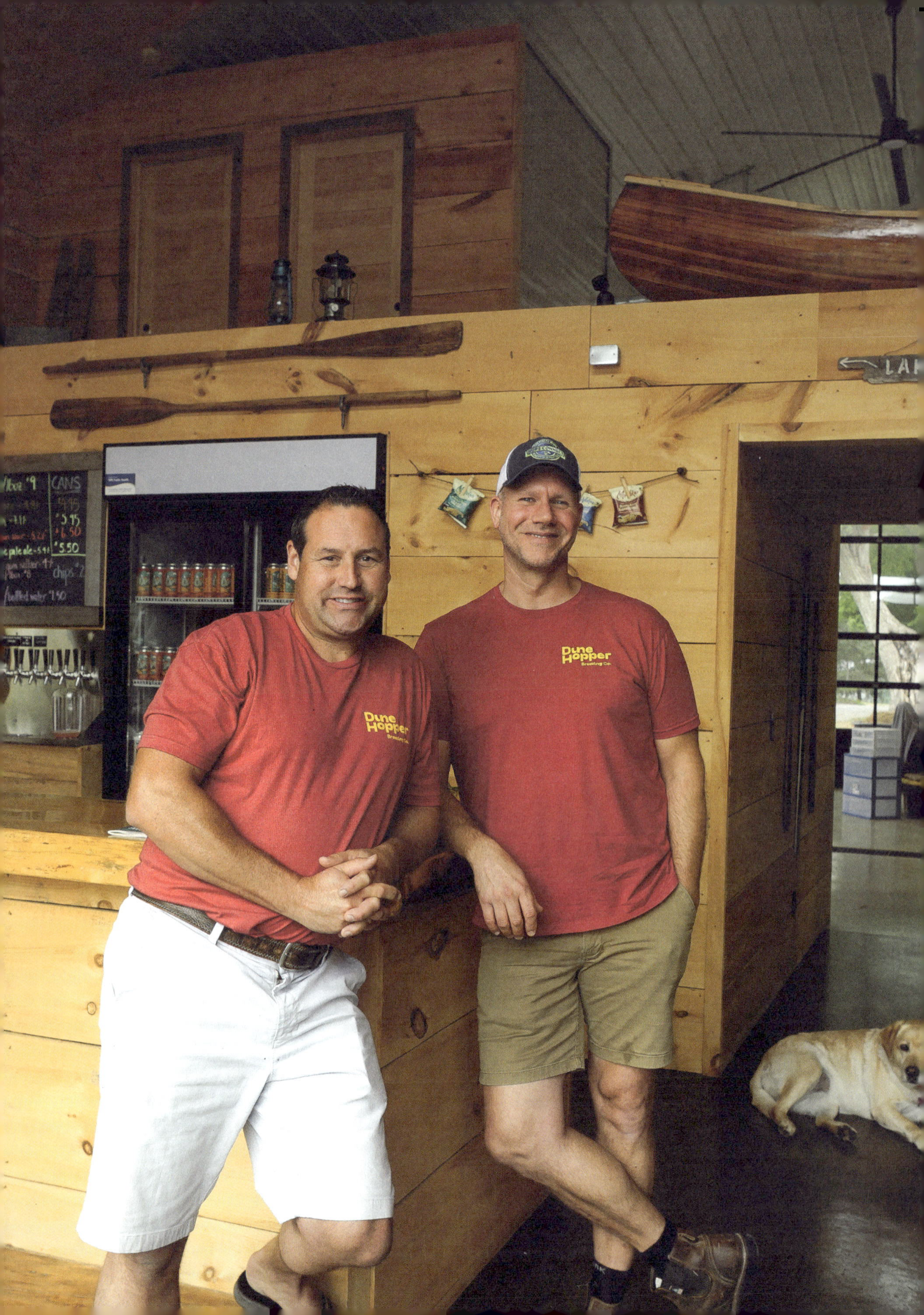
Dune Hopper
Brewing Co.
Dune Hopper
Brewing Co.

Dune Hopper Brewing Company, Bloomfield

Dune Hopper is a provincial park-themed brewery located near Sandbanks that has become a gathering spot for West Lake locals.

GREG EMM, COLIN VANDERMEULEN

Colin: I had a job working in corporate purchasing in the automotive industry, and I got to travel a lot, especially around the US. I also went to Korea, India, a few other places. In the US, in the early 2000s, craft beer was starting to take off. I'd be down in Virginia, Illinois, Ohio, and I remember having beer down there that was totally different than Labatt Blue. It tasted amazing. Then I'd come back here to Ontario and craft beer at that time was IPAs that tasted like pure bitterness, nothing else. So I thought, well, I can't get the US beer here, so I'm going to try making it.

The first thing I did was dump a bag of concentrate in a pot, mix it with some water, bring it to a boil, and then throw it in a bucket and add some yeast. I had no idea what I was doing. I mean, I was stirring this stuff while it was fermenting and it turned out drinkable, but not good. But I had fun, so I just kept doing it. And I think by my third or fourth brew, I was building the cooler mash tun. I entered a lot of homebrew competitions and did pretty well; I took Best of Show with a pumpkin beer at the very first fermentation festival at the Crystal Palace in Picton.

My first brewing job was at Signal in Belleville. Part of the reason I took the job is that I'd been thinking for a couple of years about opening my own brew pub one day. And then the owner at Signal messaged me out of the blue, asking me to come out for lunch. I did, and he offered me a job in the brewery. I thought about it for a couple of days, and I decided it was a perfect opportunity to learn how to brew on a professional scale and basically get a paid education in how to run a brewery. By then I knew Greg wanted to open a place too and it all just kind of worked out.

Greg: I knew this is what I wanted to do with my property and I was looking for a partner. A colleague of mine at the Belleville Fire Hall—Ryan Turcotte of All My Friends—and I started talking and it turned out we both wanted to do the same thing. He was partnering with Bill and Rob to open up a brewery. So Ryan introduced me to Colin, because Colin makes amazing beer. That was in 2020. I started chatting with Colin, because I didn't know what the hell I was doing with making craft beer. I bought a small Spike system and Colin came and helped me out. I used to pick his brain—I'd ask things like what kind of malt he was using.

My dad owned a pub in London, England, one of the Red Lions. So he loves beer—he especially loves Colin's stout. My British grandmother, my dad's mom, she worked in the pub in England, and when she came to Canada, she started home brewing. It was horrible, but she drank it anyway. I still have some of her equipment. That's why I first thought I wanted to do this one day.

Colin: I started brewing at Dune Hopper in late July 2023. I don't remember the exact date, but I do remember that the very first time I fired up the brew system, six or seven other brewers came to hang out. It was great. I was trying to use this whole brand-new system I'd never brewed on before. And there was Nick and Greg from Slake, Rob and Bill from All My Friends. The first beer I brewed was Tent Pitcher, my lager. I figured it would take the longest, so I did it first.

In transitioning from home brewing to commercial brewing, the concepts are the same. Learning how to operate pumps and purge a tank and do all that was the biggest adjustment. With the system we have, I could keep up with a fair bit. But I also know that as soon as we empty a tank, we have to fill it.

I'm not looking at the LCBO. I've dealt with the LCBO in the past, and while it's a good sales outlet, they take a good chunk of money. And being so small, we can't compete with the pricing of bigger breweries.

Greg: The brewery is on the footprint of an old barn. September 1, 2023, was our official opening. Everything was last minute—the last coat of shellac on the bar, hanging up the lights. What's actually been a big deal for me is the response from the local community. It's been amazing—we actually have regulars now. We want to be a family-friendly place. Bring your dog, play outdoor lawn games. If the kids are happy, I think the adults will be happy. Hopefully they'll stay and enjoy it. We want to keep building on what we have, to be the place for the community to come and watch a hockey game. Beer is a social beverage.

HOPS CONNECT
YOUR PARTNER IN CRAFT
Tito's
Handmade
TEXAS
6-1.75L
BOTTLES
10.5 LITERS

Dune Hopper Brewing Co.

COME ON IN!

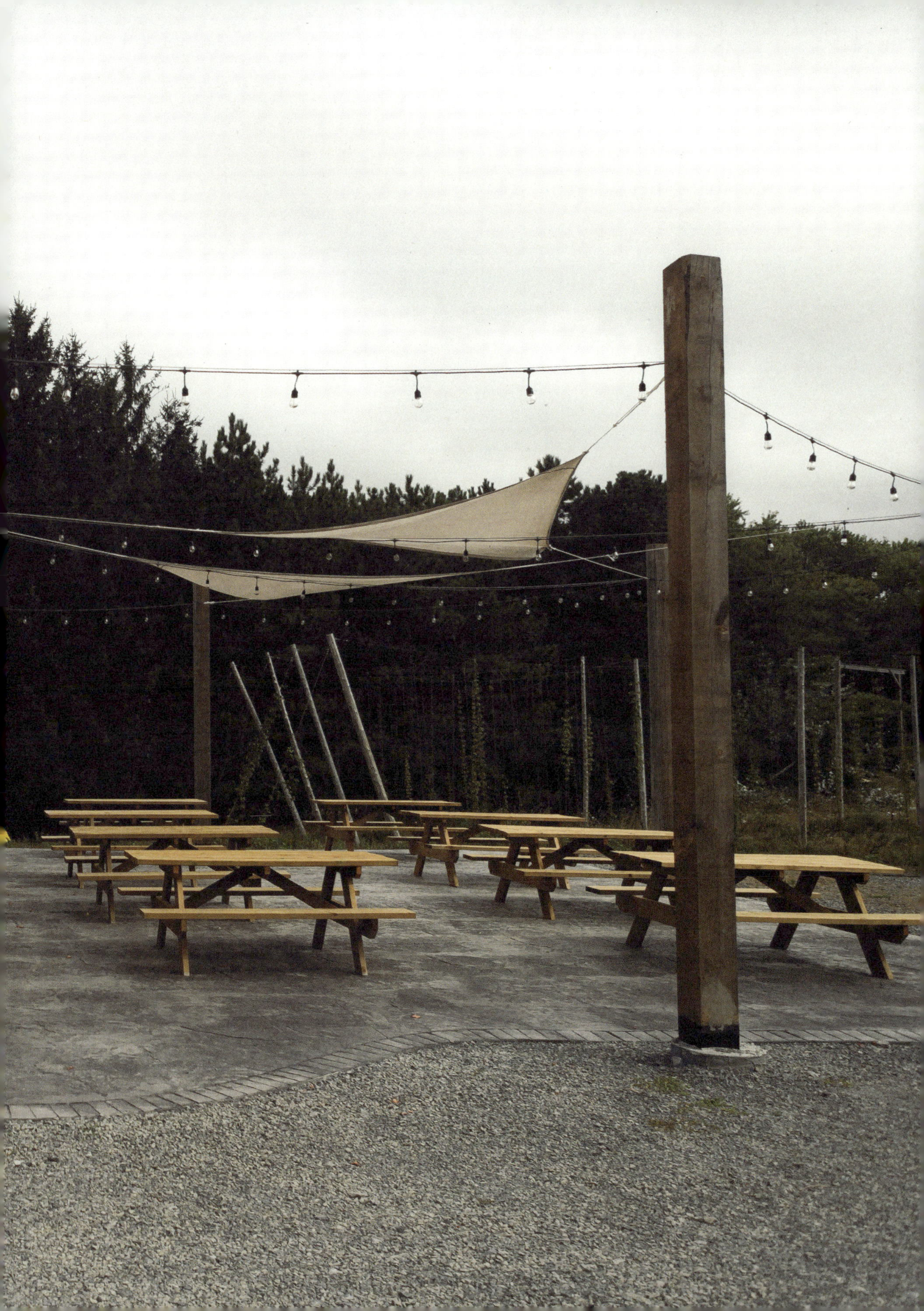

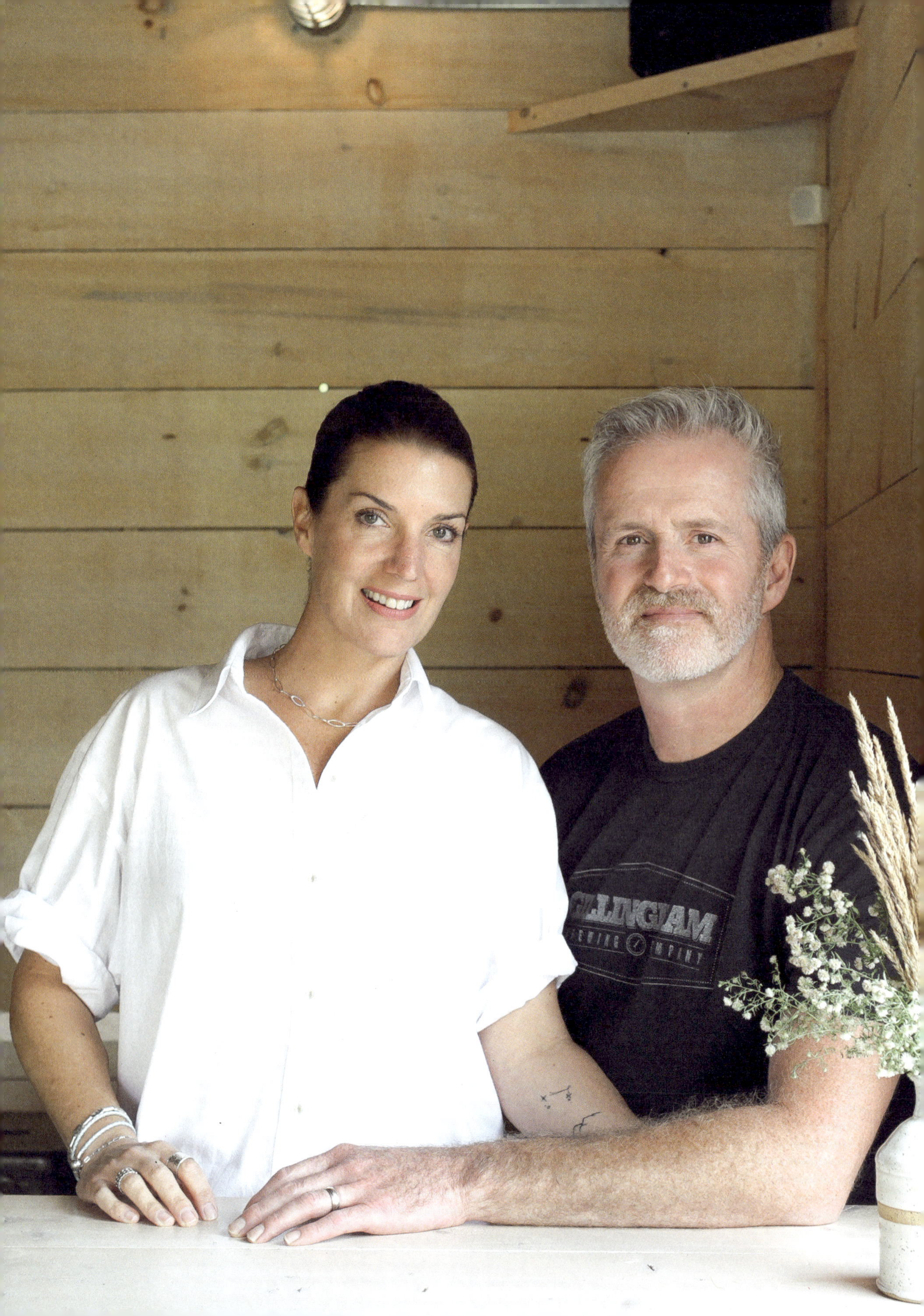

Gillingham Brewing Company, Bloomfield

Gillingham Brewing is a multi-award-winning brewery that offers a social taproom and beer garden with rotating taps featuring brew styles inspired from all over the world.

ANDREW GILLINGHAM, CHRISTINE GILLINGHAM

Andrew: When I first got into beer, the only craft breweries were Brick or Amsterdam. The Granite existed, but it was a brew pub. I was buying European beers at the LCBO, which was really expensive, and I decided it couldn't be too hard to make, so I'd try to make beer and save some money. I was reading a popular science magazine at the time about people building at-home brewing systems—three-vessel brew houses, heated RIMS systems, the whole bit. I figured I could build my own, so I started, and it took me about a year and a half. I built a three-vessel, 10-gallon brew rig in our house. I didn't know what I was doing at all. My first batch of beer almost took the paint off the walls.

Christine: Andrew's a bit of a mad scientist; he's always concocting something or creating something or building something. When he intially started brewing, it was in my kitchen, and I lost all my pots to beer. And then it got to a point where we were like, okay, no, go and find a new space and buy your own equipment.

Andrew: I worked in advertising, and I enjoyed my creative work and loved my career, but I knew I couldn't do it forever. I was really passionate about making beer and I was committed to learning about the process and mastering it. It takes a long time to make a beer that's actually drinkable. But every now and then, I'd make one and I'd think, wow, that actually tastes like something I might buy off the shelf. Back then, there were only two or three books you could read to learn what to do. The rest of it was trial and error, and sometimes my beer tasted like Band-Aids and I just wrecked everything. I think that's a good way to learn how to make beer, because you run through all the problems, you do everything the wrong way at least once, and you come to realize what you need to do to move forward. My dad is a wine and cider judge, so he's got a sophisticated palate. He helped me identify tastes and flavours early on. And still to this day, if I'm not sure about something, I'll let him try it to get his input. Christine's always in the mix too; she's also got a great palate.

Christine: When Andrew started making beer, he was very much inspired by his dad's knowledge and his success. Before they opened Domaine Darius, Dave made wine at his house in Pickering. We used to visit on Sundays and his dad would be old-fashioned pressing his grapes, filling his carboys, making his own wine. His entire basement was taken over by the winemaking process. It became my favourite room in the house. We'd go there hoping to grab a straw and sit in his cellar room and have our own little party. It was so much fun, and a lot of inspiration came out of that. Conversations around making alcohol

IPA
ESB • ALE
LAGER • PORTER

ILLINGHAM
BREWING
CREATIVELY BREWED. SPONTANEOUSLY CRAFTED.

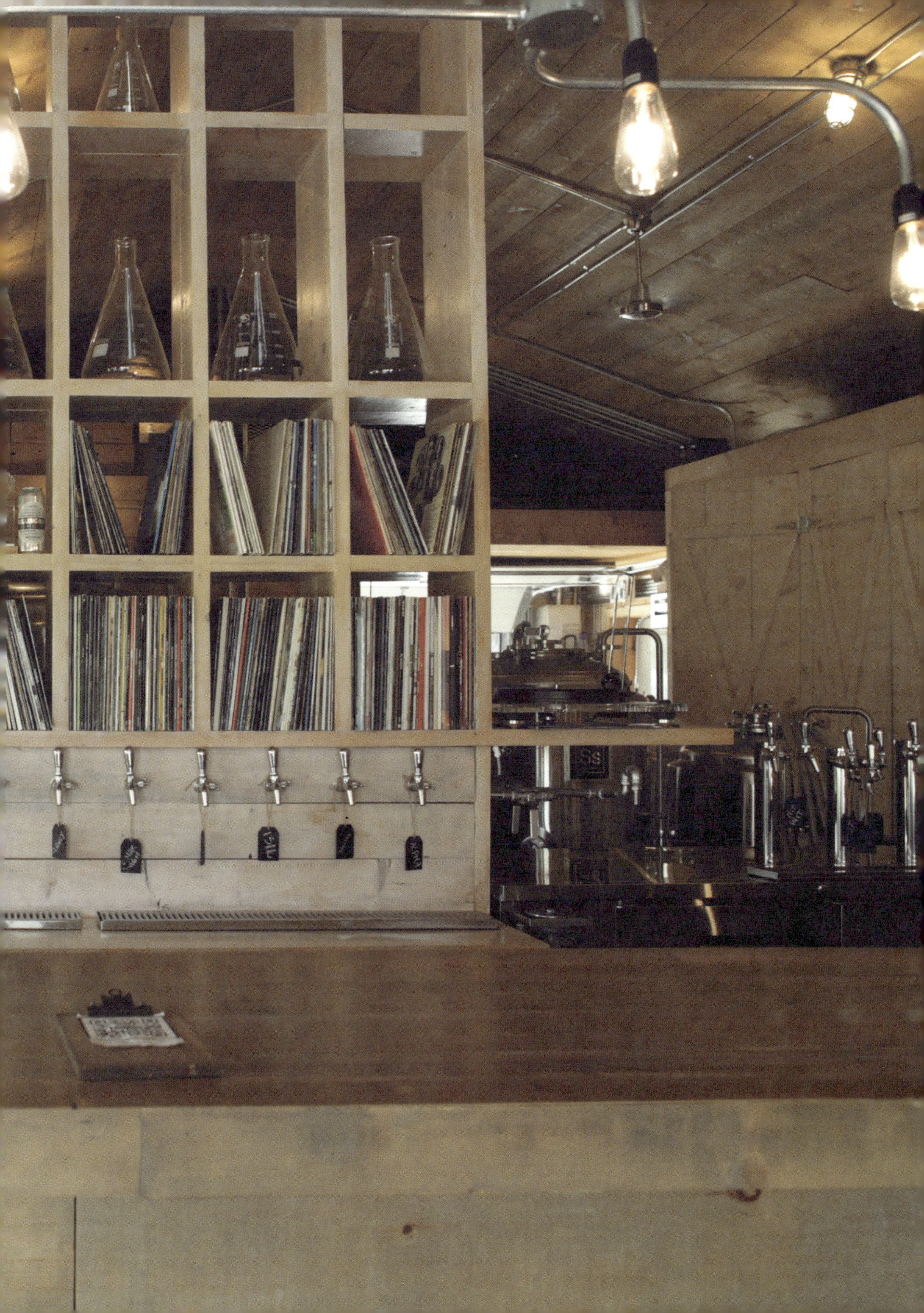

brought Andrew and his dad a lot closer; it was another hobby they could share. Andrew always looks to his dad for inspiration and support, and I admire their relationship.

For a brief point, we thought we might try to open a brewery in Toronto. Our careers were similar—we met when we were both working at the same ad agency. I moved on to work in marketing, and my last job was at Canada Post leading the ecommerce marketing team. I used to travel a lot with my job, and I was already missing a lot of time with family. Our daughter was under 10 and she was growing up so fast. Time was precious and I was missing it. Andrew was trying to manage his full-time job and being Mr. Mom at the same time. I got off a Porter flight one night, and I remember it clearly like it was yesterday. I got in a cab and texted Andrew: *Pour me the biggest glass of wine. Let's sit out in the backyard.* And we sat on our back porch, and I said, "There's got to be a plan B. I don't know if I want to keep doing this anymore." I don't know if it was a mid-life crisis, but I looked at Andrew's passion for brewing and saw how much he was evolving. I mean, every conversation was about beer and making it, and he was trying to do the best he could. So I was like, hey, we could do something with this. I've been in marketing for over 20 years. With our skill sets and his brewing talent, we could become business owners. We could take a leap of faith. So we did.

Andrew: We're super fortunate. My parents own the property the brewery is on. We've got over 50 acres of farmland, and honestly, it's pretty spectacular. You'll notice one thing, though: The brewery's here and the winery is way back there. That's a stipulation. My parents said, "The brewery cannot be close to the winery in case your beer's horrible." We did think about buying another property, but eventually, we'll get a little bit more involved with the winery. What that looks like, we still don't know. I mean, that's definitely the succession plan, which we're really excited about pursuing when the time comes.

Christine: Our businesses are separate operations, but it's wonderful to be on the same property and to have both wine and beer in the family. We've been coming here to visit Andrew's parents since they moved here full-time. This was farmland when they bought it. They did everything themselves. Built everything, planted their vineyards, built the beautiful gardens. They're so talented and extremely hard-working, both of them.

We opened in May 2019. It was all trial and error back then. Our first year in business was us just really trying to figure out how to settle into the County, understand the business needs, and work out the kinks. Transitioning from corporate careers to entrepreneurship isn't easy. And then the following year we were like, okay, we're excited, I think we're in for a good year. And then the Covid-19 pandemic hit.

Covid was good for us, from a business point of view. We built a patio, which fast-forwarded our business plan by a couple of years. We launched our website, and we tried to capitalize on as much as we could. We were, like everybody, I'm sure, working night and day, trying to figure it out and stay alive.

Andrew: We went through some big growth—we expanded our equipment three times after opening. So our biggest thing now is adjusting to the demand for what we can make.

Christine: We never really get a day off, and even when we're away on holiday, we're still thinking about the business: how we can improve, what we need to achieve to grow, how we can provide memorable experiences for our guests.

Right now, we're small, but we're growing, which means we're both really involved in every little detail. We're so fortunate to have the staff that we do every year; in peak season there's seven of us in total, and they all bring something to the table. We really do work as a team. This brewery is everything to us and we have no plans to stop now. Full throttle ahead!

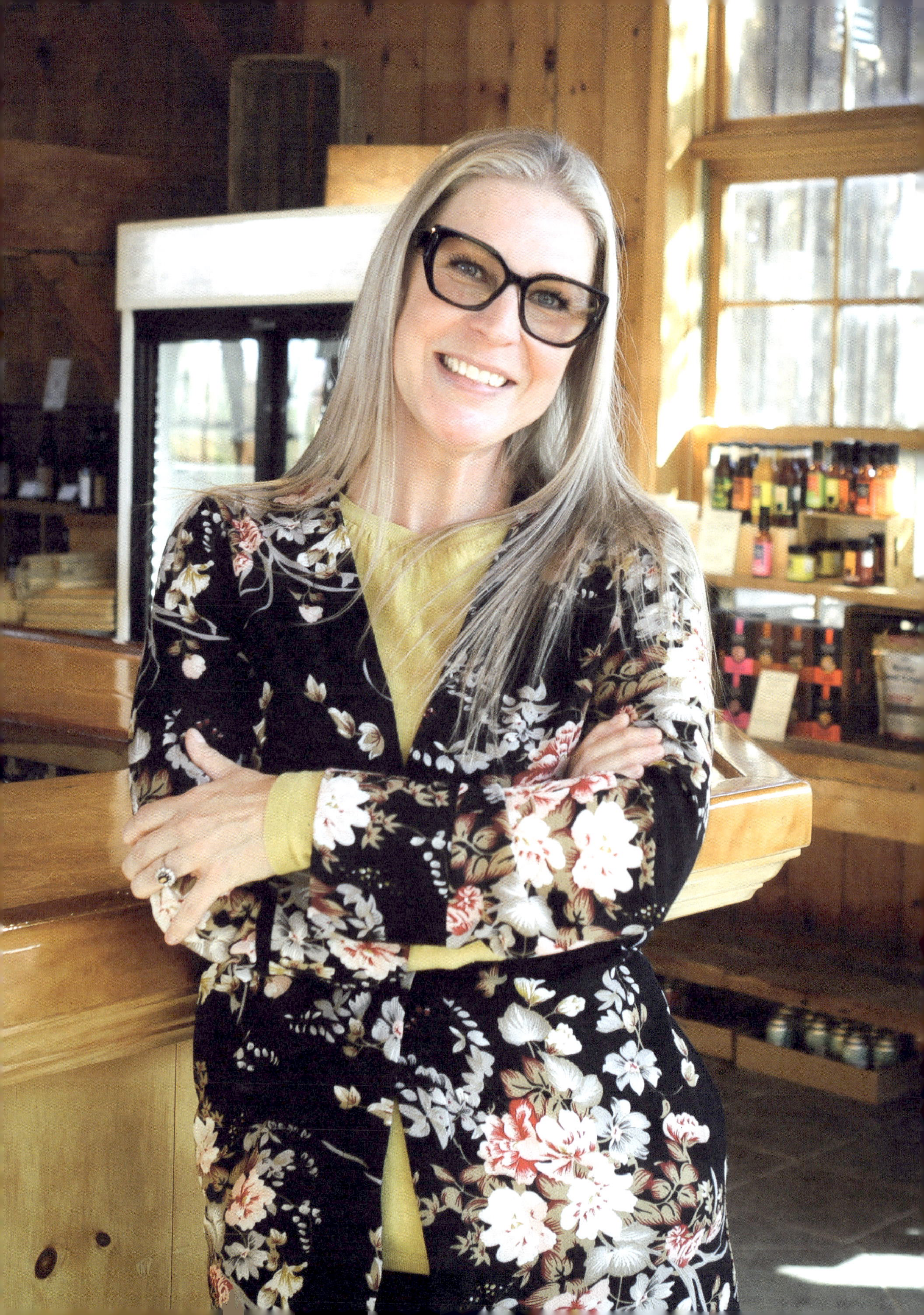

The Grange of Prince Edward, Hillier

With some of the oldest, most extensive vineyards in PEC, The Grange is recognized for making low-intervention, terroir-driven wine.

MARLISE PONZO

In high school, I majored in dance at the Etobicoke School of the Arts, and I auditioned for and got into a professional dance company, the Canadian Children's Dance Theater (now the Canadian Contemporary Dance Theatre). Dance was literally my life.

For a year after high school, I studied photography, film, and media arts, but I didn't love it. It just wasn't my heart. I dropped out of university, went to New York, and did an intensive at the Martha Graham School. I would push myself and push myself when training. I'm a perfectionist. Some of it is just intrinsically me wanting to do really good work and work really hard. Eventually, I went back to school for fashion design. I did an internship before graduating at Wayne Clark. Wayne found out I'd studied photography, so I started photographing all his designs for his seasonal lookbooks. He got me a few other photography gigs with an ad agency his friend ran.

I also worked in restaurants and bars—you had to make a living while you were doing all the other things. I worked my way up the managerial chain very quickly within restaurants in Toronto's theatre district: the Red Tomato, Fred's Not Here, and the Whistling Oyster among them. I went to Crush Wine Bar on King Street when it first opened. I remember sitting in those high tops in the front window, and I was just blown away by the space. There was nothing really like it in that area at the time. It was one of the first wine bars, if not the first. I was sitting in the window enjoying a great bottle of Brunello when the sommelier, Eric Gennaro, came over. As we chatted, he called me out that we had been friends growing up at Pine River Camp; we shared some good laughs. I soon dropped off a résumé, went for an interview with the owner, Jamieson Kerr, and then I worked there for eight years.

I didn't know much about wine. My mom is Buddhist, so she doesn't drink at all. But my grandfather made wine, so I tasted it a lot when I was younger. My grandfather always laughed about giving me my love of wine because he'd have it gurgling in carboys in the basement—and once I might have tried a few of the carboys before they were ready to be exposed to air. I also learned a ton about wine from Eric. He paid such attention to detail: the region, the producer, the terroir, the label artwork. And he really loved passing that on. Crush paid for half of my sommelier certification and my grandfather paid for the other half.

Albert started working at Crush around the same time as me. He'd studied jazz music at Humber College and had no formal experience in a kitchen, but he was falling deeply in love with all things culinary. He started staging for free, then got hired on months later. We were both in different relationships at first but became good friends. And then it started becoming a little bit more. That was kind of it for us. We were in love.

During our years at Crush, we got married, bought our first house in Mimico, and we travelled a huge amount, learning about wine and food. Albert's family is from Rome and Sardinia. Wine is so transportive in the sensory memories of experiencing a wine, even if it's just a jug of an indigenous varietal made by a grandpa and sold on the side of the road. But when you bring it home and drink it alongside a meal from the market, you're creating a memory you can travel back to. I have a really strong olfactory response to things. So for me, wine is a sense of travel—wine is a taste of the soil, of a place, of how the sunshine hit the vine and how the rain fell and how the wind aerated the vineyards.

For one of our first dates, I brought Albert to Sandbanks in my red rusted-out Chevy Cavalier. I packed a picnic from Cheese Boutique with a beautiful bottle of wine from the Maremma. Throughout our relationship, the County kept drawing us back. Albert had a great job at Le Sélect Bistro as the executive chef, and had been there for 11 years, but there was this draw. And then Albert heard from Pina Petricone, of Giannone Petricone Associates; they were working on a beautiful boutique hotel owned by Greg Sorbara that was being restored in PEC, and she thought it would be a great fit for Albert. She set up a meeting with Greg and Sol Korngold, the project manager and GM. Greg invited Albert to cook for his whole family at their house and insisted I attend. So Albert cooked dinner and they asked me lots of questions about our dreams, our hopes for Albert as a chef, about Albert as a person, about myself and our growing family, about wine, about what I love about PEC. It was a wonderful evening. And the next day, Albert got a message from Greg saying everything last night was "simpatico." He said, and I paraphrase: "It's unanimous, we loved you. We loved your wife, we loved the food. So it's a go!"

I got into working with wine here from a production standpoint, and it's now been five years. I manage all the events, which grew from two weddings my first year here to upwards of 35 events this past season. Being able to give people a beautiful experience with great food and authentic wine in this historic, enchanting venue creates a lifelong connection between them and The Grange. I'm also the sales manager, which makes me the point person for our sales team across Ontario with LCBO and licensee accounts, and for our PR company and our social media manager. I also help lead marketing and off-site activations. And, of course, I'm the resident sommelier, writing tasting notes for new releases, technical sheets, and helping with staff education.

I love tasting with the team and absolutely love when I can teach someone something new about wine. When I express what I'm tasting in a wine and perhaps why that's special, and that resonates with someone—that's the best. We've been under new leadership for the past couple of years, and it's breathed a lot of energy and life and investment into the team, the vineyards, and the winemaking program. Jonas Newman is our winemaker as of the 2022 vintage. Michael Leskovec, our president and CEO, is a great leader and is really supportive, which makes it possible for a mom of three with a farm and a husband who works a lot of hours to hold the position I have. Mike Peddlesden is back with the team—he actually did some of the original vine plantings at The Grange in the early 2000s. He has deep County roots, having started Peddlesden Wines (now Casa-Dea), which was one of the first vineyards in the County to plant vinifera. I always want to pick his brain. There's so much passion and excitement and forward thinking, and we push each other and inspire each other. I'm proud to be a part of it.

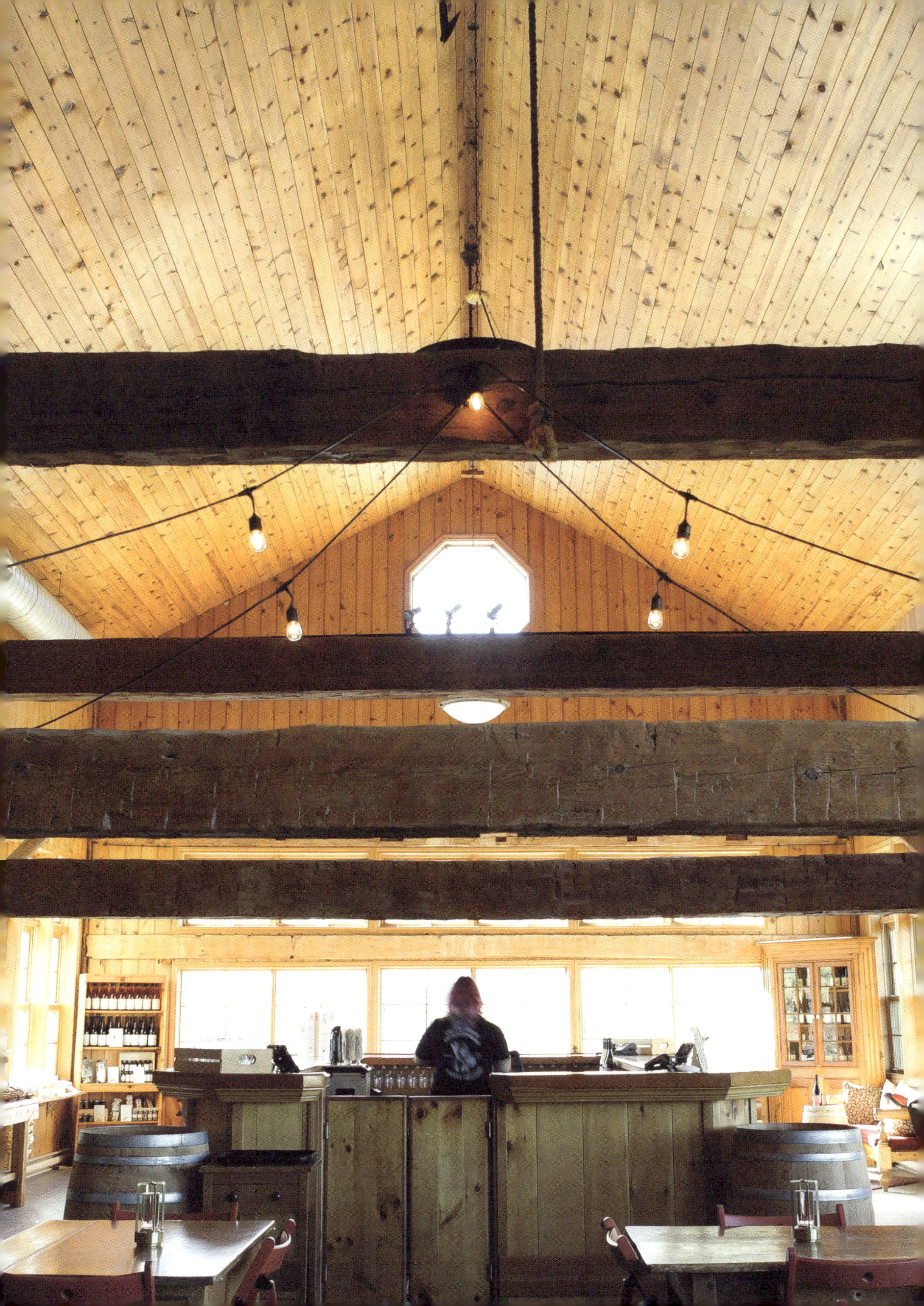

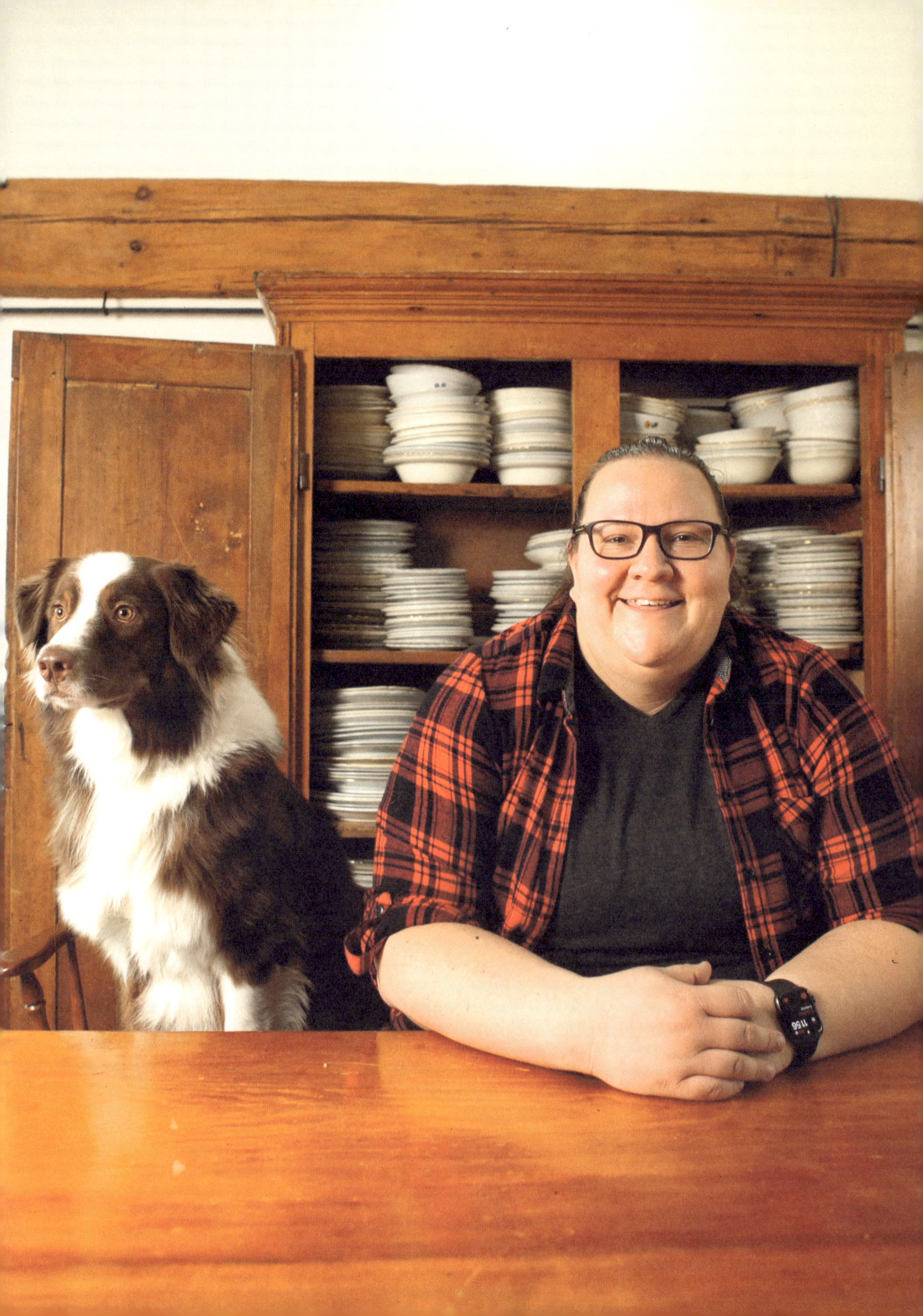

The Grange of Prince Edward's Tomato Fritters with Pesto Aioli

KEIRRA REID, HEAD CHEF

This recipe comes from a time when I worked with a Greek family at their food stall in St. Jacobs Market. I learned so much from them with respect to keeping things fresh and seasonal to enhance the flavours of a dish. I started to appreciate a lot about Greek food and discovered these traditional tomato fritters called tomatokeftedes. They usually have mint, oregano, and are served with tzatziki, but this recipe is my local spin on them.

Tomato season is one of my favourite times of the year, with the local smell of tomatoes on the vines! It also reminds me of one of my first experiences in the County almost eight years ago at the Heirloom Hurrah Tomato Tasting and Vegetable Extravaganza put on by Vicki's Veggies. I'll never forget the opportunity to taste over 100 kinds of tomatoes. It's really a special experience. After moving to Prince Edward County two years ago, I helped create the food program at The Grange of Prince Edward, and I am in the process of creating long-lasting relationships with hard-working local farmers and producers. When tomato season came around, it only made sense to combine my love for Greek cooking and fresh local tomatoes.

Naturally, I put these tomato fritters on the menu and guests loved them. While the prep time does need some patience for the best flavour, it is so worth it to enjoy some of the best produce the County has to offer. Best when paired with a glass of wine and shared with friends on a warm summer evening.

Prep time: 30 minutes (plus up to 2 hours for resting batter)
Cooking time: 6–8 minutes
Servings: 4–6 as an appetizer (makes about 20 fritters)

Ingredients

Fritters
5 cups ripe local tomatoes (or about 2 lbs)
1 tsp salt (plus 1 tsp salt for batter)
1 cup crumbled Lighthall feta (or any other)
1 large red onion (about 1¼ cup), finely diced
¼ cup fresh basil, chopped
½ tbsp fresh oregano, chopped or 1 tsp dried oregano
1⅔ cups all-purpose flour
4 tsp baking powder
½ tsp freshly ground pepper
vegetable oil, for deep frying

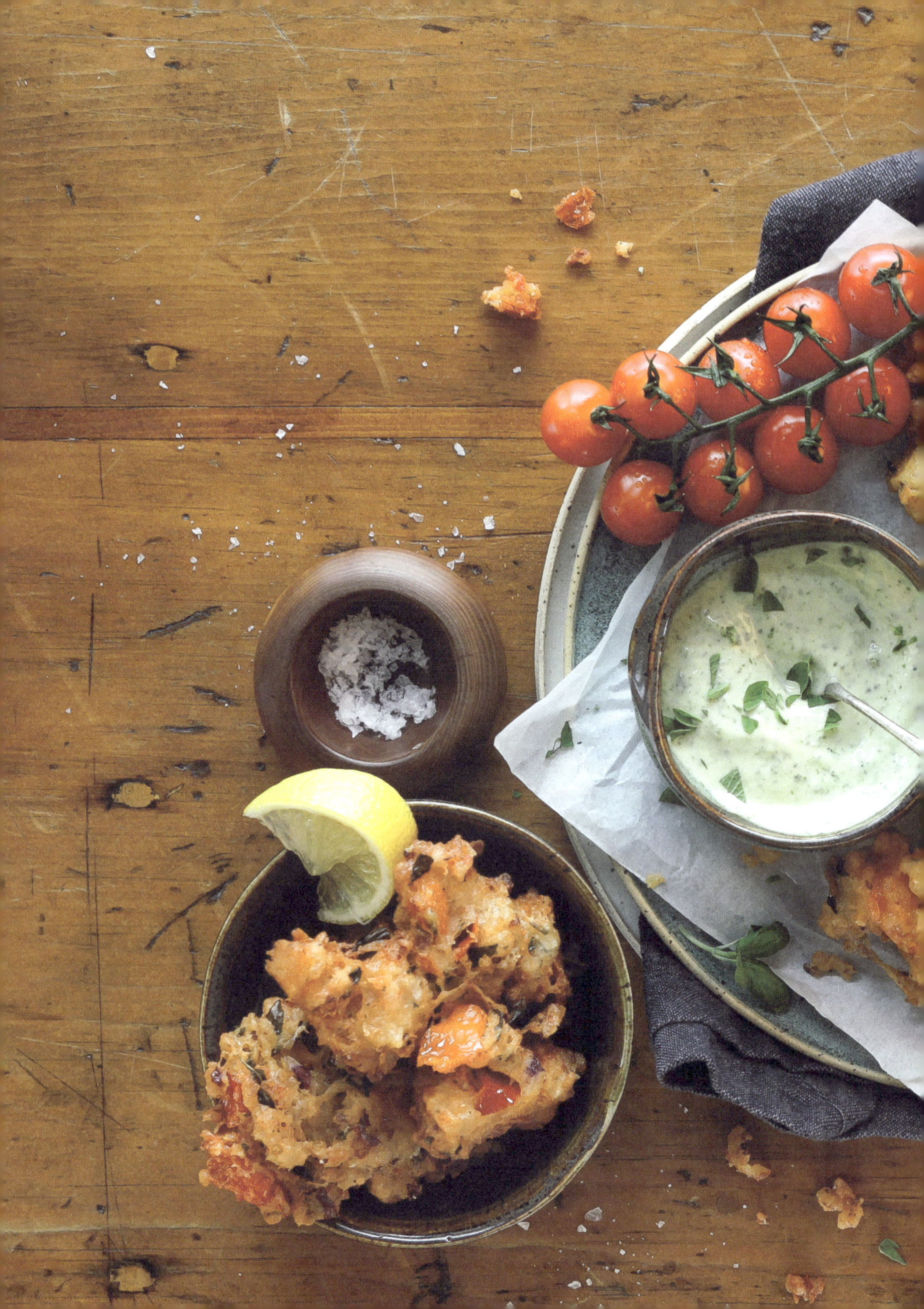

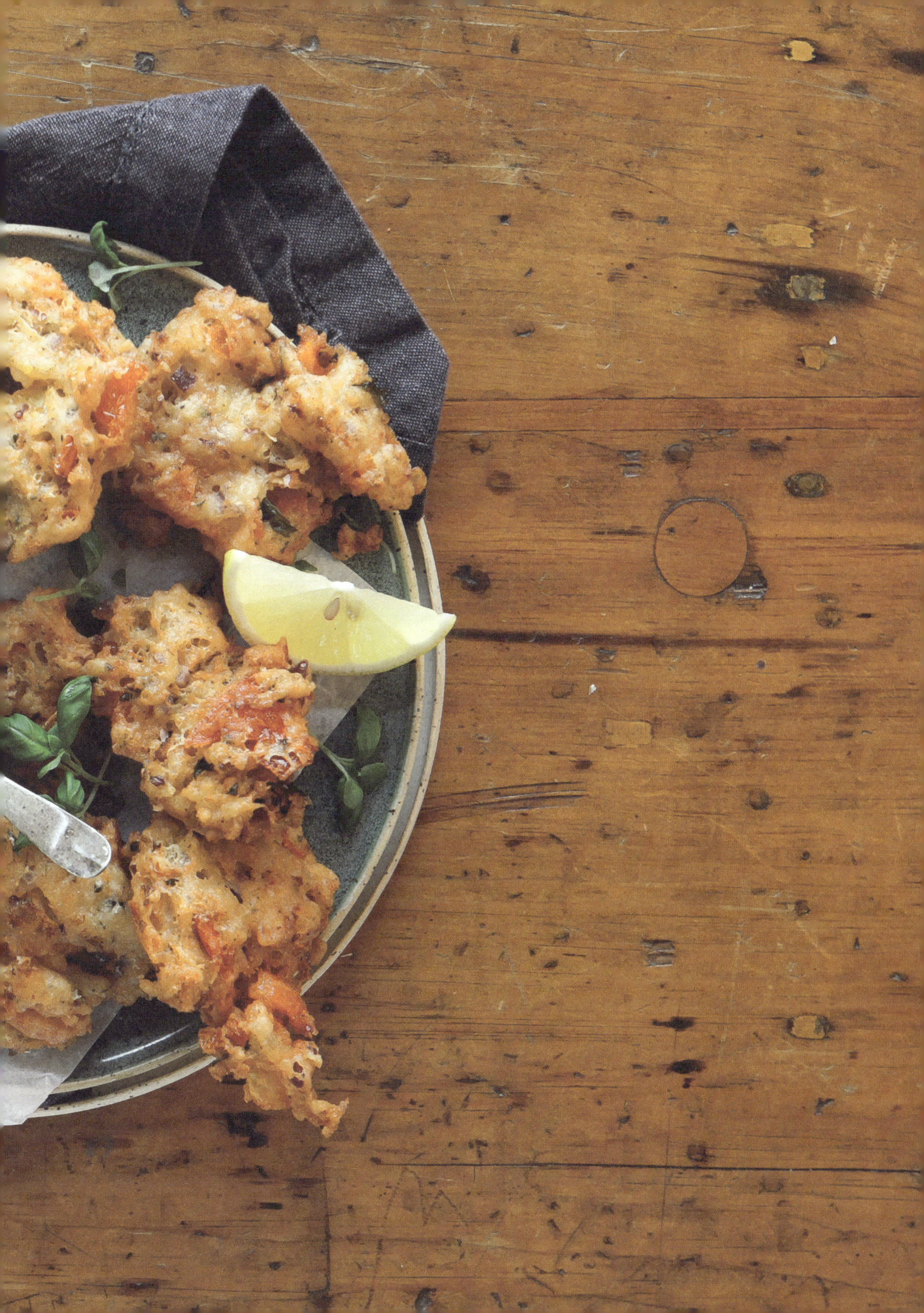

Pesto aioli
2 cups fresh basil, coarsely chopped or torn
1–3 cloves garlic, coarsely chopped
½ cup spinach, coarsely chopped
¼ cup olive oil
to taste salt and pepper
1 tbsp freshly squeezed lemon juice
½–1 cup mayonnaise

Method

Fritters
Set a large colander over a bowl. Remove cores from tomatoes. Using clean hands, firmly crush tomatoes into a coarse pulp to loosen seeds and juices; sprinkle with 1 tsp salt. Drain at room temperature for 30 minutes. Discard juices.

In a large bowl, combine feta, onion, basil, oregano, and drained tomatoes.

In another small bowl, combine flour, baking powder, and 1 tsp salt and pepper.

Add flour mixture to tomato mixture, stirring with a wooden spoon until combined and firm enough to form into balls, adding a little more flour if needed. Cover the bowl and set aside in the refrigerator for at least 30 minutes or ideally for 2 hours, allowing flavours to blend. (Can be made the night before, covered, and stored in the refrigerator).

Pesto aioli
In a blender or food processor, add basil, garlic, spinach, and about 2 tbsp of olive oil. Blend until combined, then slowly add remaining olive oil while blending into a smooth, thick consistency; season with salt and pepper. Add lemon juice and pulse for 2 seconds. Spoon pesto into a bowl; fold in ½ cup mayonnaise to combine evenly. Add up to ½ cup more mayonnaise or until desired consistency. Refrigerate until ready to serve. (Can be prepared up to 2 days ahead).

Assembly
Add oil to a deep fryer and preheat to 365°F degrees (or add 3" of oil to the bottom of a heavy saucepan and preheat to medium-high heat).

Shape dough with spoons into patties or balls, gently lowering each fritter into the hot oil, being careful not to overcrowd. Cook for about 2–3 minutes on each side until golden brown. Drain well and serve while still hot with pesto aioli.

Chef's Notes
Variations: This recipe can also be made with gluten-free one-to-one baking flour (like Bob's Red Mill Gluten Free 1-to-1 Baking Flour).

Pesto aioli with cheese (or nuts): Add ⅓ cup finely grated Parmesan cheese or pine nuts when first blending basil, garlic, and spinach with olive oil, if desired. I like to serve it nut and dairy free at The Grange.

Drink Pairings

These smooth and easy offerings are the perfect way to prep for your next bite: Keint-He Portage Pinot Noir 2021, The Grange of Prince Edward Estate Pinot Gris 2023, Midtown Pilsner.

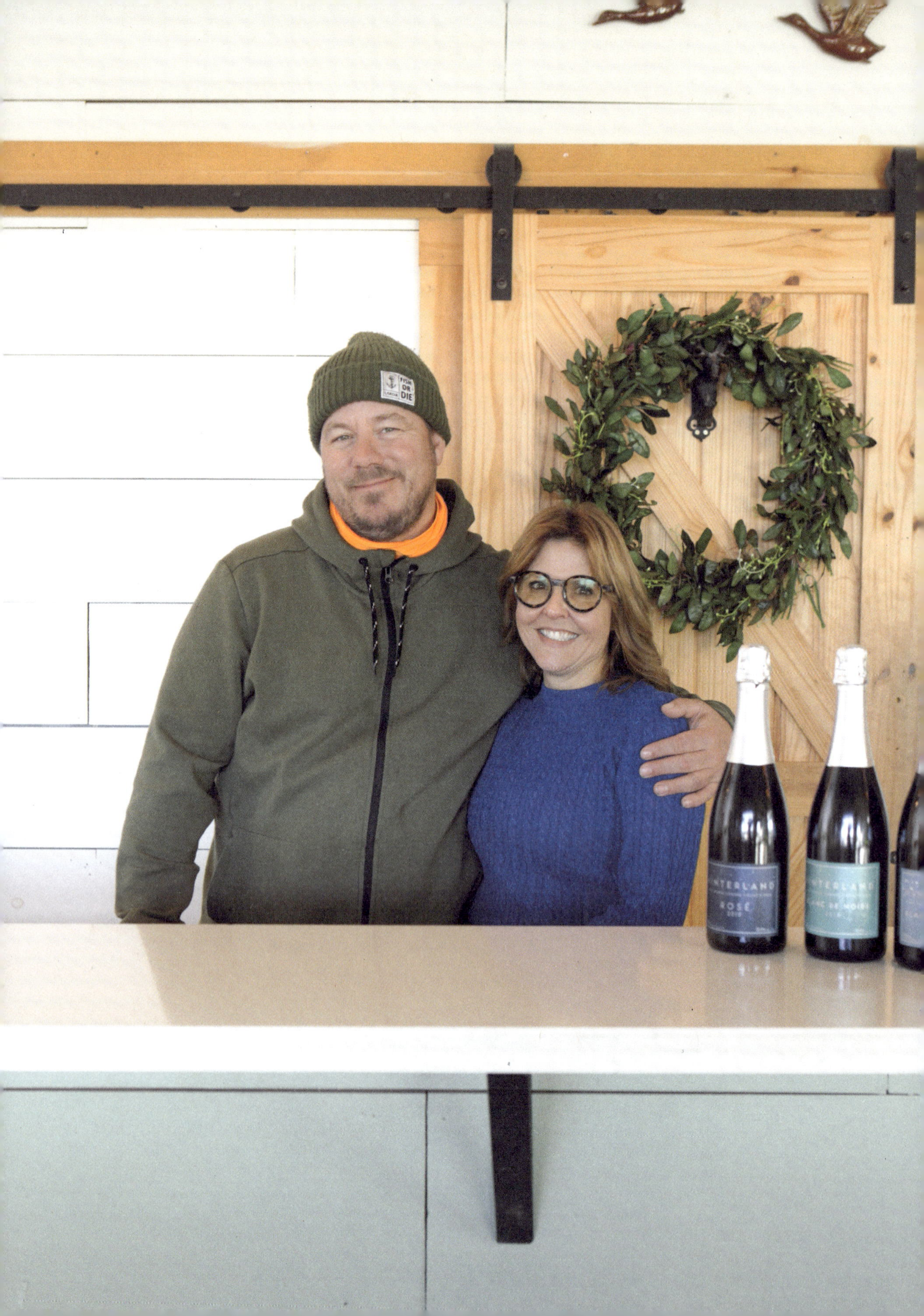
FISH OR DIE
ROSÉ

Hinterland Wine Company, Hillier

From Ancestral to Charmat to Traditional Method, Hinterland covers the full spectrum of sparkling winemaking for every occasion.

JONAS NEWMAN, VICKI SAMARAS

Vicki: One day, when I was 18, I told my parents I wanted a vineyard. And they both said, "Do you have a fever?" I studied botany and plant pathology and earth sciences in school, but then I felt like I had to make money—even when you kind of know what you want to do, there's no way you know how you're going to get there. So I decided to find a job that would pay me as much money as possible. I got into pharmaceutical sales. I met Jonas while bringing clients to Scaramouche. I said, "You're 27 but you're already maître d'. Where are you going next?" And he said, "Well, actually I want—" and this should have been foreshadowing, because I interrupted him, which has lasted throughout our 17-year marriage, to say, "because I want a vineyard." And he said, "That's exactly what I was going to say."

Jonas: I wanted to get out of Toronto. I like being outside. Canadian wine was starting to become more of a thing in my world—I was starting to see Canadian wines as something special. I had my favourite producers from Niagara, and I'd heard about guys like Mike Peddlesden and Geoff Heinrichs and Lanny Huff putting in serious acreages in the County. Niagara was out of reach, but we could buy land on a credit card here back in 2003. We bought our property from Gord and Judy Benway. Rob Benway still lives two roads down and farms everything around us. I think we were winery number seven. We did nothing in 2004 and then we planted in 2005, and then we came to the realization that we were going to have to make wine somewhere. We pulled the floor out of the barn, repaired it, put all the windows in, put in electrical, put in plumbing, painted, and all the rest over time. We made our first wines here in the milk house in 2007—310 cases of wine. It was the fucking best. A mint vintage.

Vicki: I remember one winemaker drove by, and he didn't even get out of his truck—we were outside picking our grapes before everyone else because we were set on making sparkling—and he said, "You guys are crazy." And we were like, "Maybe you're right, maybe you're wrong." We made a good decision for our vineyard. We weren't so busy trying to make the next Burgundy. We asked ourselves, what can our vineyard make? I think it's sparkling. We're going to stay in the lane of what we can do.

Jonas: We made some still wine in 2007, and then in 2008, we made none. We just decided to go whole hog sparkling; 2008 through 2012, we made no still wines. I think we're going back to doing 99% sparkling again. The thing is, you start buying equipment for certain styles of wine. It wasn't really practical for us to go out and buy a whole red wine setup too. So we decided that we'd specialize and try to get really good at sparkling.

Vicki: If all of Ontario bought only County wine for two weeks, we'd be sold out. We wouldn't have enough. That's how little we make. And that's why our focus now is on supporting our neighbours. Our equipment is available to use by anybody who wants to make sparkling. Of course, we're going to cost share—we did have to borrow a quarter-million dollars for equipment—but we're not doing it to make a profit. We believe in this region's sparkling wine—we believe in it so much that we're willing to create our own competition.

Jonas: Grant Howes, the beverage pioneer out here, is responsible for our Whitecap. The first year I made an inquiry to a grower about getting some Vidal. And I never made a deal, never committed. I was actually out hunting when I got a call about a delivery; Battista from Hubbs Creek was here working on his wine, and he unloaded the truck for me. Anyway, someone dropped off a couple thousand dollars worth of Vidal and we were like, what are we doing to do? So we fermented it and it worked out beautifully and it was tasting amazing, but we didn't have any tools to do Charmat. So Grant and Jenifer of The County Cider Company took it in and force carbonated it for us. I mean, we were barely open. It wasn't VQA, but it was a bubbly experiment. In 2010 we started doing Charmat properly. And that's thanks to them.

Vicki: Early in the Covid-19 pandemic, we had time to examine what we were doing. We were doing everything ourselves. We were exhausted, but we were selling wine. We either needed to back away or go into another gear. So we decided to go into another gear. We hope one of our kids would like to take over eventually. Maybe we don't want this life for them, but we want to give them the opportunity. In 10 years, they'll be old enough to make an informed decision.

Jonas: For perspective, we don't make as much wine in Prince Edward County as a medium-sized winery in Niagara. And a medium-sized winery in Niagara is a blip on the world wine scene. So we have to focus on quality and we have to help each other out in order to be noticed. The unreasonable, unbalanced amount of attention County wine gets from critics, international and otherwise, means we've got something special going on. There's something in this dirt for sure.

Vicki: And something special in the air and the sunlight and the water. I love the fact that this is a mixed-activity place. If you're here for a couple of days, you can go hit beer and wine, cider, and spirits. You can see art. You can pick your own fruit. Sandbanks, North Beach—you can go to Presqu'ile if you want to venture out. This is a playground.

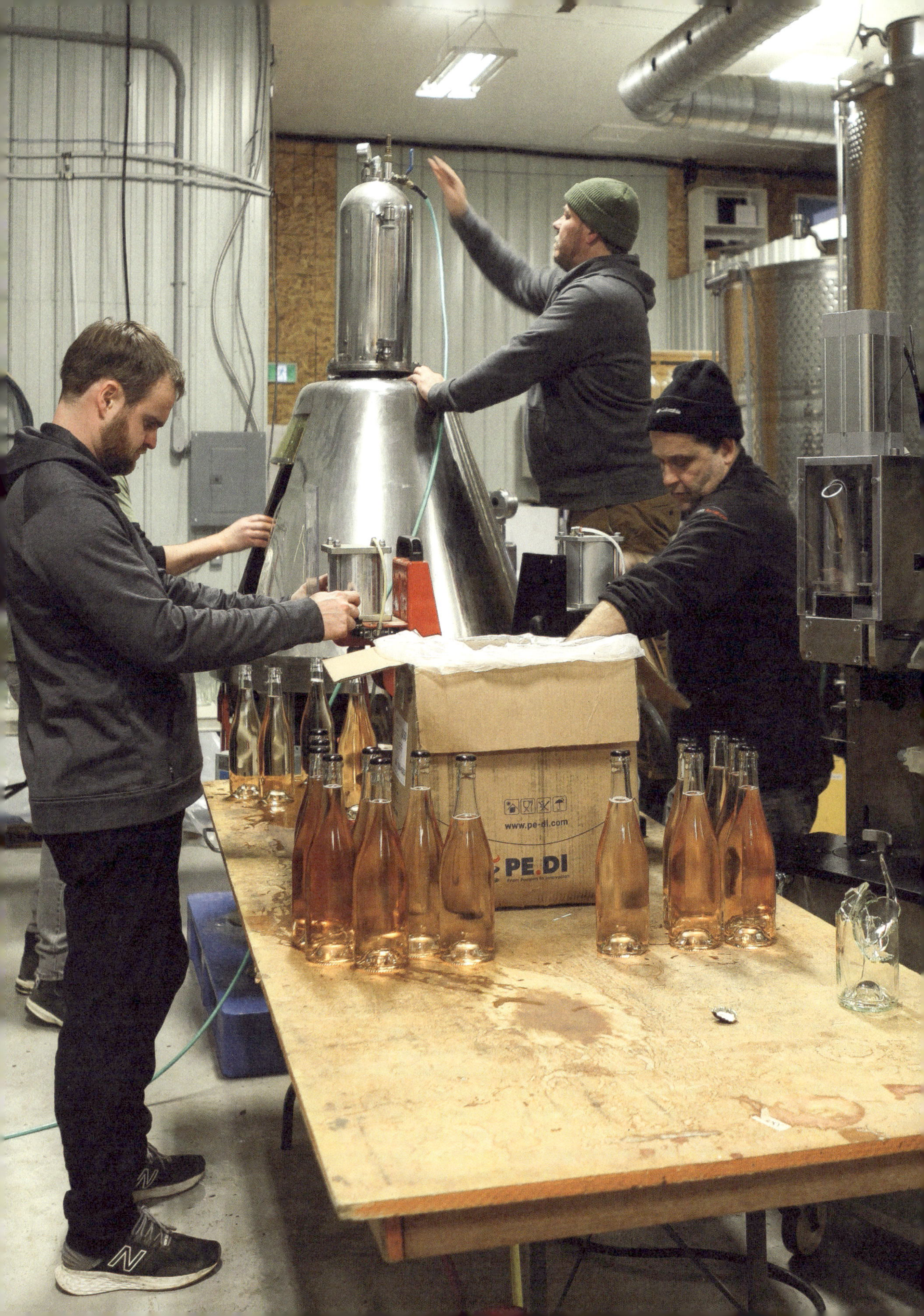
www.pe-di.com
PE.DI

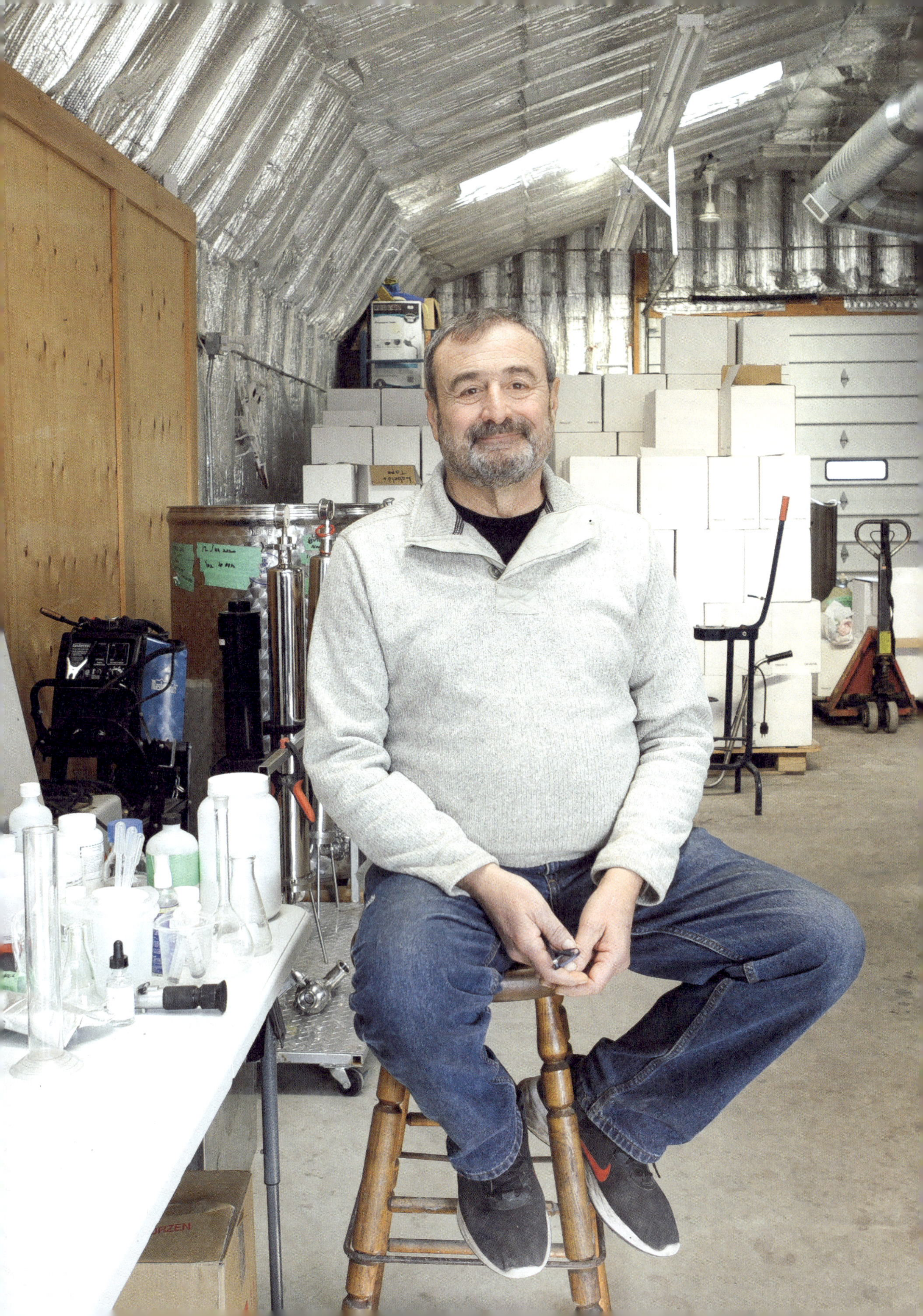

Hubbs Creek Vineyard, Hillier

Hubbs Creek planted their first block of vines in 2002, and since then they've produced Pinot Noir, Pinot Gris, and Chardonnay in a modern European-style vineyard.

JOHN BATTISTA CALVIERI

Fortunately, I'm not reliant on this winery to pay my salary. I had what I call a real job: I worked at the University of Toronto with electron microscopes. If I had to start over again without the real job, I would definitely have a pizza oven. Twenty years ago, when we were one of the first to plant a vineyard, funding was difficult to come by. People thought we were crazy. Honestly, I did not expect this to become a tourist region. I thought we would be making Pinot and Chard, then shipping them off to Montreal and Toronto. My dream for a winery is one that makes terroir-driven wines just like the great wine houses of France and Italy. It was very much like that here initially; there was no tourism, and we were steady at about 20 wineries. But then—especially after the opening of the Drake in 2014—we saw an increase in the number of wineries.

Years ago, I took a leave of absence from U of T to live in Italy in order to learn to read and write Italian. I was immersed in food and wine culture, and I thought, wow, I can raise my whole family on five acres. However, I was naive—it's not possible in Canada because of how the industry is structured. In Europe, a 2.5-acre vineyard can support a family. It's just a different approach. One example is the 6% LCBO tax; even if I sell a bottle through my winery, I still have to pay it.

Richard Karlo introduced me to Dan Sullivan of Rosehall Run and Dave Gillingham of Domaine Darius. I was living in Toronto but they still took me on as an honourary member of the Pickering Wine Guild. Boy, did I learn a lot. I learned to have a thick skin; the club members were brutal if you didn't make a good wine. After all, some them were real members of Wine Judges of Canada. During club meetings, our bottles of wine were numbered; they didn't have our names on them. So let's say it was a Pinot night, and if your wine was terrible, you would get trashed. I'd be in the corner going, Jesus Christ, they trashed what I thought was a good wine. It was a bit of an eye-opener, but it made you really think about what you were doing. That's why guys like Dan and Dave make good wines—they learned that when you're doing blind tastings, it really is different. Criticism is hard sometimes, but it's important. If you're afraid of criticism, don't get into the business.

We've been growing grapes since 2002; we're one of the oldest vineyards in the County. I grow Pinot Noir, Chardonnay, and Pinot Gris. These three European grape varietals do well in our terroir because of our soil types and because the number of growing days is similar to those in continental Europe. Once you establish a following, Pinot Noir, Pinot Gris, and Chardonnay sell well; you'll have no problems moving them. At times, people complain that I only have three varieties, and I say, "Well, they do well here. Why would I grow something iffy? One hundred yards down the road the soil structure is so different that Pinot will taste totally different there."

What makes good European wines is the focus on terroir; it's important to winemakers where their wine comes from. I'm trying to make a craft wine that reflects the County, Hillier, and Hubbs Creek; I'm trying to make terroir-driven wine.

I have 41 acres total and six high-density acres under vine, with about 18–20,000 vines. Spring comes from the moment those vines start to bud until you harvest. You've only got one shot at growing and making those grapes into wine. So if you lose that, you could be out of business. There's very little margin for error. I learned to farm by trial and error and a lot of mistakes. I wish I'd planted my narrow rows at two metres by one metre instead of five feet by four feet. Initially, the philosophy was to plant narrow rows like they do in Burgundy, but because of hilling up to cover the grapes in the winter, it's just brutal. That's why there's basically no more super-narrow vineyards, your classics, left in the County. There's the odd one here and there. I prefer two metres between the rows by one metre between the vines. This allows enough room for narrow vineyard tractors like I have. In addition, you still have high enough density to reduce the crop load per vine, which increases fruit quality. Another nearby vineyard is 10 feet by 5 feet. That's more of a North American approach, because land is cheap here, relatively speaking, compared to Europe—try buying an acre of land in Tuscany, good luck.

The beauty of vineyard and tractor work is that it's like fly-fishing. You're only doing one thing. You're focusing on not killing the vines. All you're thinking about is that one job. It's real therapy. The downside of wine-growing happens when you get hit by hail, frost, or downy mildew, a type of mould. Also, you can't take a holiday when you're in the middle of the season, when there's a ton of disease pressure everywhere, and you're living on pins and needles till August. In other words, the downside is that I can't play as much as I'd like.

For me, wine is wine-growing! I love how Pinot Noir and Chardonnay really reflect the vintage. I'm not blending anything that is allowable under VQA rules; we are permitted to blend up to 15%. For example, our 2017 and 2019 vintages are big and bold, while our 2015 is lighter. But they're all still Pinots. They are reflecting vintage. Now, if I wanted to, I could make them all the same, add a little Cab, a little this. There we go. Big wines everywhere. But then the art of winemaking, or the art of growing wine, is nonreflective of our terroir.

I think it's in our nature to be creative as a species. Philosophy is important. If you make wine as an art form more so than as a business, you might be surprised how much more the County would flourish. Unfortunately, it's difficult to balance the two. For some people, it's a business and terroir is not that important. Keith from Closson Chase and I talk about this all the time. I'm less than one-tenth the size of Closson Chase, but Keith treats me as his absolute equal. Being small or big doesn't matter for many of us. We are all so willing to help each other out. We work together, and if there's an issue, we call each other. Many of us are now getting up there in age. In fact, that's a concern we're regularly discussing. When we age out, who will take over?

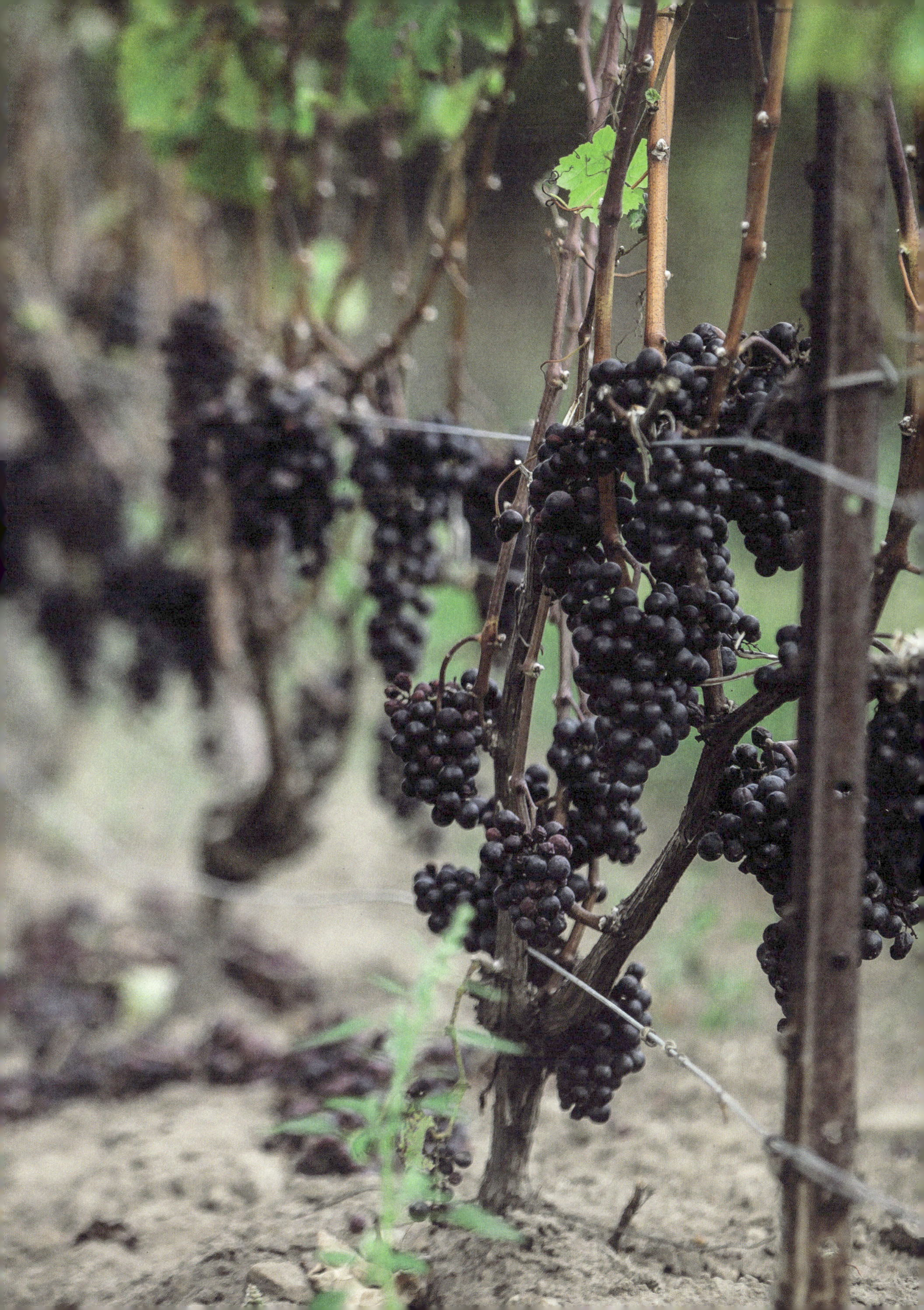

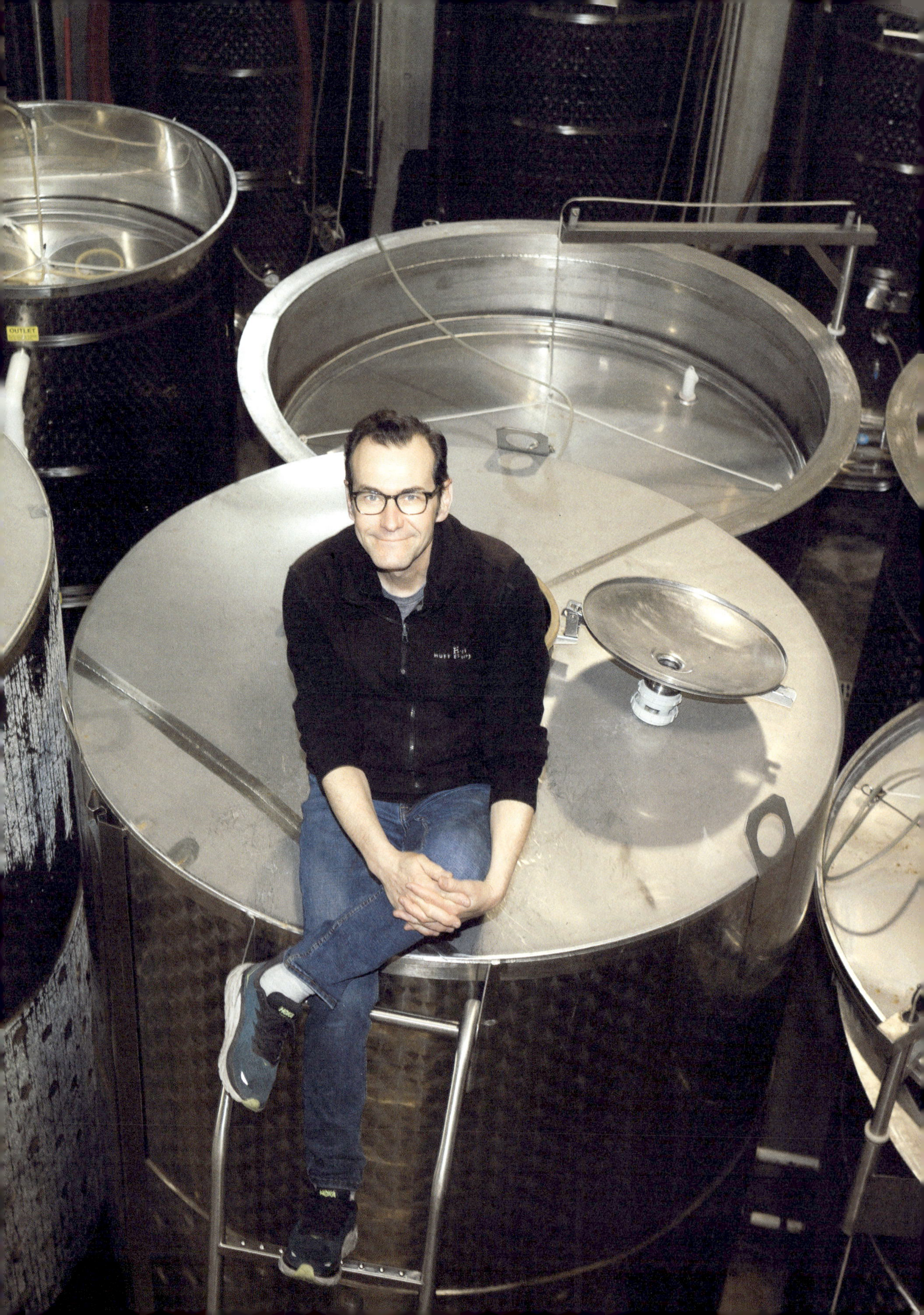
OUTLET

Huff Estates Winery, Bloomfield

With a state-of-the-art facility and a tasting bar overlooking the vines, Huff Estates has long been a staple of the County wine scene.

FRÉDÉRIC PICARD

When I was young, I wanted to work for Doctors Without Borders, but in France, the exams to become a doctor are extremely difficult and I was a bad student. I went to business school instead. I did my last year in Montreal, and I got to know Canada a little. After business school, my dad died, so I took some time off. I told my mom I wanted to see the world and she connected me with my uncle's friend who needed help on his farm in Saskatchewan. For two months, I drove a tractor all day. It gave me time to think.

When I returned to France, I knew I wanted work that was connected with farming, but I also liked chemistry, so I went to Burgundy and studied wine. Afterwards, I travelled and made wine for three or four years. I went to South Africa, Chile, and the US. Around that time, my uncle's friend decided he wanted to invest in a French vineyard. It was 2002 and land prices in southern France were very high. We had a good budget but not enough to buy a winery for €20 million. Instead, I met Jenn and moved to Canada.

I found a job in Niagara with winemaker Jean-Pierre Colas at Peninsula Ridge. While I was working there, Lanny Huff came to visit—he knew the owner—and he said, "I want to start a winery in Prince Edward County and I need a winemaker." The owner said, "I've got this young French man who's looking for a job." So Lanny asked if he could show me the County. I visited PEC in November 2002. There was two metres of snow. It was −12°C. I said, "You want to make wine here?"

I decided to give it a go for five years. We started with minimal equipment, a few tanks and a press. I was a little bit picky, because for me, it was important to start with good tools. When Lanny built the winery, we designed the production area together. Our first vintage was 2003. There was Chardonnay, Merlot, and Pinot Gris. I think I've got pictures of me with my first two barrels in 2003 in the big empty cellar.

At the time, everyone in the County went to the Waring House. We spent Thursday, Friday, Saturday nights there. In two months, we met everybody. We were young, we were 30 years old, just hanging out drinking. It was fun. It was like being part of a family, because no matter where you went, you knew someone. We had a good time because of that—it felt like it was the beginning of something. I will never forget how when I arrived, people were so nice, and how quickly we became part of the community. My English was terrible and nobody spoke French here, but it was still fantastic.

Some people like my wine, some people don't—that's life. But I'm happy here. I love Canada. This is a country I always wanted to live in. I'm Canadian, and I'm super proud of it. The first time I saw my wine in a restaurant was at the Merrill Inn (now the Merrill House). I went there for dinner with Jenn and our Chardonnay was on the wine list. I remember feeling very proud of that. In 2007, we won for best white wine in Ontario.

That was an achievement. It's not really about the medal; it's a reward for all the hard work. Sometimes I think I would like to go somewhere else, to see what it's like, but I'm happy here.

I called the County "the lab" for the first 10 years, because none of us knew exactly what we were doing. We weren't sure how to make good wine, how to grow grapes, how to grow more than a minimum of one ton or two tons an acre in this environment. We were like pioneers. So it was kind of a laboratory of learning about which grapes do the best, that kind of thing. Lanny has always been open to experimenting, even though it's a big investment for the winery.

I'm very lucky to have a good boss. Lanny is very generous with me. When I arrived, I wanted to do sparkling wine right away. That wasn't an easy thing to do. I wanted to do a dry rosé. There wasn't a lot of it in Canada at the time. Lanny let me go ahead and do all that, which is amazing. He's also a good businessman—that's why he built a hotel and a gallery. And I think he's always wanted to do well because he's one of the only winery owners to be born in the County.

I'm happy I stayed here because if I had left earlier, I wouldn't have seen what's happening now. When I arrived in my 30s, I wanted more things happening. I wanted more people, more restaurants, more breweries, more bars. It's about life, right? So I'm happy to be here and I'm happy the way it's changing. We have plenty of new places and it's fun as always.

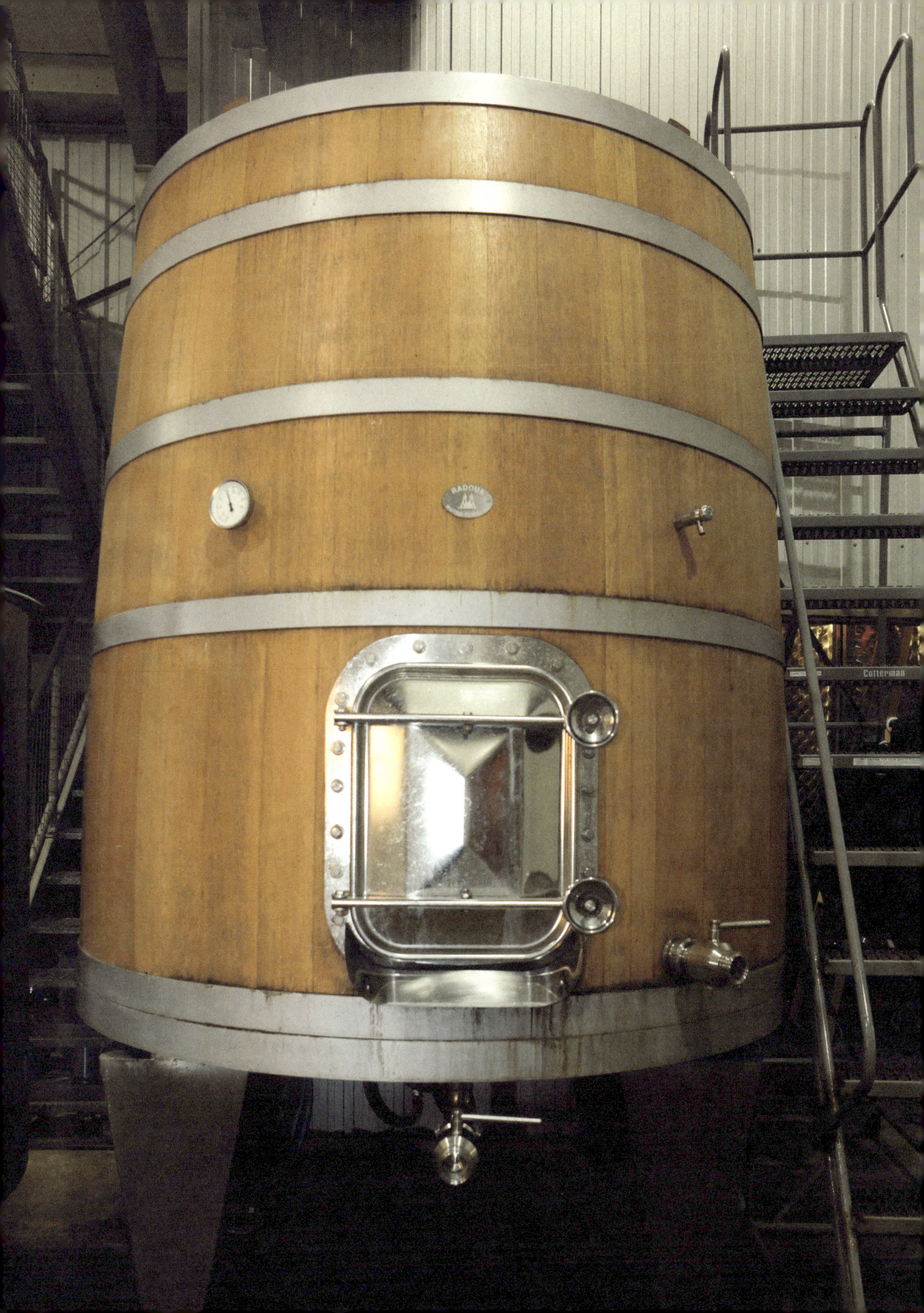
Cotterman

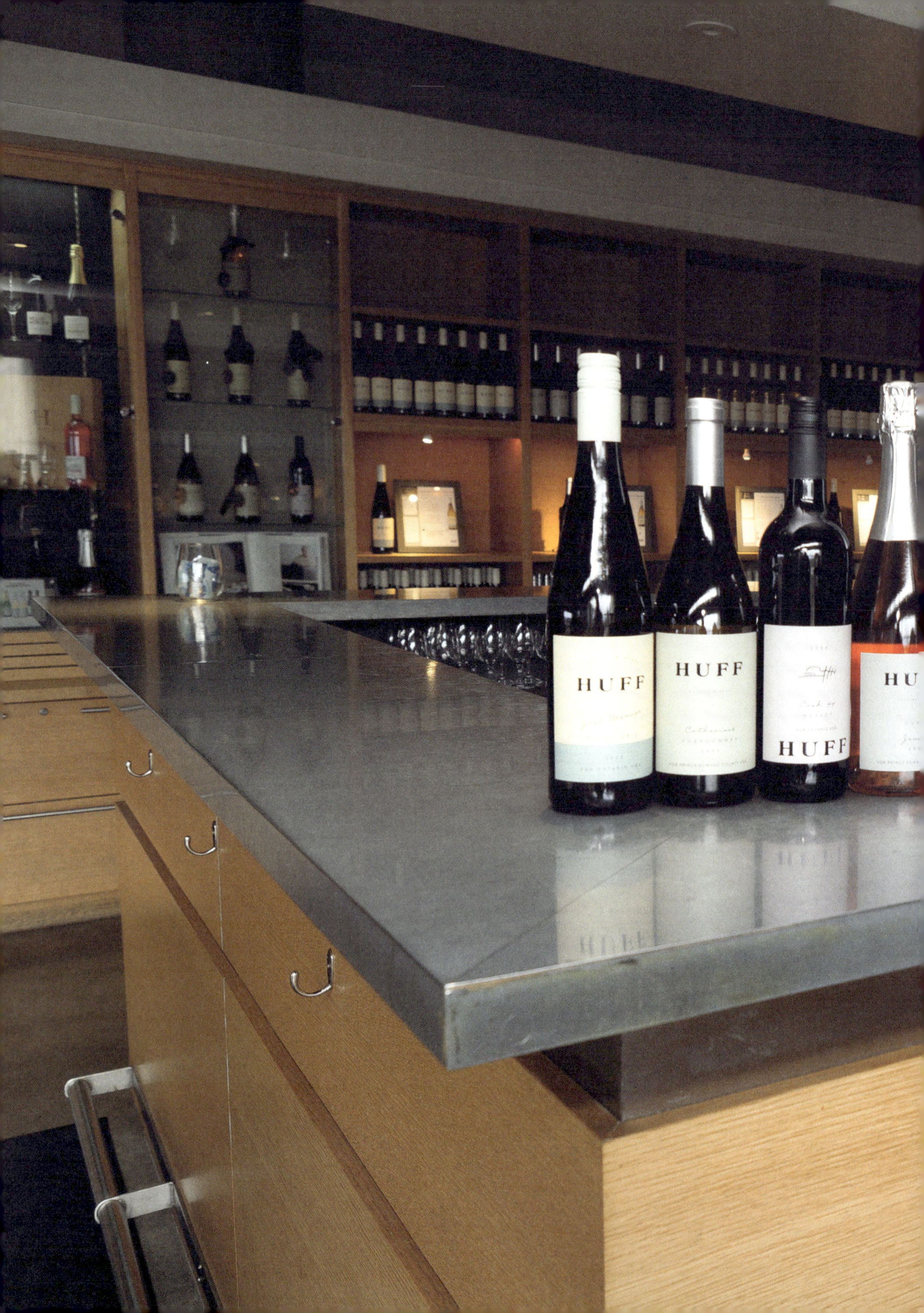
HUFF
HUFF
HUFF

$45
$40
$27
$22
WEEKENDER $19
CHARDONNAY $35
$21
$22
HUFF
HUFF
HUFF
HUFF

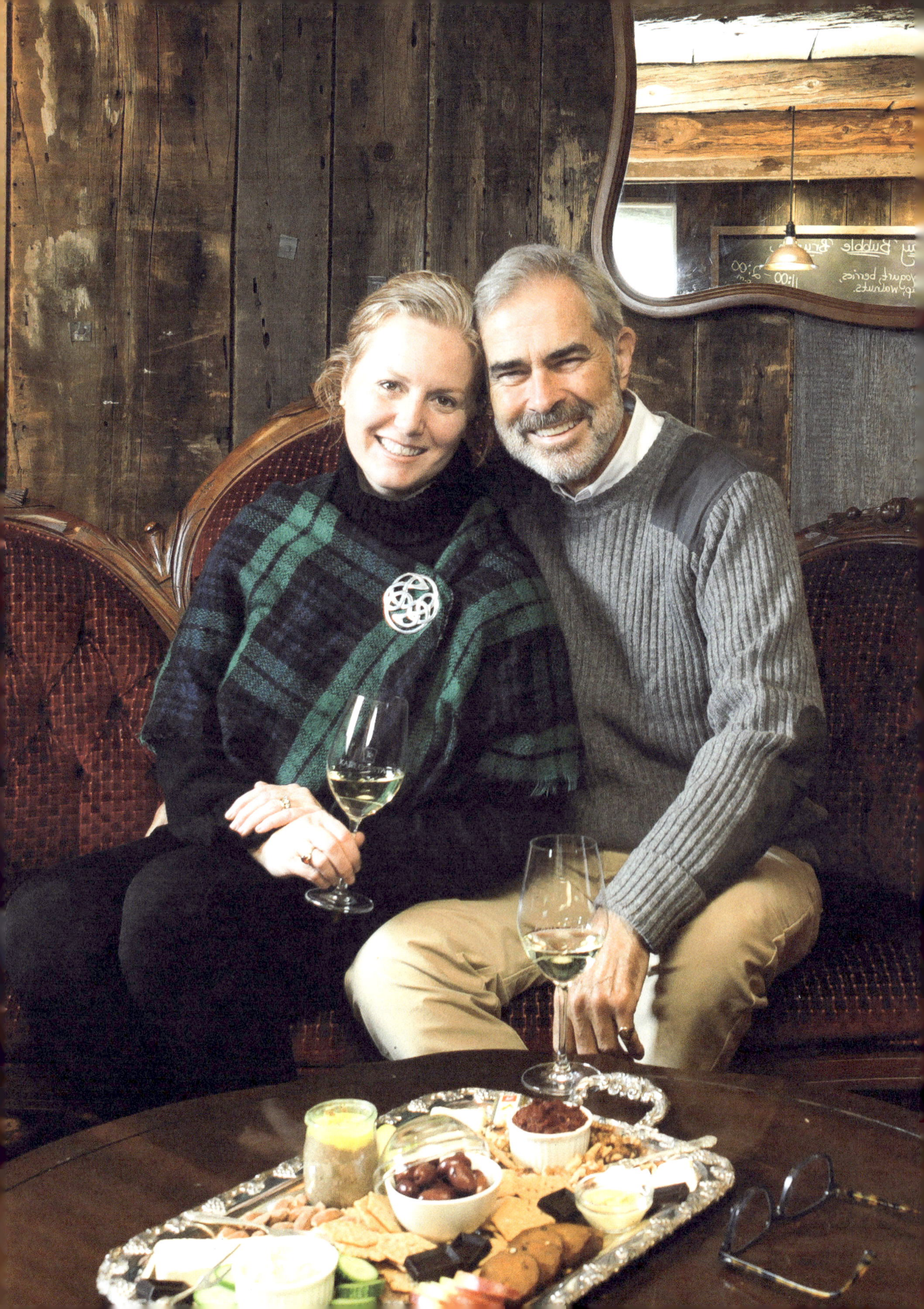

Karlo Estates Winery, Wellington

Located in an old post-and-beam barn, Karlo Estates is the world's first certified vegan winery and was named on VineRoutes Magazine's *"Top 10 Wines of Ontario" list.*

SAXE BRICKENDEN, SHERRY KARLO

Sherry: Richard's dad made wine. Richard realized if he helped his dad, he would get some wine to share with his buddies. Eventually, Richard made his own wine, and when his dad tasted it, he said, "You know what? You're better at this than I am. You make the wine." So Richard started making all the wine for the family. And then, of course, he made way too much. It was always good to be his friend.

He entered it into competition with the Amateur Winemakers of Canada and ended up getting a silver medal at the national level on his first try. Someone then suggested he join the Pickering Wine Guild. The guild is basically wine enthusiasts teaching each other how to make wine and tasting each other's wines blind so they can help each other get better. A few County winemakers came out of that guild—Dan Sullivan of Rosehall Run was the first to come searching for land out in the County, and then he invited the guild to come out for a tasting. Richard immediately fell in love with the County.

It took over a year and a half for us to find the property we wanted. We started driving around the County with a picnic basket and a bottle of wine, looking for the ideal place. One day we drove past this barn and saw a For Sale sign. As Richard turned in, a spike sticking out of the farm gate ripped a hole in the tire. After calling CAA and realizing we had an hour to wait, we knocked on Joe Stevenson's door. Joe was the third generation of the family that owned the place, and he offered to show us around. It was exactly what we were looking for: about 100 acres, south-facing slope, calcareous limestone clay loam soil, beautiful Hubbs Creek running through the vineyard, and a barn with a gable roof line or "hip barn." All the tomato crates we still use to display our wines are from the original farm's tomato production. The winery's speakeasy is the old milking parlour. The centre barrel room was the calving stable and our granary art gallery was, you guessed it, the granary.

We started planting in 2006. Since it takes three years to get a half crop and five years to get a full crop, we had time to meet people and have some fun parties. We had a life. Today, we have 14 acres under grape. Once the grapes come on, we're fully engaged. We did our first vintage in 2008, we opened the doors on May 22, 2010, and hit the ground running, because we couldn't afford not to.

In January 2014, Richard came home from a boys' weekend with a cough that wouldn't quit. After many tests, it was discovered he had stage 4 colon cancer and it had metastasized. He didn't want to tell anyone; he preferred to use the time he had left to help me learn how to run the business because he wanted to make sure his family was looked after.

Richard died on November 26, 2014. The funeral was a good distraction; it grew from a private family gathering into the Drake Devonshire calling us, offering to do a wake for

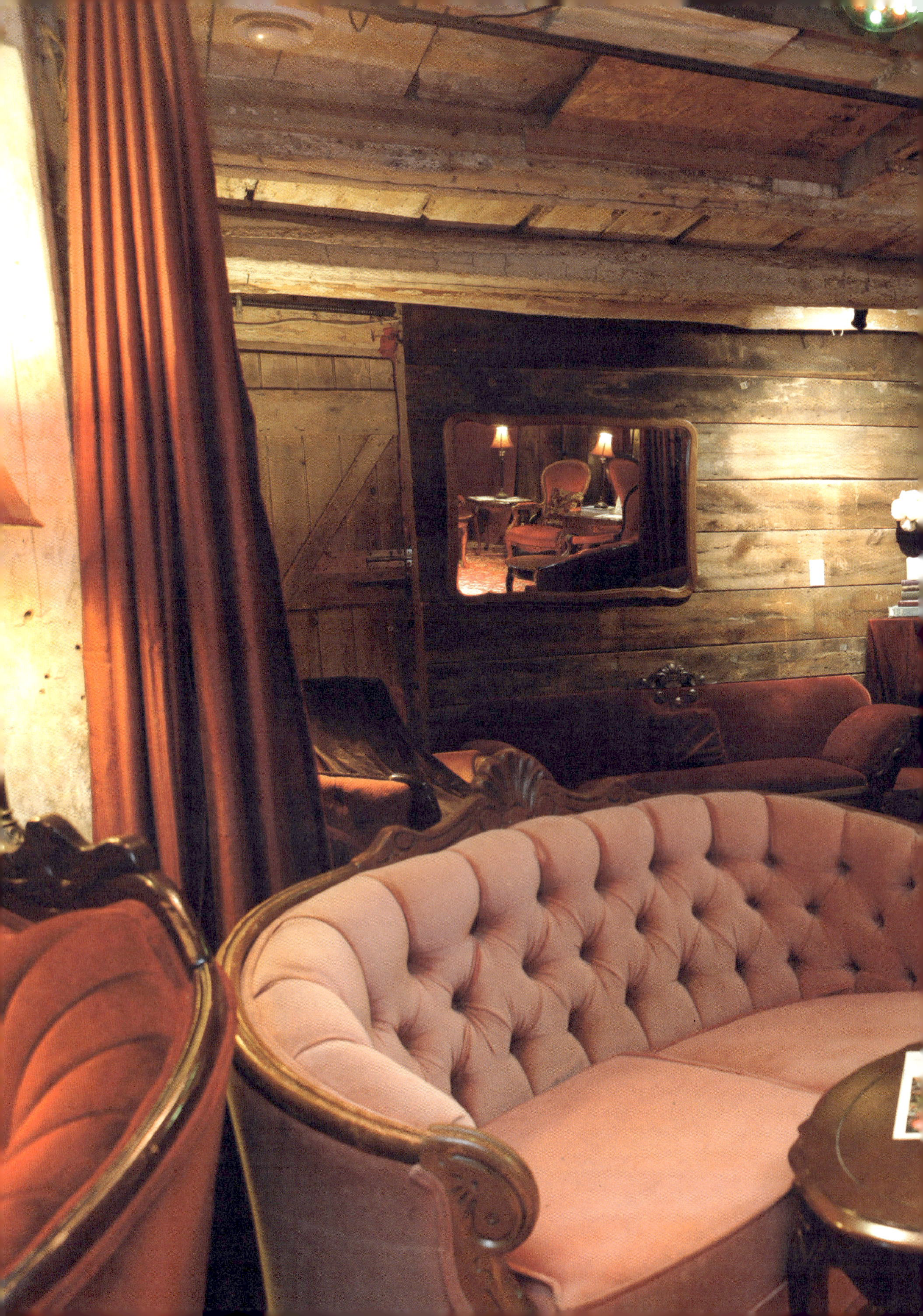

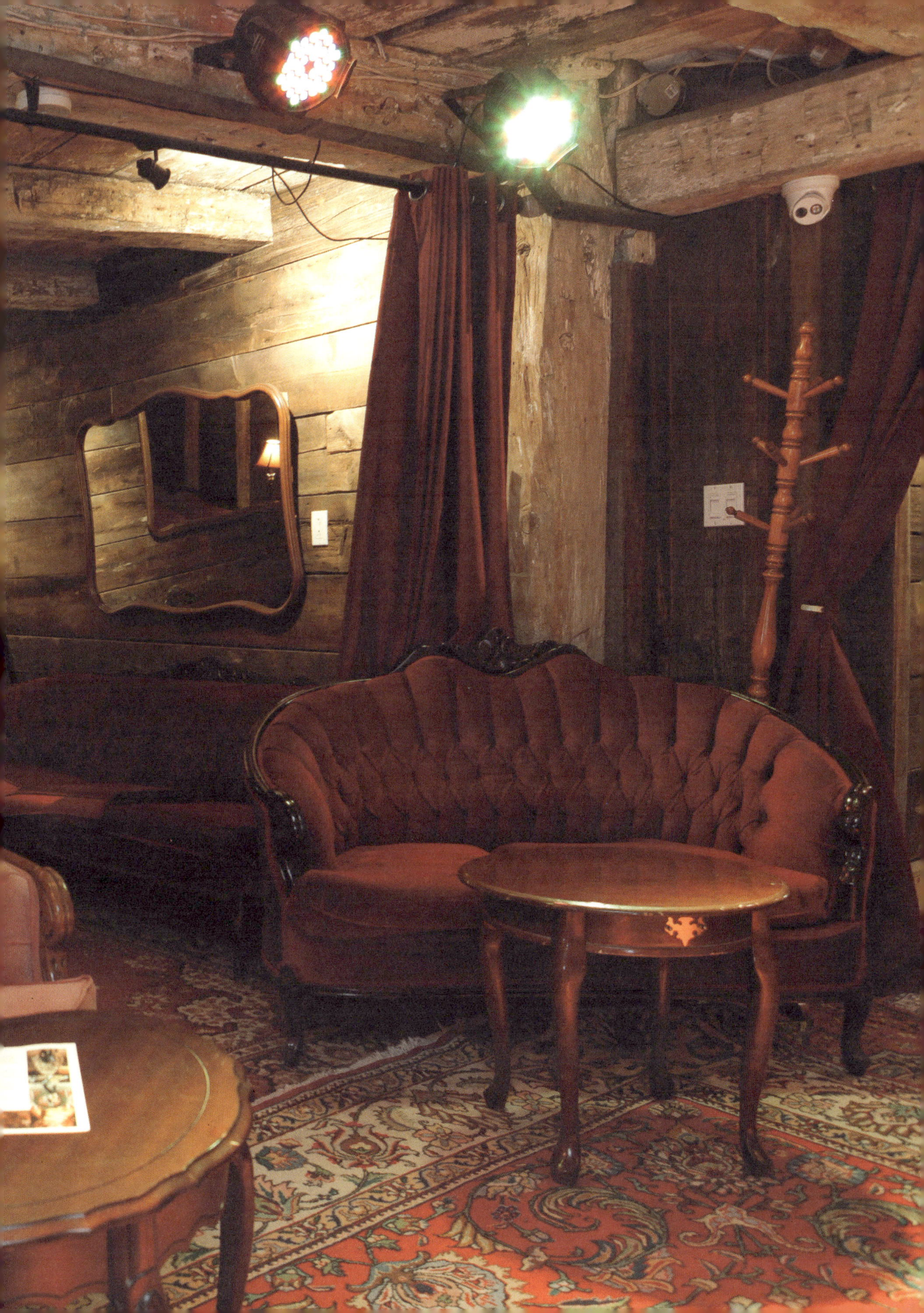

him. And then the Drake calling us back saying they had so many people register that they had to move it to the Essroc Centre. The Essroc Centre figured out how to do the licensing to serve our wine because they knew it was so important to us. It was so incredible how everybody in the community showed up, like a big extended family.

Afterwards, all the winemakers and the wine judges came out to help, and they tasted through everything; they told me what had gone off. I'd been doing marketing and PR and designing labels. I didn't know how to make wine. I felt like after Richard died, everyone was watching me, wondering what I was going to do. Is she going to fold? Is she going to keep the winery? What's she going to do?

Saxe: Sherry is being her usual understated self. She lived through hell watching Richard lose his mobility and die. It's bad enough to lose your husband, but in this case, her husband was also her winemaker and her CEO. He had all the numbers in his head. They decided to move up their wedding date because he didn't want her to have any issue inheriting the business they had co-founded. Sherry pulled the wedding together in just a few weeks. Only close family knew Richard was dying. Imagine all their friends coming over to them and saying how happy they were that they had the rest of their lives ahead of them. It takes a special and determined woman to wake up the day after Richard's death and say, "Okay... we can do this." She didn't want to feel like he had died in vain.

But the story of Richard, Sherry, and I is tightly entwined. The three of us were on a dating website in 2001 called Lavalife. What we had in common was wine as a passion. I had met someone and I was taking down my profile when I noticed Sherry had winked at me a couple of weeks earlier. I responded and explained why I was taking down my profile. She said, "Yeah, I've met someone who is courting me by taking me to Prince Edward County to look for vineyard land to build a winery." I responded, "You've got to go with that guy!" We never met, but we did correspond from time to time.

After Richard's death, in the spring of 2015, Sherry invited her Facebook friends to a wine tasting taking place in the Distillery District, two blocks from where I lived in Toronto. I thought it was about time I met this redhead. So I walked into the event never having seen or spoken to her in person; this was 13.5 years after we first met online. All I knew was that she looked beautiful and I liked her sense of humour. I was smitten but we didn't get a chance to talk, so after tasting my first Karlo wine, I brought her a box of Soma artisanal chocolate to pair with her port-style wine. A couple of days later, we booked our first date.

After dinner at the bar at the Drake Devonshire, we went for a moonlight walk in the Karlo vineyards, and she told me Richard had made a wine called Quintus. I'd founded several companies in the consumer electronics industry and was an avid wine collector—I got my diploma from the Italian Wine Academy in San Gimignano in 1996—but wine certainly wasn't my day job. But when she said Quintus, I thought, I'm no wine amateur; this is my chance to show off a bit. I said, "Oh, so it's five of the Bordeaux varietals in one bottle?" And she said, "Yeah, that's what it is."

I continued. "You know what you should do? You should make a wine called Sextus. I went to Viña Carmen and met Jean-Michel Boursiquot in 1995, the guy who rediscovered the Bordeaux Grande Vidure or Carménère (I started name-dropping—the works), blah

blah blah." I was showing off on the first date. And Sherry was politely listening to me mansplain. "Oh, you don't say... oh, that's very interesting."

Then she asked, "Saxe, do you think you can identify that vine right over your shoulder?" I said, "Well, no, but by the smirk on your face, I would say it's probably Carménère." She said, "Yep, it's the only commercial planting of Carménère in Eastern Canada. Richard and I bought the property with the express intent to produce Sextus." Since then, when she's talking, I just shut up, because she's several steps ahead of me.

The dean of George Brown's culinary college named us the "best-known winery that's not in the LCBO." We've declined offers to list at the LCBO because we sell out every vintage direct to the consumer at the farm gate, through restaurants, or online.

I think one reason we've got epic talent like our executive winemaker, Derek Barnett, and winemaker, Spencer Mayer, is because we don't say, "No, you can't make that one. It's not profitable enough." We have learned that to make something extraordinary, we just have to stay out of the artists' way.

I feel like Richard is a brother, after being here for nearly nine years and seriously tripping into stuff that Richard did and thinking, oh man, that was the right thing to do. Sometimes, if I'm disagreeing with Sherry on something, she stamps her feet and says, "That's what Richard used to say!" I'll be thinking, "Thank you, brother!"

Sherry: We achieved Richard's dream of producing Sextus in 2018, and again in the 2020 vintage. It's not easy. It's a blend of all six of the original Bordeaux grape varietals—Cabernet Franc, Cabernet Sauvignon, Merlot, Malbec, Petit Verdot, and Carménère. It has rarely been made since the phylloxera epidemic of the mid 1800s. Suffice to say there is an unusually powerful motivating force driving us—to make sure Karlo Estates is something Richard would be proud of.

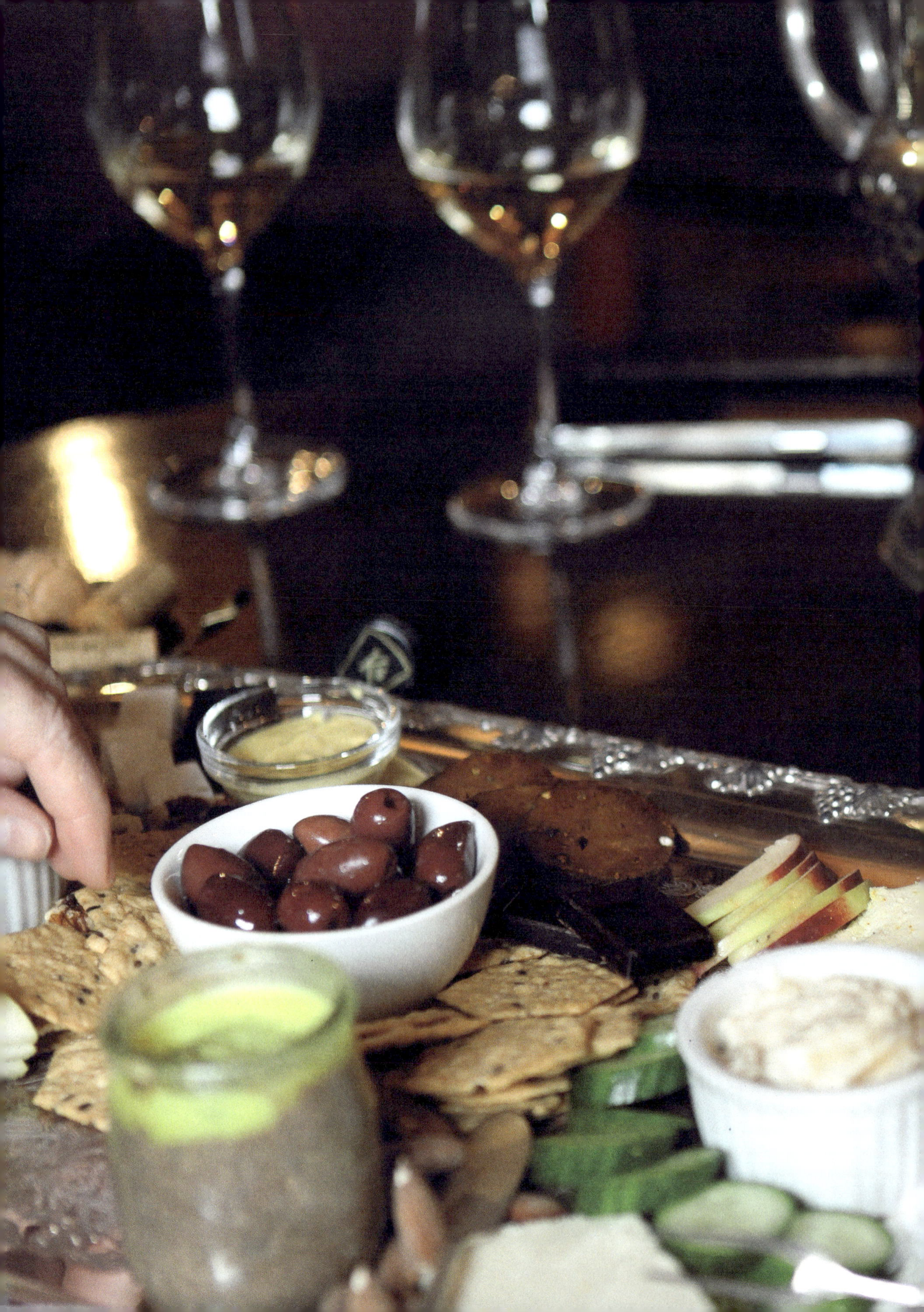

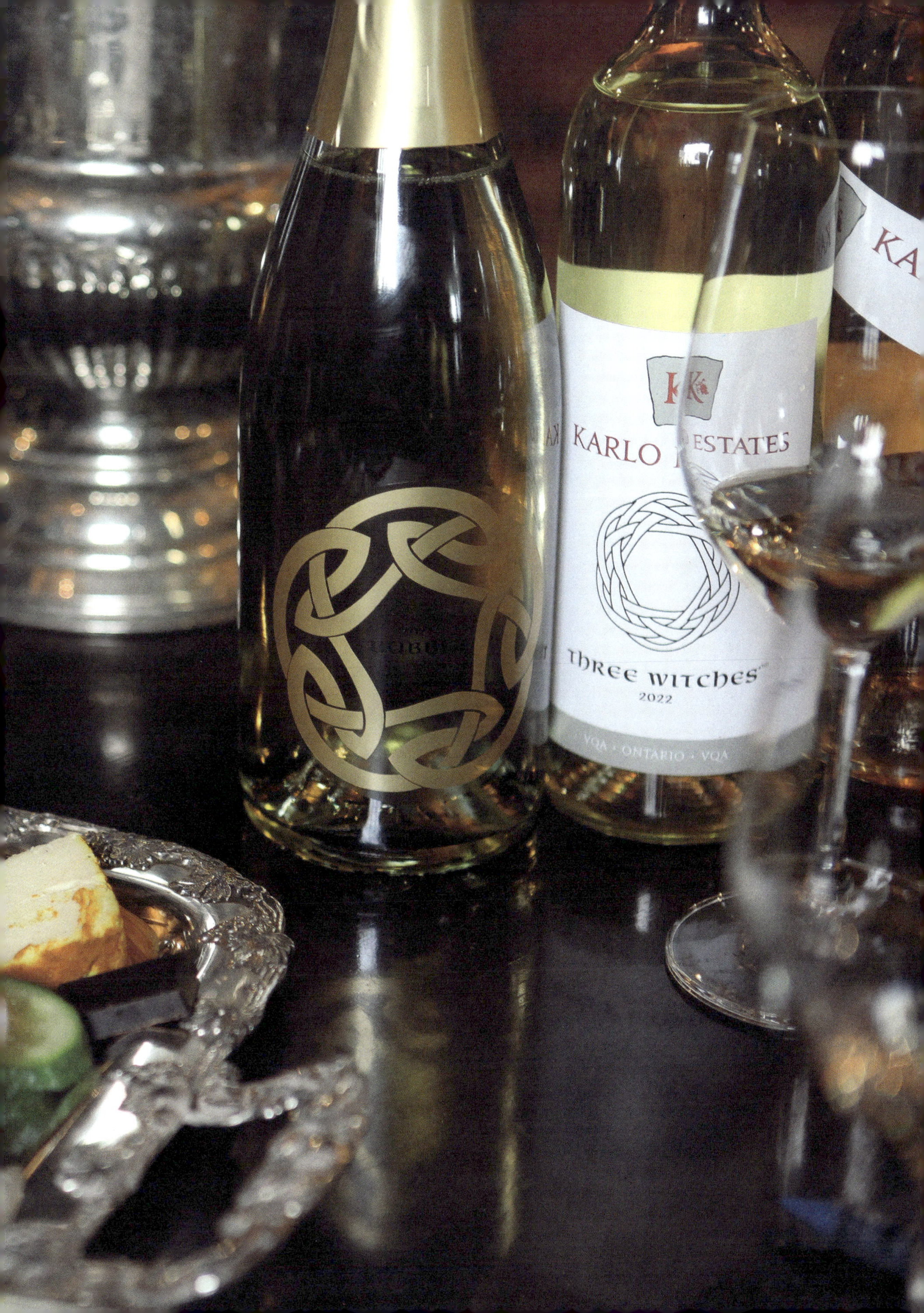
KARLO
ESTATES
THREE WITCHES
2022
VQA • ONTARIO • VQA

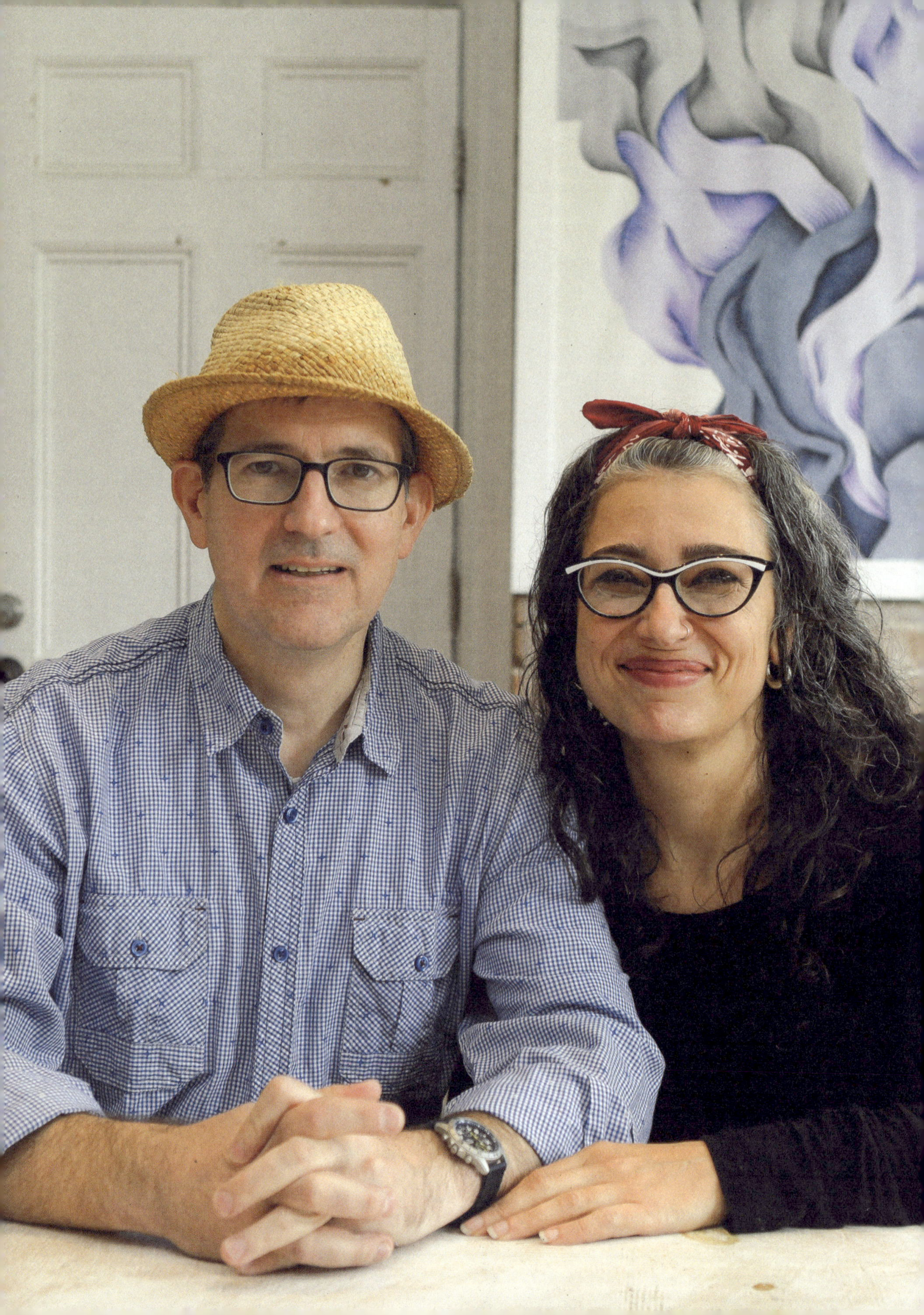

Kinsip House of Fine Spirits, Bloomfield

Kinsip is an estate distillery where spirits are fermented, distilled, and barrel-aged on their farm using homegrown and locally sourced ingredients.

MARIA HRISTOVA, MICHAEL WATERSON

Mike: Kinsip is a made-up word; we get to pour the meaning into it. It's a family undertaking, and then there's sipping spirits. Plus the idea of also appreciating a sip. It was evocative of what we like about spirits and family.

Maria: I was born in Bulgaria. My family's been distilling for many generations, and I grew up in an orchard that had previously been a vineyard. The vines were over 100 years old, so my grandparents slowly started taking them out. They planted a lot of apricot trees because in Europe people drink the thing that's from their region. And so where my mom grew up and where I was born, the thing they drank was apricot eau-de-vie. I never thought I would get into distilling, but here we are.

Mike: Part of what appealed to me is that there was a lot to learn. Both Maria and I, from an engineering perspective, appreciate the technical aspects of distilling over other beverage alcohol. At the same time, we're able to move new products through the production cycle pretty quickly. I also develop medical devices, which require clinical testing—there's a long cycle of planning and executing, getting things done. Here, we don't really worry about having too much inventory. We can sell it and then we can make new things.

Maria: We went back and forth between Montreal and Toronto for quite a while, and I'd noticed the sign for the County on the 401. We started coming here in 2007 or so, so it was still very early on. And then my daughter was born in 2010, and Michael's sister and her husband had a child in 2010. They lived in Ottawa at the time, so we started meeting here. At one point, we thought that we wanted to buy a place here together. We wanted our kids to be close to each other. We got a real estate agent and we kept driving around to visit properties. And finally I was like, "I am after that house, that distillery." Eventually, our real estate agent said, "You know what's up for sale? The distillery. With the house!" It felt like a once-in-a-lifetime opportunity. So we bought it.

We were fortunate to retain both the retail manager and the initial distiller for a while, so there was some continuity. That was really helpful because it also gave us a slower start into figuring out what we wanted to do and how we wanted to do it.

When the Covid-19 pandemic started, we shut down the production of any spirits, and then in a week's time, we figured out how to turn over all of our production into hand sanitizer. Mike is amazing at figuring stuff like that out. I spent a lot of time sorting out packaging and labels and making sure it was all approved. My parents were here helping us crank out hand sanitizer for the hospital, for local retirement and nursing homes, the police, hospitality. It was wild.

Mike: The type of apricot rakia Maria's family makes in Bulgaria is called kaisieva. I really like that Kinsip is also very grounded in this place, the County. The previous owners of our property, Peter and Sophia, had also been very inspired by the European notion of local spirits—that as you go through different countries in Europe, there are very local kinds of spirits that are part of each place. That's what motivated their choice of still. You have to make some decisions about what you're going to try to do. We've taken that a step further in terms of using grain from our own farm and using local botanicals.

The Nymans work the farm for us, so we divide the farm each year. Some fields they farm for themselves, and some we decide: this one rye, this one barley. We produce a single malt using our peat—one of the largest deposits of peat in the province is a kilometre down the road. It's very special to be able to do that here. It means that we have to malt our own barley, because it's essential that the smoke is introduced before the grain is dried in the malting process.

We want to figure out barrelling in a way that's repeatable. Pete and Marla Bradford were here as coopers for quite a bit and we learned a lot from them. We continue to work the barrels ourselves now, and we char the red wine barrels in which we age our signature rye whisky.

We're at a stage where we need to grow beyond the County. We're pushing into more distributors and working with dozens of gourmet and gift retailers across the country to bring the County to the rest of Canada.

Maria: We both still have full-time jobs. It's tough for small distilleries in Ontario because the taxation climate is so terrible. We pay 10 times as much tax as wine does, so we keep scraps from every bottle that walks out of here. We're trying to figure out how to deliver a premium product and to run this sustainably. So much of our success depends on how many people come to the County and, in turn, how many people visit us here.

I value the notion of physical labour and connecting to what's on our table. I grew up watching my parents work and working alongside them, and I think that it's been very important for my kids to see us do the same thing.

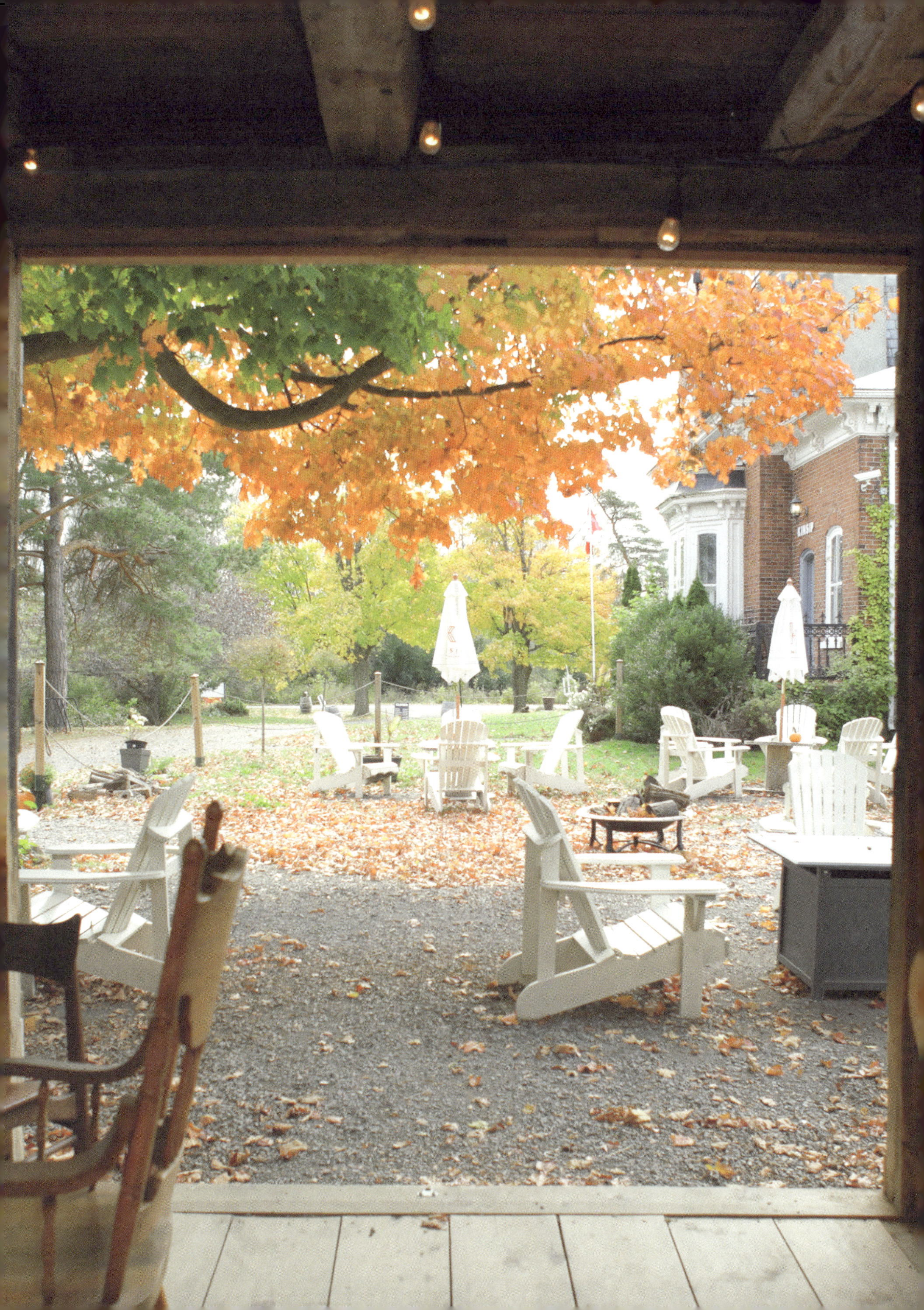

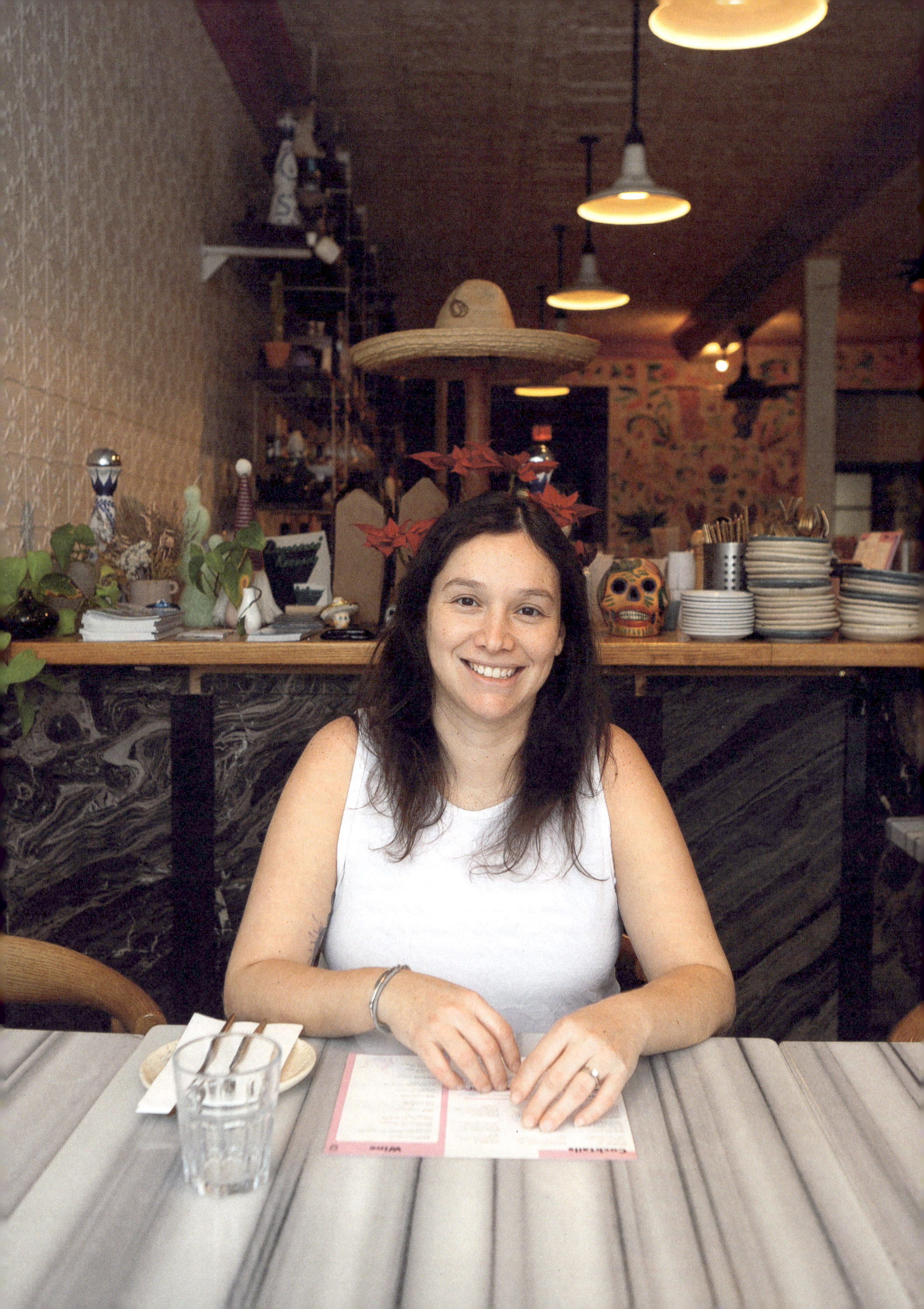

La Condesa's Cheese-Stuffed Meatballs with Chipotle Cream Sauce

Celebrating the beautiful cuisine and culture of Mexico, La Condesa is a vibrant Wellington gem.

SAMANTHA VALDIVIA, OWNER AND CHEF

Albondigas, or meatballs, are a traditional, approachable Mexican comfort food. Canned chipotle peppers in adobo sauce are smoked jalapenos in a rich tomato sauce, easily found in the Latin section of most supermarkets. These creamy, cheese-stuffed meatballs make for delicious bites that even kids will love.

Prep time: 15 minutes
Cooking time: 20 minutes
Servings: serves 4 as a main or 6 as an appetizer (makes 16 meatballs)

Ingredients

Meat
650 g medium ground beef
½ large white onion, finely diced
3 cloves garlic, finely chopped
3 tbsp panko (regular or gluten-free)
2 eggs
4 dashes Worcestershire sauce
1 tsp dried Mexican oregano
2 tbsp kosher salt
150 g mozzarella cheese, cut into ½" cubes
¼ cup vegetable oil
1 cup chicken stock, to deglaze pan

Chipotle cream sauce
150 ml can plum tomatoes
¼ white onion, finely diced
2 cloves garlic, finely chopped
1 cup 35% heavy cream
125 g cream cheese (about ⅔ cup)
2–3 canned chipotles (or to taste), coarsely chopped
½ tbsp kosher salt
½–1 cup chicken stock
sliced avocado and chopped cilantro or microgreens, to garnish

Method

Meatballs
In a large bowl, mix ground beef, onion, garlic, and panko. In another small bowl, beat eggs, Worcestershire sauce, oregano, and salt. Add egg mixture slowly into beef mixture, stirring until evenly combined.

Using a large spoon, divide beef mixture into 16 equal portions, about 1½" in size. Press your thumb into the centre of each portion; press a cube of cheese into each indentation. Form each meatball to seal cheese into the centre; roll into balls. (Can be prepared up to 1 day ahead and refrigerated. This also allows the meatballs to firm up before frying.)

Sauce
In a blender or food processor, purée tomatoes, onion, garlic, cream, cream cheese, chipotle, and salt together until smooth. Set aside.

Assembly
Heat oil in a large frying pan over medium-high heat. Add meatballs, cooking in several batches without crowding, until evenly browned on all sides but not fully cooked. Remove meatballs from pan; cover to keep warm. Add 1 cup chicken stock to pan, scraping in any browned bits from the bottom of pan. Add puréed sauce mixture; continue to cook over low heat, stirring constantly, for about 10 minutes, adjusting texture with remaining chicken stock to desired thickness.

Return meatballs and any accumulated juices to the frying pan with sauce, stirring gently and constantly, turning meatballs occasionally for another 3–5 minutes or until just heated through.

To serve, spoon meatballs and sauce over rice or pasta, garnished with sliced avocado and chopped cilantro or microgreens.

Chef's Note
Appetizer variation: Instead of coating the meatballs in sauce, fully cook meatballs in a frying pan, and set aside and cover to keep warm. Add 1 cup chicken stock and sauce mixture to the frying pan over low heat, scraping in any browned bits from the bottom of pan. Heat for about 5 minutes or until heated. Adjust texture with additional chicken stock to desired thickness. To serve, spoon sauce into shallow serving bowls; top with meatballs and garnish with sliced avocado and chopped cilantro or microgreens.

Drink Pairings
The unique flavours in these beverages will bounce against the creamy richness and spice: Hinterland Borealis Rosé, Parsons Brewing Two Left Feet Gueuze.

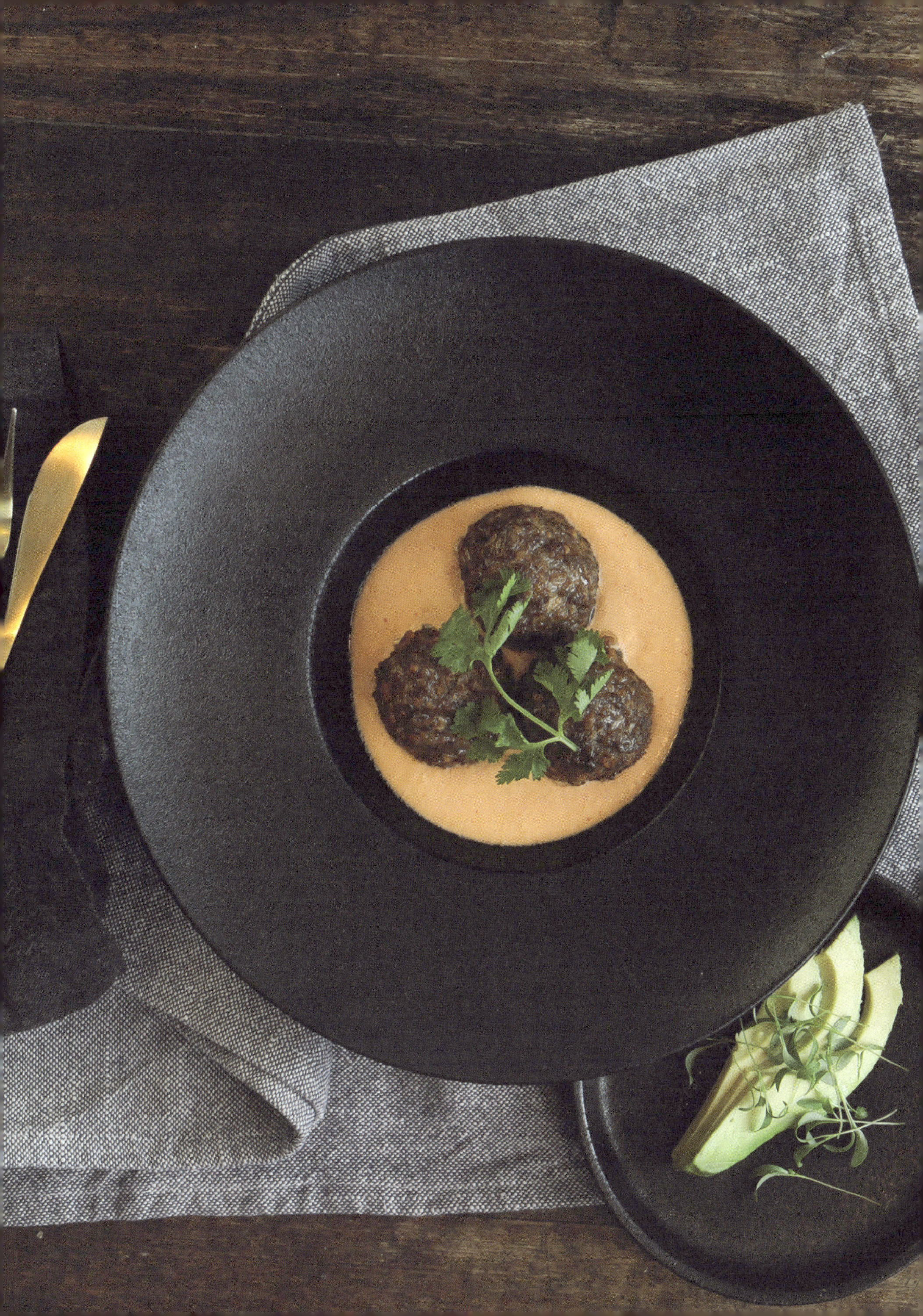

Cab Franc
Lacey

Lacey Estates Winery, Hillier

Lacey Estates is a family-run winery that prides itself on low-intervention, terroir-inspired wines.

KIMBALL LACEY, LIZ LACEY

Kimball: My parents were weekenders at the start. They bought the house next door back in 1982, and then the surrounding 60 acres came up a couple of years later and they jumped on that right away, when everything was cheap. They didn't want anyone building anything over here. They wanted no neighbours. They would leave Toronto on Friday at 9 or 10 o'clock at night, even later sometimes, just to avoid the traffic, and then head home Sunday.

After high school, I went right into working in the brokerage industry. I spent 15 years in the brokerage industry, based in Toronto and travelling all over. I met Liz in 1988 through a mutual friend at Herschel's Deli in Toronto. Liz was working at Royal Bank, doing commercial leasing. After a buyout, I got a really good severance. So we decided to sell the house in Toronto and move up here.

I've always been interested in wine. My parents were into wine as well—they loved it. I would say winemaking comes from my dad's side because, being part Portuguese and all, winemaking comes from the heart. Dad and I went to a seminar at Peddlesden Wines—now Casa-Dea—about starting a vineyard. Afterwards, we looked at each other and said, "Yeah, we can do this." No farming experience, nothing. I started working at Peddlesden that year and started planting here that year as well.

We went straight into farming. Liz looked after our three children and worked in the vineyard too. On weekends, family members would come up and help. The first weekend in 2003, we hand-planted our first 200 plants and it was the hottest day of the year. By the end of that weekend, we all looked at each other and thought, we're crazy. The next weekend we got a little auger to dig the holes. And now we've got a big auger on the back of a tractor. So life's gotten a little easier.

When I was working at Peddlesden, the winemaker at the time started showing me how to make wine; I did that for four years, and at the same time I did the grape and wine certificate program through the University of Guelph. I left Peddlesden—I think it was Carmela Estates at that point—in 2007. I got a call from Deborah Paskus, the winemaker down at Closson Chase, asking me to come down and see her, and she asked if I wanted to join the team. I spent the next 10 years as the associate winemaker at Closson Chase.

We've got roughly 10 acres of plants. The whites are Frontenac Blanc down in the front, Pinot Gris, Chardonnay, Riesling, and Gewürztraminer. For reds, we've got Capron, Pinot Noir, and Bacco Noir. The Frontenac Blanc is a hybrid, the Baco is a hybrid. The rest are all vinifera. We basically planted stuff we like drinking.

Liz: Our kids are all different. Emily, our youngest, started helping out when she was four, and her job was to drop the plants in the holes. And then at 14 she was driving the tractor, and then at 16 she was helping her father make wine. Our son's a computer programmer, so this isn't his thing. Our older daughter's in retail. So eventually maybe two out of the three might come back.

Kimball: Our daughter Emily is the assistant winemaker at Southbrook Vineyards. She went through Niagara College and graduated in 2018. She talks to me about all the different pieces of equipment she uses down in Niagara and is always telling me what I should get. And I'm like, "How much is it?" Only $44,000. I just laugh. She suggested that we make a rosé using Pinot Gris, skin on—it was skin-contact wine before it became popular. We surprised her by naming that wine after her. It won an award too. It's important that she's out doing her own thing now—she's got to make her name and then she can come home in 10 years and kick me out.

I love the smell of the grapes as they're coming in, the smell of the ferments. I get excited about different types of aging and keeping stuff in barrel longer than a lot of people will. With my Chardonnays, I've got one that's six months in barrel. Some of my Cab Francs and Cab Sauves I've left in barrels for three or four years. I play around with stuff like that. I taste them about once a month to see where they're at, or more often, depending on when I'm looking at bottling. If I'm getting closer to bottling, I'll taste more often. I line all the glasses up on the table and taste the barrels and figure out what's going to be blended with what. One of the big things that pushes me with the wine is that I'm a big food person. I love to cook. But I'm my own worst critic, so I'd rather be a winemaker than a chef.

When we first started out, I was nervous about the wines and how people would react to them, because it was something new that I was doing and because of general insecurity. I've worked through all that. I don't get as nervous about the wine now because I know it's good.

The last few years, I've been in the tasting room more often, and I like hearing comments from people about our wines. I find I'm healthier than I was when I was in the brokerage industry. Owning my own small business and paying down the mortgage, seeing how people react to the wines—those are big motivators right there. The difference between the County and Niagara is that Niagara is usually busy year-round, and one of our biggest barriers to growth is that we're not.

Liz: Kimball's been forced into the tasting room these last two years due to family health issues. He's normally in the back—he's very quiet, shy. We don't have any employees, it's just us running everything. It's tiring, especially when you live right next door. We've been married for 34 years, so we don't always agree. When we close for the day, at the dining table, we're still talking business.

Putting that Open flag out and seeing everyone show up, including the mayor, and friends and people Kimball had worked with at other wineries—we made it. When Kimball was working over at Peddlesden Wines, unbeknownst to him, everyone made a bet that this city boy wasn't going to last one season in the vineyard. Twenty years later, we're still here.

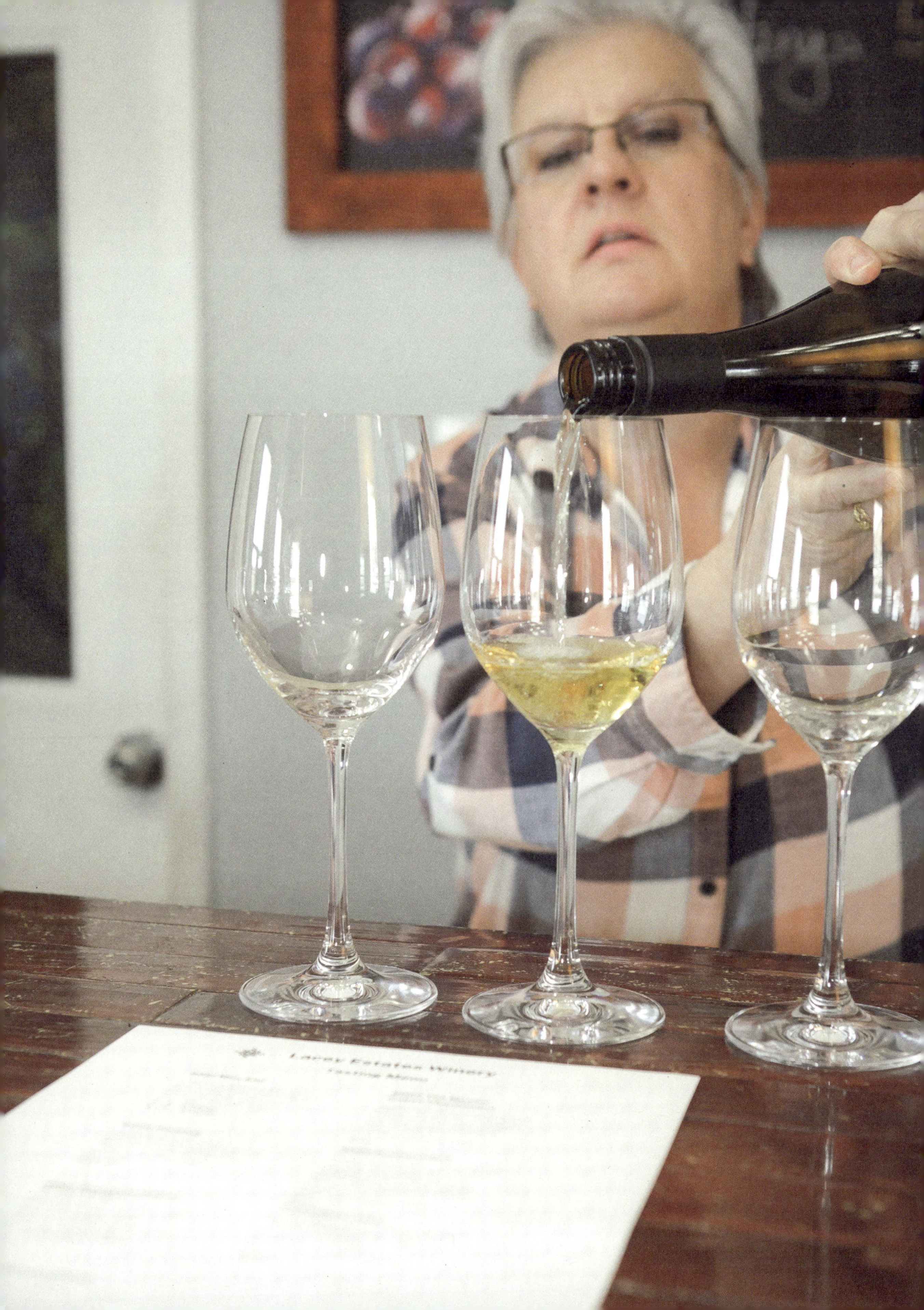

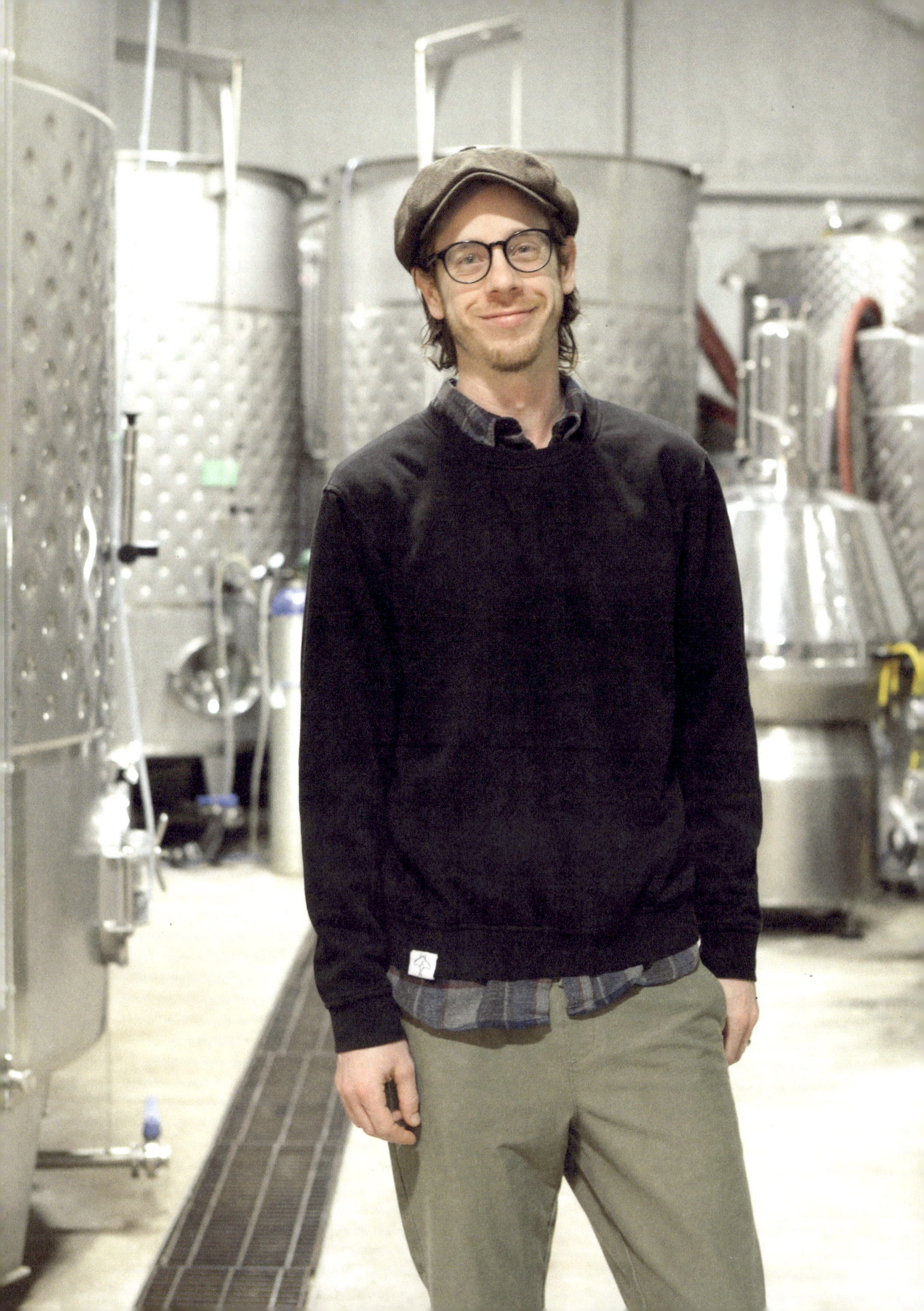

Lighthall Vineyards, Milford

With 60 acres of vines, Lighthall also produces its own sheep's milk cheese on site, with both cheese and wine reflecting the farm's natural terroir.

CHRIS THOMPSON

I was really into cooking from a young age. Chef was my original career goal, but working in kitchens for 10 years changed my mind. All the people across the counter were making twice the money and working half the hours, so I figured I might try that. I did some construction and factory work too, which actually turned out to be really good prep for winemaking—it's quite industrial, a lot of plumbing, a lot of forklift driving, a lot of fixing things. I met my now-wife, Megan, and moved to Toronto to be close to her, and I started working at a wine bar called Quanto Basta, a little Italian place kitty-corner to the Summerhill LCBO. I had worked in fine dining settings with wine before, but that job was really my proper crash course in the wine world.

I decided to take a Wine 101 class at George Brown; I thought I might as well learn something that would help me in my job. And then the more I learned, the more I got into it. Wine is based on history, which is why I find it so interesting. It's not just a beverage. To understand wine, you have to learn about history, language, culture, geography, soil—different rock types and mineral content and chemistry and microbiology.

My third time visiting the County was to play music at the Acoustic Grill; this was after Megan and I started dating. A friend of hers lived in Picton, so we made a weekend of it. I remember texting her friend and saying, "I don't know if I have three hours of material that's polished. Do you know anyone who could open for an hour?" And she said, "Yeah, I'll ask my friend Jeremie Albino." So Jeremie came and opened for me, which is hilarious because our musical careers have taken quite different directions since then. By the end of that weekend, Megan and I decided to move out here.

I wanted to work directly in a winery or brewery but couldn't find anything right away, so I started at the County Canteen. We were living at Point Petre, and a friend forwarded me a Facebook post from Elis, the only employee at the time other than founder Glenn Symons, saying that Lighthall was looking for help in the tasting room. I emailed Glenn my résumé and within 15 minutes he'd emailed me back to see if I could interview the next day. Megan had our one car at the time, so I longboarded down Royal Road; it's an old gravel road, and it took me half an hour. I arrived drenched in sweat because it was late July. Glenn watched me walk in, sweating and holding a longboard, and he was like, "Who's this kid?"

I started in July and by Labour Day we had sold out of wine. Glenn had a 2017 Chardonnay and 2017 Pinot Gris, and something else that had been ready to bottle since March of that year. He just hadn't bottled it because he was so busy. I started helping in the cellar and he took me under his wing. I was a sponge. A lot of it came really naturally because it's quite industrial work, but you do need a good palate. It was a good marriage of my skills.

Tonnellerie
MONTGILLARD
BOURGOGNE
VGS FG MT
500L 23

①23 MR/P/P CBF

Early on, I took over the Charmat program, so that connected me to other winemakers, like Keith at Closson Chase. I got to know Fred at Huff. And we did stuff with Broken Stone and Hillier Creek and Sugarbush and Long Dog—and half the County, it felt like.

I think when I started we had 16 acres and did about 1,500–2,000 cases of wine. Around that time, we also got some investment. Now we're 62 acres of vines and over 5,000 cases. We have a separate retail space with a retail manager and a full team of retail staff. We have a separate cheese building with a cheesemaker and cheese-making staff. We have a whole warehouse with all of our inventory. I have some cellar staff. We have a vineyard manager taking care of all our different vineyards with all of his vineyard staff. We have a general manager, we have all these department heads. It's a completely different landscape from when it was just me and Glenn and Elis on the weekends and Patrick making cheese. Five years is a while, but it's also not that long.

In 2020, our seasonal workers were set to fly in from Thailand to staff the vineyard. The same guys have been coming for eight years; they had a connecting flight, Bangkok to Tokyo, Tokyo to Vancouver, Vancouver to Toronto. Airport security stopped them: "Sorry, Tokyo won't let you pass through." This was right at the beginning of the Covid-19 pandemic. No one knew what the hell was going on. And because of the time difference, we had no idea. They were trapped at the airport overnight, had to find their ways home, and then get in touch to tell us they weren't coming.

So we had no vineyard staff. It was me and a ragtag crew: Chris Bonham Carter, Matt Palmer, lots of people who worked in food and beverage, which is very different from working agriculture. We started with a crew of 15 and by the end of the two weeks there were 4 people left. By the end it was me and Glenn's kids who had come home for the summer, and one or two others who stuck it out. It was a good crash course in vineyard management.

I think the appeal is staying true, as much as possible, to the vintage, so long as you can still create a balanced and delicious product. I'd rather intervene a little bit if it's going to make something that's more delicious or more balanced. I don't want to be too dogmatic about things. The old adage is "wine is made in the vineyard." The winemaker just has to not fuck it up. If you've got crap fruit to start with, and it's horribly farmed, it doesn't really matter what you do to it in the cellar, it's going to be average at best. Conversely, you can have amazing fruit and ruin it. So that's the challenge.

By the time we got to the 2021 harvest, Glenn was starting to burn out. He had been doing this for 13 years, seven days a week, non-stop, and he kind of hit a wall. He said he was thinking about moving out east and asked if I'd be interested in taking things full on. And that was kind of it. The 2022 harvest was my first full harvest running the show, and our Pinot Gris won double gold, best of all its categories. But that wasn't just me—we have a solid team and most of the credit goes to the vineyard team. They brought in good fruit and I didn't ruin it.

We're still a ways off, but I'm trying to work on getting the sustainable winemaking material certification for us and seeing what we can improve in the vineyard from a vine health perspective and with the soil. When you've got 50 pots on the stove, it's really hard to be laser-focused on each one. I'm looking forward to having fewer pots on the stove so that we can fine-tune and do things better.

Available for tasting:		Available for purchase:	
FLIGHT $18	Short Flight $13	SINGLE VARIETALS:	BLENDS
Untamed	Harrison	Kingston Black $16-	Blush $
Harrison	Savvy Pomme	Yarlington Mill $14-	Cans
Savvy Pomme Sparkling	Sparkling	Dabinett $12-	Untamed
Blush	Blush	Harrison $11-/$20-	Hopped
Sour cherry	Pommeau	Savvy Pomme $10- Sparkling	Sour Cher
Pommeau		Savvy Pomme Still (750ml) $19-	

RARE TASTING SPECIAL 15% of
Blush, Dab., Harrison (SAVE 6

Loch Mór Cider Co., Hillier

Loch Mór produces award-winning, small-batch sparkling dry cider crafted with apples picked from their 10-acre orchard.

SARA BOYD

I first tried cider while living in London. In the UK, people go down to the West Country for weekends, to Cornwall and Devon and Dorset, to visit the cider orchards. When you're living in London, it's easy to travel around Europe. So you can go over to France and try French cider. We went to Saint Sebastian and tried Spanish cider. When we were in Berlin, we tried German Apfelwein. I'm a curious drinker—I like to try new things.

Gary's work transferred him to Texas, and when we relocated there, I was shocked by the lack of cider in the stores. It didn't even occur to me that the cider we were used to drinking didn't exist in the same way outside the UK or Europe. We thought we could make it ourselves, but Texas isn't an apple-growing region. It doesn't get the cold, and you can't buy decent apples or get decent juice.

We started researching apple-growing areas in North America. By that point, we were green card holders, but I really didn't want to put down roots in the States. I wanted to move back to Canada, so we went for it. BC was in the running; we're both big skiers and you can grow apples out there. It's lovely but the land prices are really high. We looked at Nova Scotia but it was a little too removed from major city centres. Quebec was a challenge because our French isn't good enough. We chose Ontario, and Prince Edward County specifically, because of the proximity to Toronto, Ottawa, and Montreal. Plus it's a VQA region. It's really pretty.

Our biggest learning curve was in actually growing the apples. Neither of us had any background in apple-growing. At the time, you needed five acres of trees to get your license, so we planted our trees in 2017. Apples are one of the more complicated types of produce to grow because they're susceptible to diseases and bacterial pressures and fungus and insects that attack trees way more than any other widely grown crop. The imposter syndrome was real back then: we didn't know how to make cider or how to take care of 3,000 trees. What were we thinking?

This used to be a huge apple-growing area, so the one thing we did know is that trees could grow here. Once the trees were in, our attention turned to building plans and getting them approved by the planning office. And then we had to figure out our tank sizes, what equipment we needed to get first, and how to set it all up.

Our kids were really young at that point and Gary was working full-time from home. There was a lot going on. I think that's when—especially in the summer, when we're working in this industry and we don't have weekends off—you feel the worst parent guilt. When friends who aren't in the hospitality industry invite me to the beach on a Saturday afternoon, my only response is, "I can't go to the beach. Can I go there in the winter when I have time?"

I think the main difference between beer and cider is that we can only make cider once a year. We need to have more storage. Cider also doesn't have a lot of research behind it. When you're a winemaker, you can get Pinot Noir or Chardonnay grapes, and you can look through catalogues to find the best yeast to use and the processes you need to follow to make wine. That doesn't exist for cider. It's a lot of trial and experimentation—so much experimentation until you stumble on something that works. That's what we've done here.

We're one of the few orchards to grow the Harrison cider apple, a North American apple that was thought to be lost after Prohibition. It was popular in New York City clubs and was often referred to as champagne cider. All the orchards were thought to have been destroyed, until a collector found a single tree near a mill in New England. People started propagating it in the 1970s. We planted some here a few years ago without having tried it, because we couldn't get any to try. The other orchards in North America growing Harrison apples right now are in Washington state and Virginia, though I've heard of people planting trees in Ontario after trying our cider. The trees grow really well here. Harrison apples are like the heirloom tomatoes of the cider world. Very few North American cider apples have any tannins, and the characteristics differ from some of the British cider apples. Harrison has a really light tannin profile to it. It's not overpowering: orange peel, leathery notes, really crisp. It's a very crisp apple, especially in our orchard. A slight astringent tannin on the end, but still really soft.

I wrote my pommelier exam in January 2020. There's no official study program or course, aside from suggested readings and learning topics, but half the exam is knowing the trees and the apples. I'd researched and planted the trees, and I had fermented individual batches. I knew my apple flavours. I had visited so many different cider regions in the world. During the blind tasting exam, you go through several rounds of three ciders to identify high flavours, identify regions, identify apples, and to pick up on faults. I was the third Canadian to pass—I'm a Certified Pommelier.

I see such points of difference between all of us local cidermakers; we serve different communities, different customers. There's enough space for everybody here. And we're all making great cider.

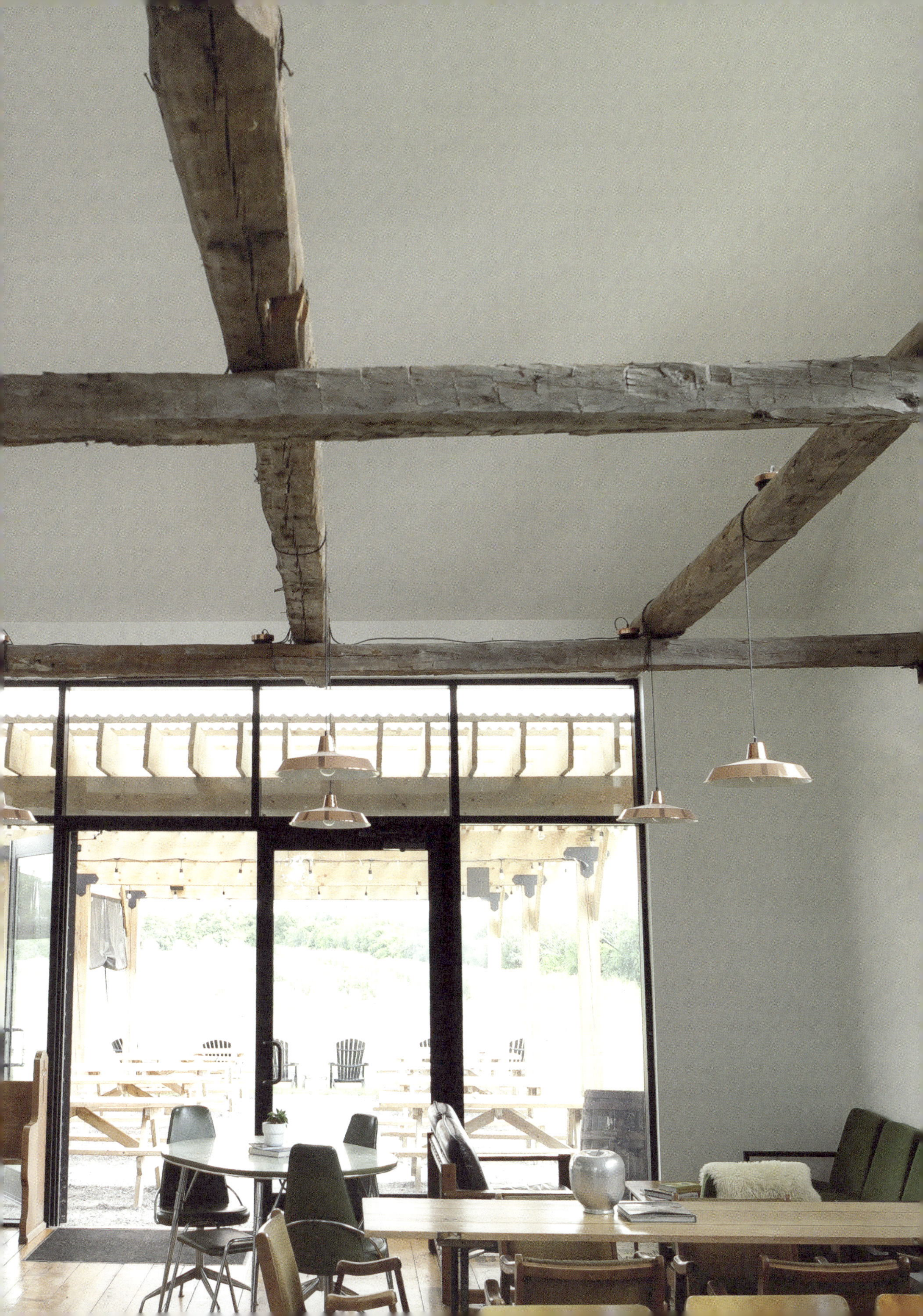

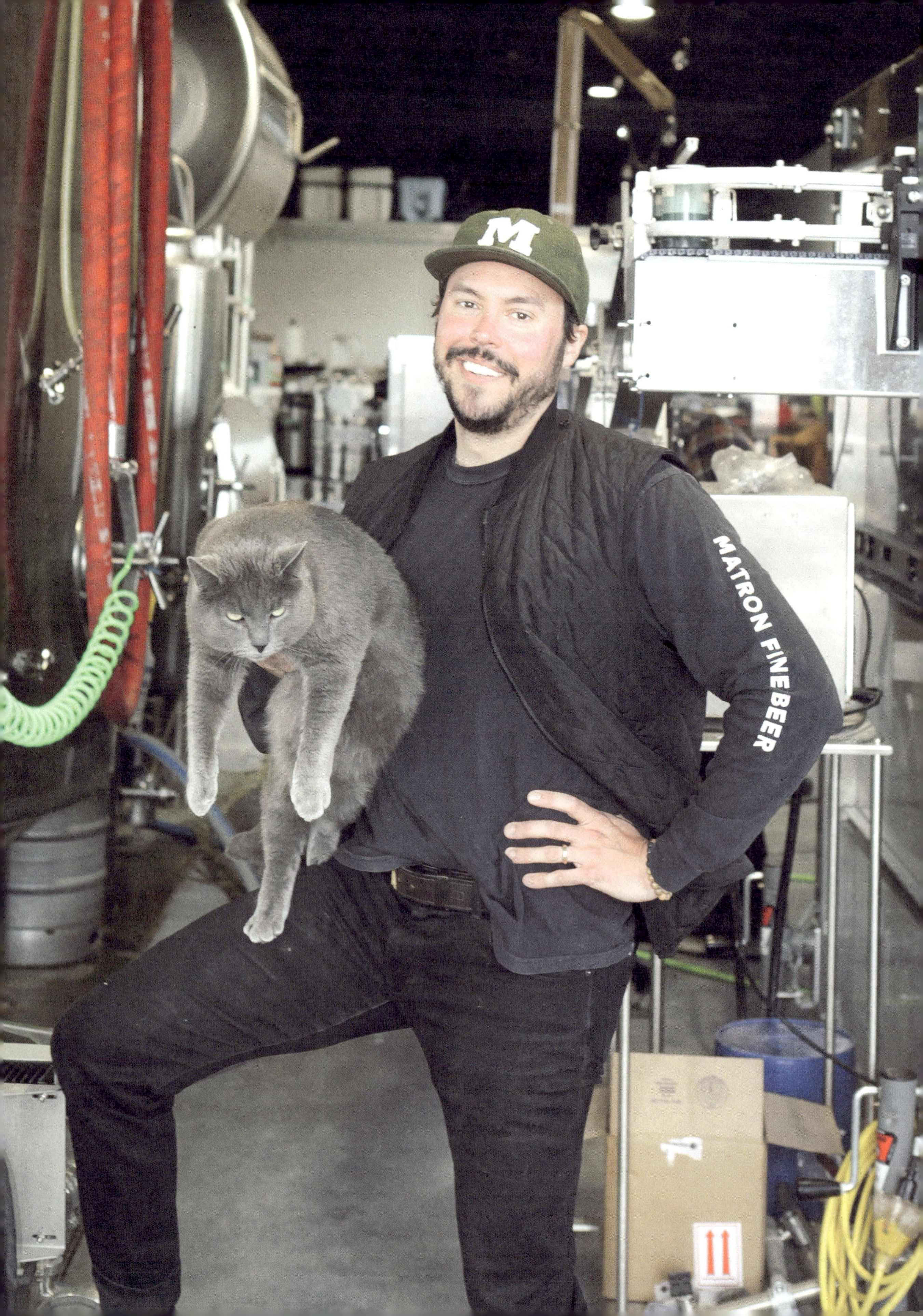
M
MATRON FINE BEER

Matron Fine Beer, Bloomfield

Matron is a brewery that expresses local terroir with balanced lagers, aromatic IPAs, and elegant farmhouse ales.

JUSTIN DA SILVA

I grew up sailing in the summer, and after university I coached sailing in the British Virgin Islands for a year. My partner, Mallory, had gotten a job at a marketing agency in Ottawa and we did the long-distance thing. But I had this thought when I was down there that I should go back and finish my university degree. And then I came back, and I was like, why did I leave the Caribbean?

I got a job at the Clocktower Brew Pub in Ottawa. The brewmaster was Patrick Fiori. He went to Heriot-Watt University in Edinburgh, Scotland, one of the few schools in the world to offer a Master's in Brewing and Distilling, so he was very knowledgeable in all things malt. Within three months of getting the job, I was learning how to brew there. Bryce McBain, who went on to work at Beau's and Halcyon—he works at Matron now—gave me homebrew equipment when he was leaving to go to the Siebel Institute in Chicago and said, "Have at it, here's the books." I started almost obsessively making beer. On the weekends when I wasn't working, I'd be making a batch in my kitchen, trying to figure it out. I kept thinking that I needed to make it better and better and better. That was really the beginning of the end, so to speak.

Mallory and I both needed a break, so we decided to quit our jobs and travel to Europe. It was nice to travel and experience so many small towns that make different types of beer we'd never be exposed to over here. I came back and Clocktower took me back part-time; I got another part-time job at Kichesippi Beer to pay the bills. After juggling both part-time jobs for a while, I started doing sales for Nickel Brook. That gave me an interesting perspective—I wasn't just in Ottawa anymore. I was on the road. I was going to Kingston, I was covering a lot of territory, doing LCBO sales, doing beer festivals. That opened my eyes to more of the industry.

I was brewing at Beyond the Pale when an individual came in and asked them about consulting on opening a brewery in Kingston. His name was Ron Shore and he hired me as a consultant. He bought a little pilot system, and his business partner had a small warehouse space, and I'd go down to Kingston on Wednesdays and cook up a batch of beer. I crafted Stone City's four core recipes. When we opened in 2014, I managed the brewery, came up with new recipes to release every week, and started doing off-site sales to grow the brand. They brought Mallory in to work on marketing, brand direction, and managing the front of house. We really took that brewery on as a project, hoping that one day we would be a bigger part of it, with our sights set on eventually starting our own. I think at one point we did 60 new beers in a year, which was a lot. Honestly, when I look back on it, it was fun, but it was stressful and exhausting trying to produce so much different work. Ultimately, it gave me the ability to experiment, to see what I like, what I want to focus on. I think we built something pretty amazing. We're still in touch with many of the people who came through that place, and I think that's a testament to the community we built there.

We won the tender on our brewing equipment, we bought a house in the County, and then we bought the brewhouse in the same week. That was another push-you-off-the-fucking-cliff moment right there—I guess we're doing this now. It's a 14-acre farm with a natural gas feed. It wasn't on municipal water, but it had a good well, and we put in another well when we bought it. We got the property in August and Matron was born. Mallory gave her notice to Stone City the day the property closed.

The name Matron is a nod to Mallory and Jes, our business partner. The beer industry is a pretty male-dominated place, and we wanted to build a brewery that was very welcoming and warm and took care of people—whether it's the customers or the employees—and the land we work on. Matron embodies that. It's maternal, but still feminine and strong. It can also be used negatively to mean "a sober old lady," which I think is amazing. We thought it was kind of cheeky, and a lot of our beer names have double entendres, so it fits.

Balancing work and family is very hard. One thing we have as business owners is flexibility over how we use our time. We finally found child care, which is a huge thing in the County. Jes had a child four days after us and she moved back to Ottawa. So she's been more remote, doing sales and taking on a bunch of the administrative stuff, because running a front of house, running a brewery, managing a property, doing all that plus marketing and social media, is a lot.

I really like days when Mallory and I can work together. It doesn't happen that often anymore, but when you've worked with someone for a long time, and everything falls into place without having to really talk about it too much, that's nice. Jes, Mallory, and I all worked together for an event recently, and it had been a couple of years since that had happened. That reminded me of our first summer being open—it was a lot of fun and we worked so well together that we didn't even really need to talk about what we were doing.

At Stone City, I was a big proponent of making fancy beers and serving them in stemware. I've enjoyed moving away from that; when we opened Matron, we decided to do pitchers. We want to make fine beer that's really drinkable.

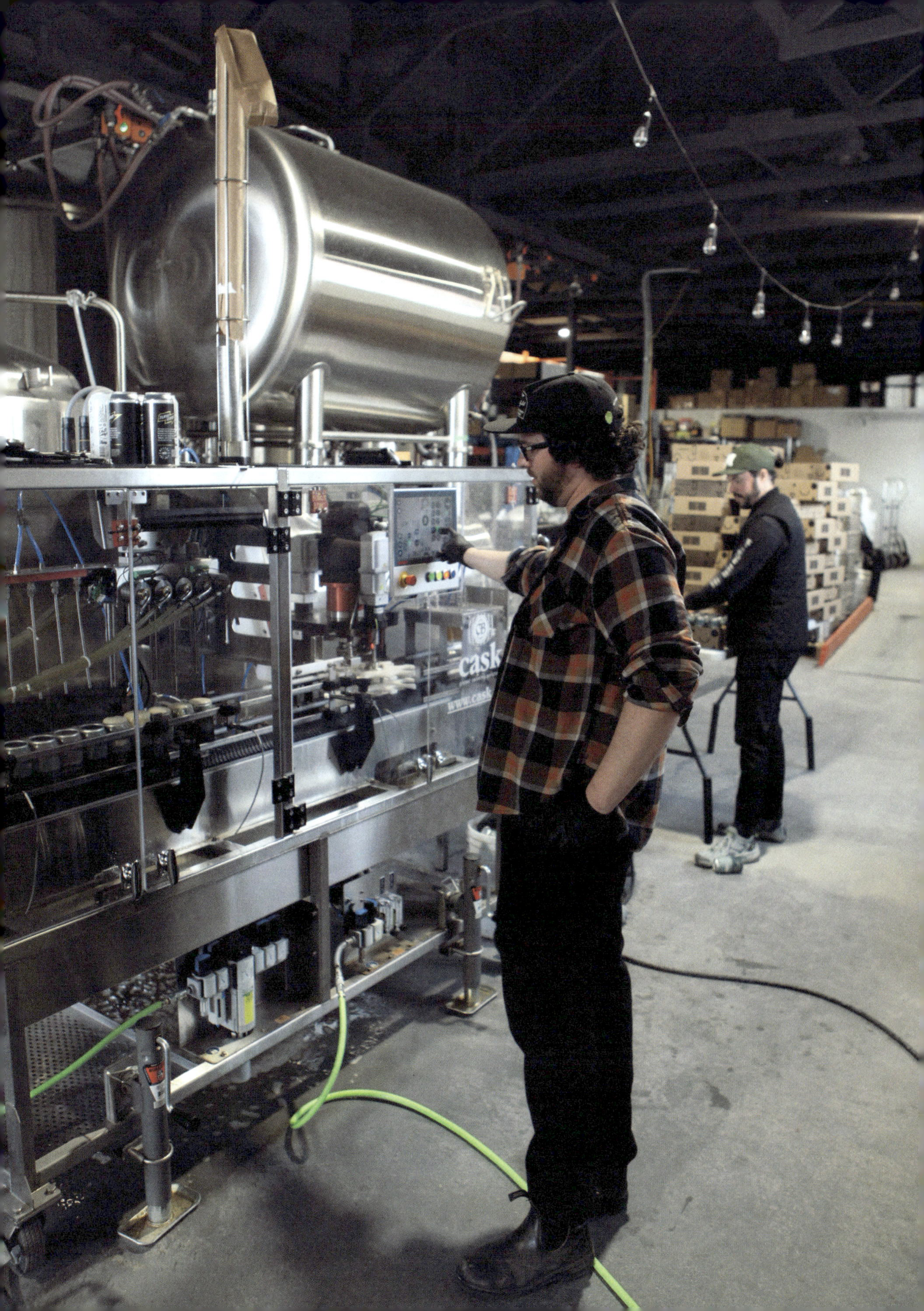
cask

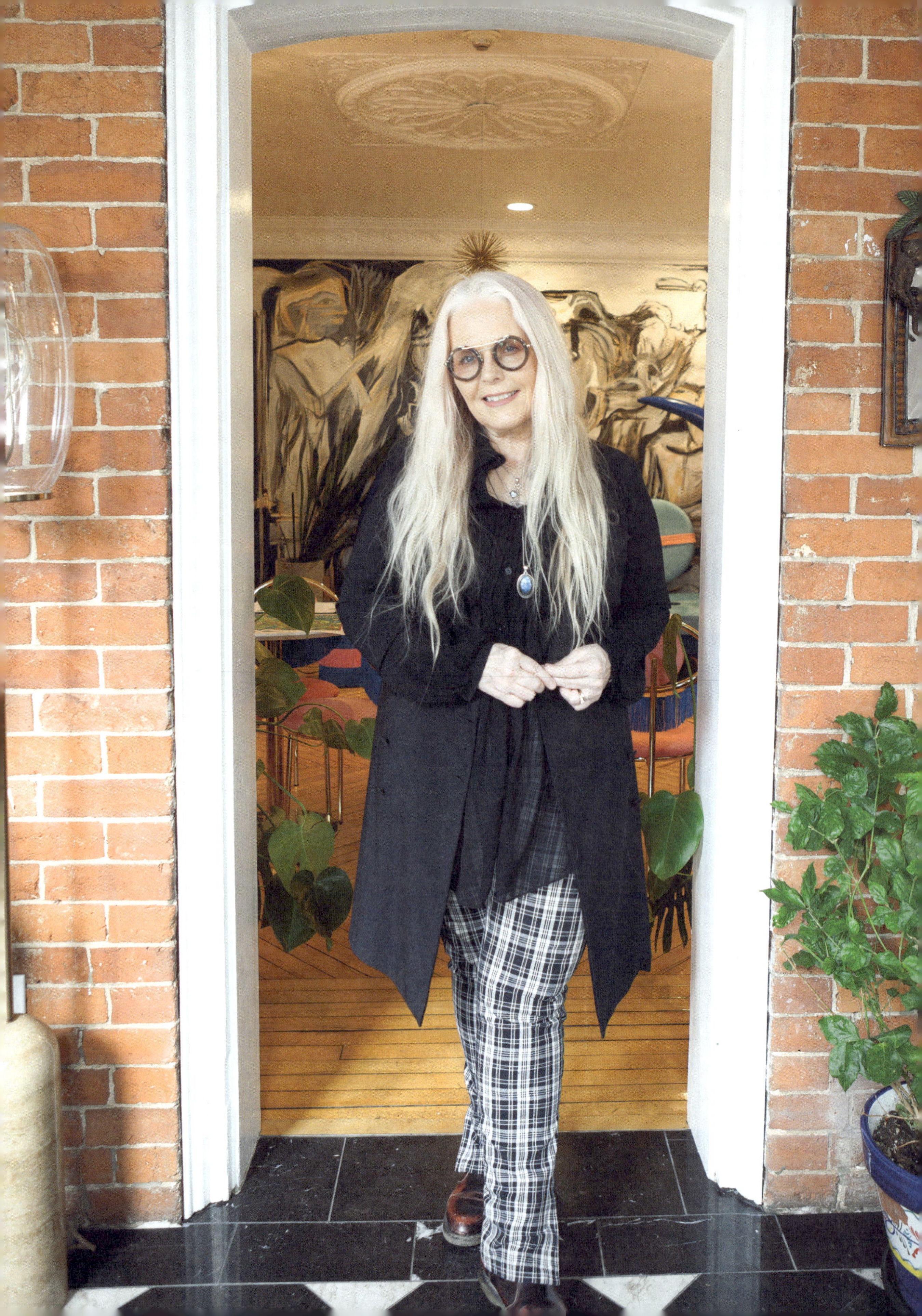

Merrill House, Picton

Built in 1878 for Judge Edwards Merrill, the Merrill House has been restored and offers boutique hotel and dining experiences.

ASTRID YOUNG

As a musician, you work in restaurants because you can't gig all the time. And even when I started getting to a point where I was making some money by touring and doing sessions and stuff like that, I still needed more to make up the difference. I got my first bartending gig when I was way underage, right out of high school, and I kept at it because it was a job I could pick up anywhere.

I thought I knew something about wine, but when you start learning about it, you realize how little you know. My wine moment came when I was working for an orchestra contractor in Los Angeles. I did all the contracts for the musicians who do movie soundtracks. We were on a break from a session at a Mexican restaurant across the road from Paramount, and we were talking about how much we hated dealing with the suits at the studio. This one guy said, "All you need is to have something in common with them, like playing golf or knowing something about wine." And I thought, well, I'm not much of a golfer. So the next day I bought a *Wine Spectator* magazine and I read it cover to cover. I was fascinated. And it snowballed from there.

Becoming a sommelier really changed my perspective on hospitality. I was a touring musician and I went all over Europe and the United States, which meant I got to visit a lot of wine-growing regions. Having a connection to the place and the people and the wine and the cuisine is just so rich and incredible. If I was in Paris and had a couple of days off, we went to Champagne or Burgundy. From Florence, we visited Piedmont or Chianti.

I came back to Toronto in the late '90s. I was going to stay for about six months and then hightail it back to California. But I found out that I had cancer and I ended up staying for another year while I went through treatment. I was looking for something to do during that time, so I enrolled in a 22-week course through the International Sommelier Guild. I wore sunglasses all the time and nobody took me seriously. But I'm pretty good at being an outlier; I just keep showing up. The interesting thing is that there's a stereotype in the wine industry; some people walk around like they're carrying some God-given secret. At the time I thought, well, if this is what it's like, I don't know if I want to be in this business. At the end of the course I thought, I've invested all this time and money, and I really do love wine. So if I really want to pursue this, I should maybe go someplace other than Toronto. That's when I moved to Napa Valley.

I immediately saw the difference between the wine people in a wine-growing region versus in a city. The wine people in the city, they've never gotten their hands dirty—that gives them an attitude. Most of them are afraid you know more than they do! I rented a little cottage in a town called Calistoga, in the north end of Napa Valley. One day, I walked out of the cottage and there was a case of wine sitting on my front step, half full of bottles.

None of them were labelled, but there was a note on top of it from the lady living across the street, who was one of the higher-ups at Beringer. She'd written: *I thought you'd be interested in these wines, they're from a Cinq Cépages cuvée tasting.*

After living in Toronto, Los Angeles, and Calistoga, there was no going back to the city for me. I just love small-town living. The interesting thing about Napa Valley, even though it has such a big reputation, is that it's very much like the County in a lot of ways; it's smaller than you think, and everybody knows each other and each other's business.

A guy I knew from Toronto had property in the County and he brought me out here. I remember him taking me to Waupoos Estates Winery. There were four wineries at the time: Black Prince, By Chadsey's Cairns, Waupoos, and Peddlesden Wines. Twenty-two years on, I predate most of the wineries. I love the fact that I can remind people of where we came from and what our roots are and who is responsible for making us who we are.

I ended up moving here permanently, even though I still wasn't really convinced that I was going to stay, but I thought I needed to figure out if it was possible. I knew some winemakers down in Niagara, so I got them to give me wine to trot around to a few restaurants here. And that's how I met everybody. Amy and Edward Shubert, who used to own the Merrill Inn, now the Merrill House. I met Kathy and David, who owned the Devonshire. I met Andrew Laliberte, who owned a place called Ruby's, where 555 now is—I met Grant Howes from The County Cider Company sitting at the bar at Ruby's. I thought immediately, these are my people!

It was all just so new here, but there was a lot of excitement, and when I discovered that most local winemakers were going to focus on Pinot Noir and Chardonnay, I was just like, oh, this is where it's at. I think Prince Edward County is a very important wine region. We're making great wines, the best Chardonnay in Canada, bar none. I've been at the Merrill since 2016, a little more than two years before Jordan Martin bought it from the Shuberts, and I feel very privileged to be be able to introduce people to local wine, to change their minds.

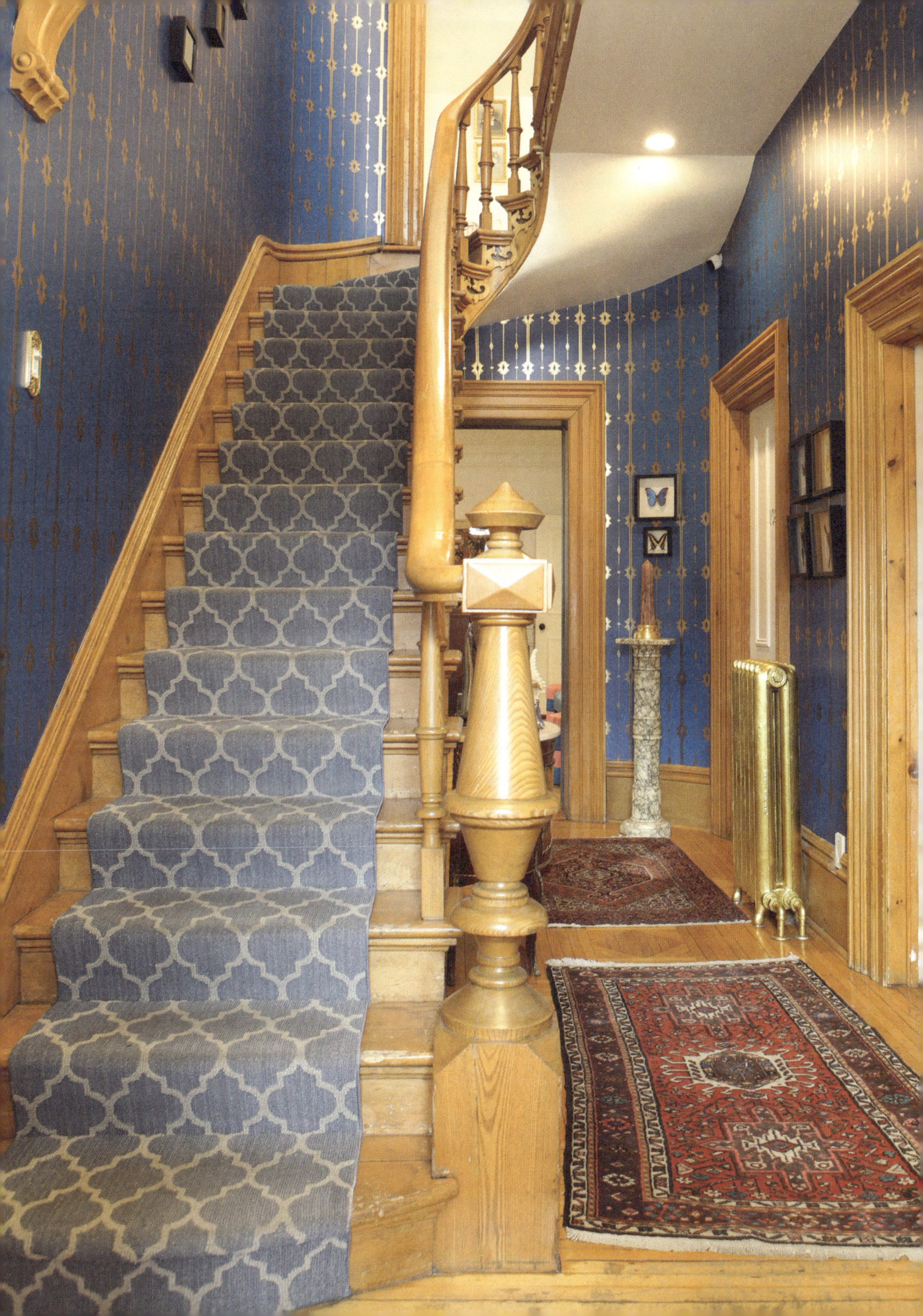

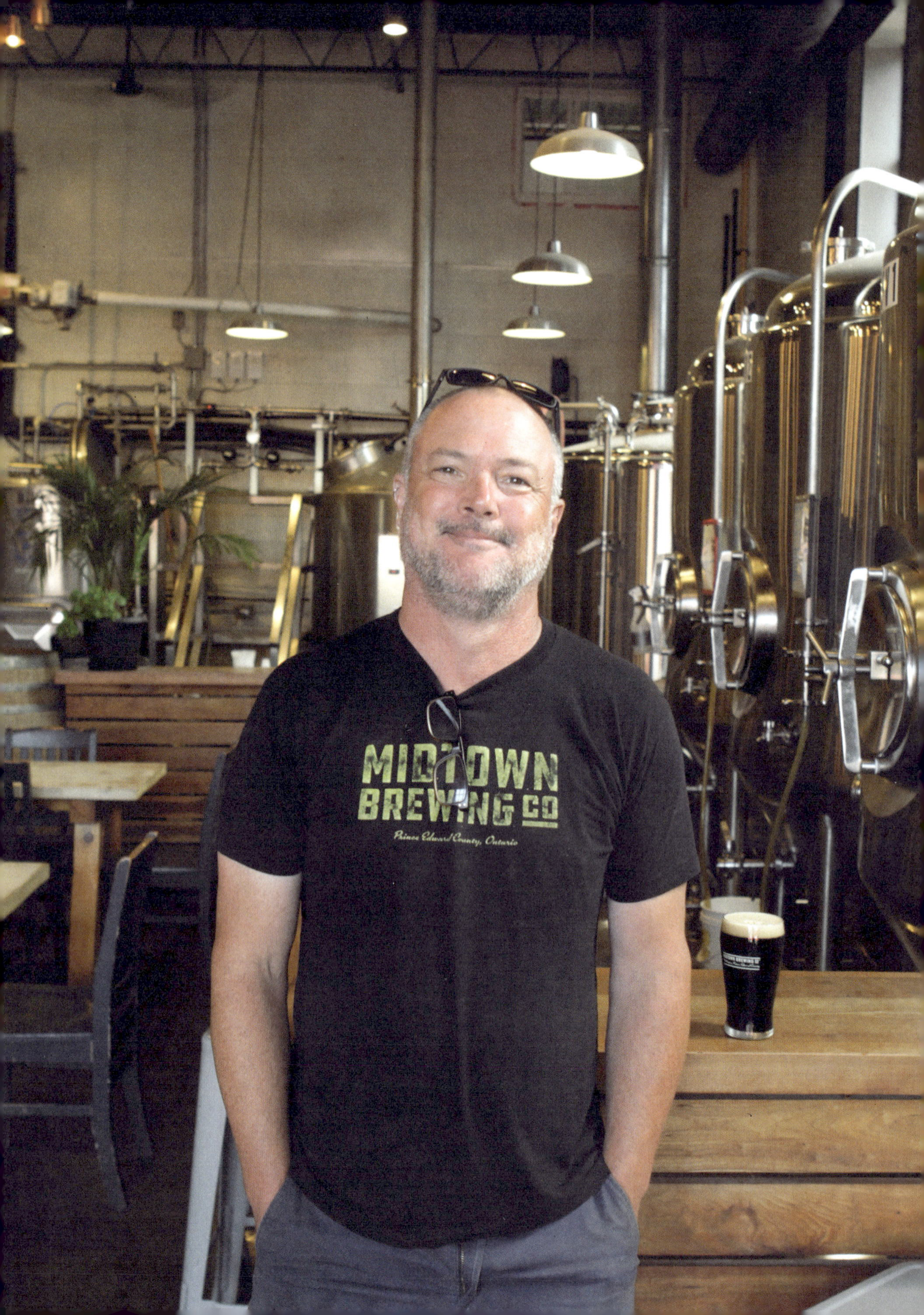
MIDTOWN
BREWING CO
Prince Edward County, Ontario

Midtown Brewing Company, Wellington

This community-minded brew pub is located in the historic Midtown Meat Company building.

SPIKE LEES

I put myself through school by working in pubs. I was going to do cellular biology. If I remember right, I wanted to concentrate on the physics that were involved in the transfer of molecules and particles through the cell membrane. And then I completely switched everything and studied photojournalism. I think I was looking for travel and adventure and I saw that as a potential route.

There were lots of cellars in London because at the time, all the tourists wanted warm English cask ale. Anyone who lived in London was drinking Fosters. There were four little windows in the pub basement, and they'd back up a tanker truck and fill up 200-gallon or 400-gallon tanks of Fosters. It was my job to sort out the casks. This happened mainly in Fuller's or Whitbread pubs in tourist areas like Covent Garden.

I was always coming and going from the UK. I ran irrigation for a banana plantation in Israel in the earlier 1990s; I ran a bar in Greece. I worked in a kitchen, and I made a lot of chicken and potatoes. Travelled around Turkey—I travelled a lot. I found my way to Canada for the first time in 1997, and it was on a visit back to Canada for my best friend Nick's engagement party that I connected with Jen. We moved here permanently after Jen and I got together.

Beer culture is completely different between Canada and the UK. Growing up, I learned the difference in flavours because my dad managed brewery depots and worked as a wine merchant. So I was aware of the British characteristics of caramel, chocolate topping, those kinds of things. I knew a good pale ale when I got one, and I didn't like what I would call stinky beer, bitters, and things like that.

For a long time, I worked as a line producer in film and television. Eventually, I took a job with a company called RTR Media in Toronto because it was the closest I could get in the industry to working nine to five. Otherwise, the hours are long and the demands are quite high. I did that for two and a half years, and then the writing was on the wall that a big media shakeup was coming. I really wanted a second career, and I thought about the times in my life that I'd most felt at home, most content. And it came down to beers, pubs, and food.

Jen and I have lived in cities all over the world, but we're both from fairly rural areas, and things changed when our kids came along. We wanted to be around greenery. My family was in England at the time, and Jen's mom lives out here, so the County made so much sense to us. We lived here for a couple of years before opening Midtown. I took the odd jobs I could find; I worked at a couple of wineries. I met Mark Andrewsky, my primary business partner, at a winery. We thought two heads would be better than one. We made some test brews, wrote a business plan, started to collect investors, and spent about a year looking for a location; we really thought we'd end up in a Quonset hut at the back of a field somewhere. Then somebody bought this place and didn't know what to do with it. We approached them and asked if we could retrofit the building. And they were like, sure, here's your lease. Go for it.

We dug the holes and smashed the floor open, which is no joke—it's 18 inches of concrete. Two slabs. Got the drains in, got them connected, then covered all of that up and did the rest. We had to cut the holes in the walls for the windows.

At that time, I think there were around 40 wineries in the County. I thought our timing was right; we were going to be one of the first breweries. But the more the merrier; every brewer out here offers different expressions and flavours because we're different individuals. My taste is completely different from Drew's at 555, from the guys over in Bloomfield, from Chris Parsons. We all make totally different beers. I think that's also part of the appeal of the community here: we help one another out. I mean, we're going to cross over in some of the styles we make, but we're all going to interpret even common beers differently.

Originally, I thought I'd be cranking out more seasonal, small-batch barrels, more cask beer. Instead, we have our mainstay flagships and we're like a tiny version of a British regional brewery. Quality and consistency is what we go for. We use real crops and natural ingredients, and things shift from year to year and crop to crop. But my goal is to make sure it's always easy to recognize the Midtown ESB.

So we're sailing in a lot safer waters right now than I thought we might. I think we also all got a little bit smacked in the mouth when craft brewers were typecast—there was this big media push around the big burly beer-drinking guy with the beard and all the tattoos. And that certainly doesn't reflect me or what I'm trying to do. I think it might have turned away a lot of people who might otherwise have been beer drinkers. I'm constantly repeating, no, I'm not a New England IPA person. I'm going to make a lager. I'm going to make bitters that are still balanced ales. These are all-natural, handmade beers that taste really good; I want to be able to sit down and talk to my friends over beer that tastes just right.

Seeing people you don't know walk out with a six-pack of beer and thinking, I fucking made that—I made that recipe, I made that beer—is amazing. One of my favourite times here is when the fireplace is going. It's February, it's dark outside, and a bunch of locals have come in on a Friday night and they're all content, and being sort of loud and noisy and fun and happy. That is really rewarding.

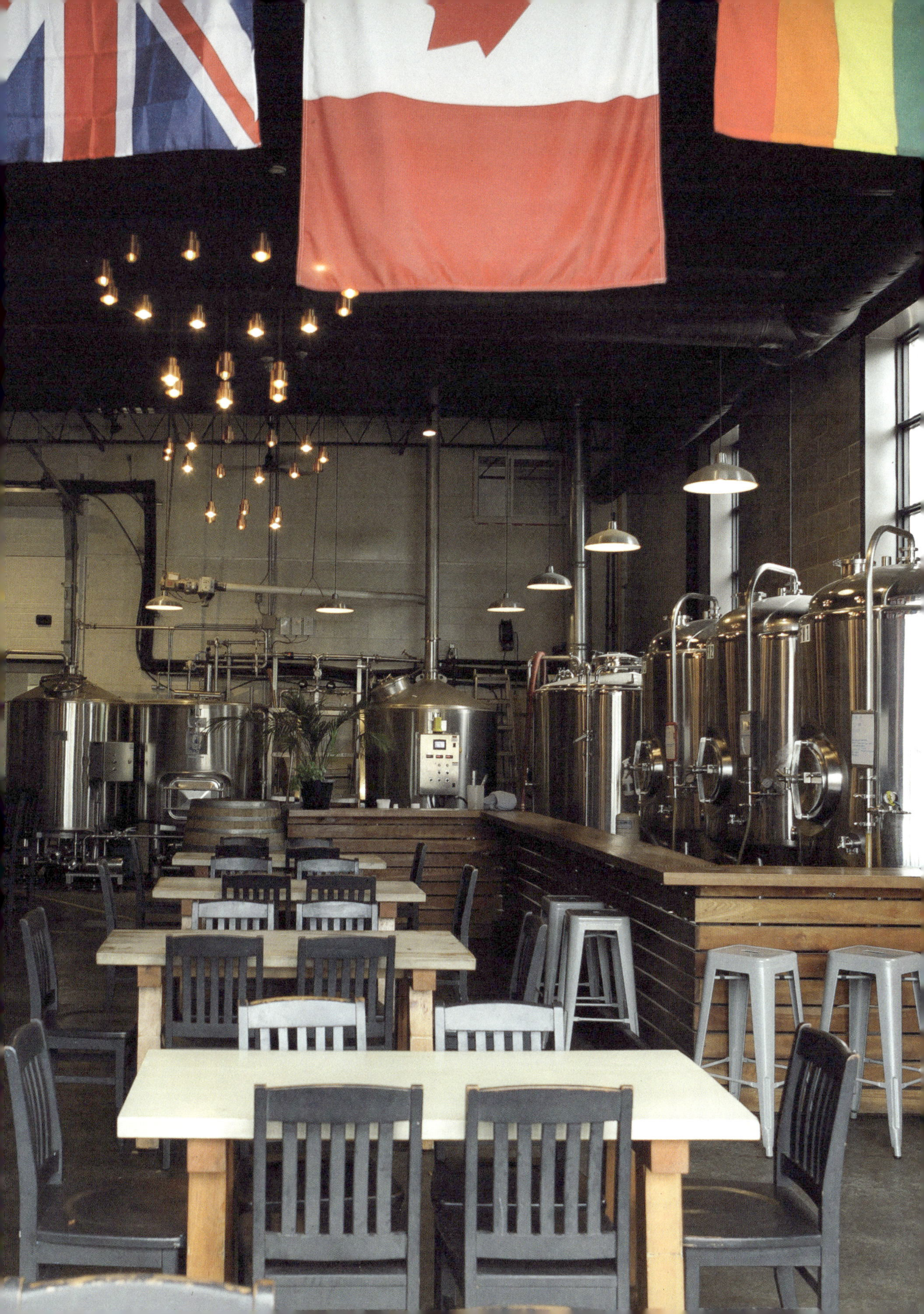

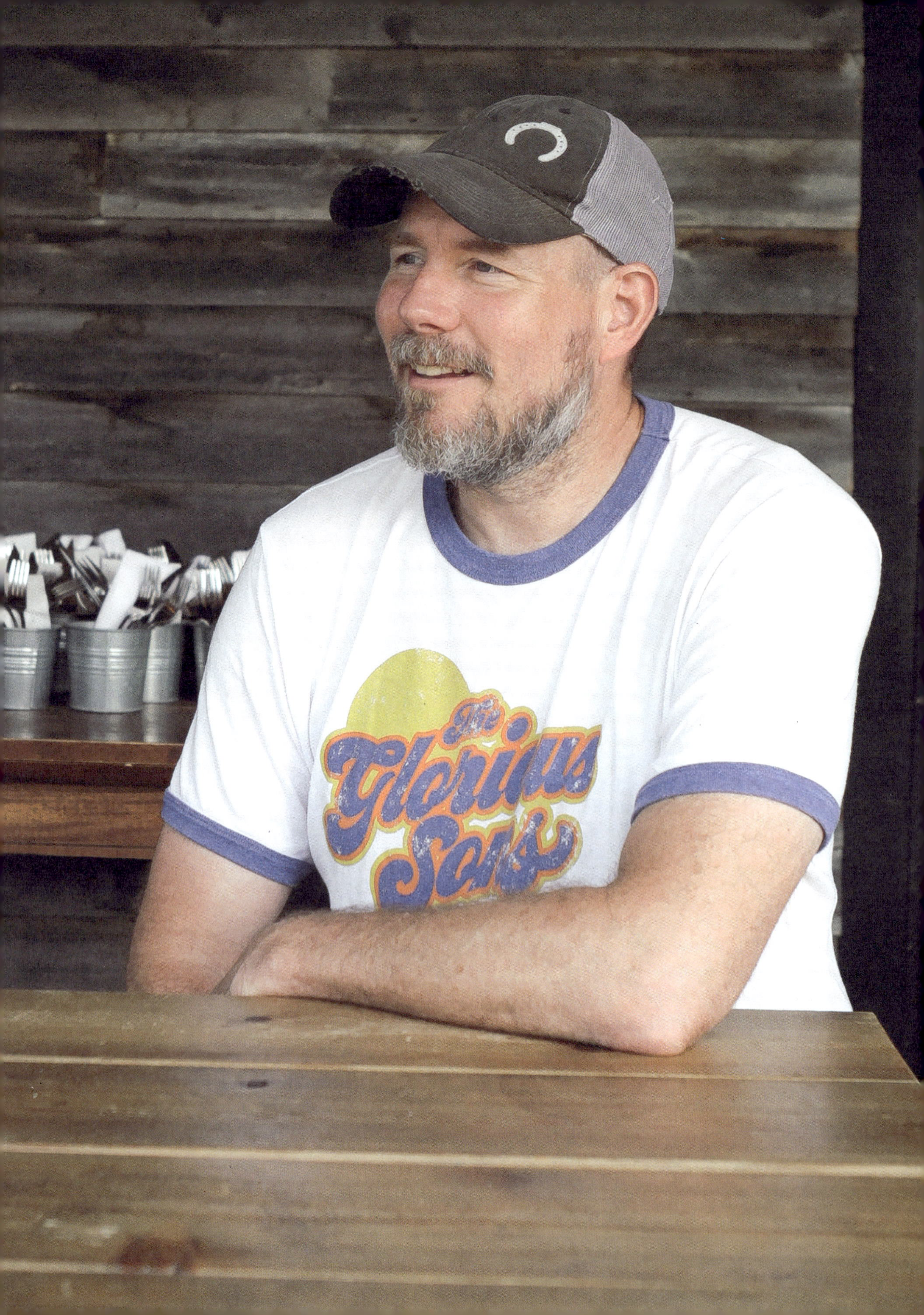
The Glorious Sons

Parsons Brewing Company, Picton

With a focus on sustainability, Parsons is a farm brewery that makes premium and unique brews.

CHRIS PARSONS, SAMANTHA PARSONS

Chris: Continental beer halls and quaint country pubs provided strong inspiration in shaping Parsons Brewing. One place in particular stands out—the small town of Polička in the Czech Republic. A little bigger than Picton, Polička has one brew pub that's also the local inn; I stayed there once while playing a friendly hockey match. We modelled Parsons on that ethos of the small-town community brewery as a gathering place for people to drink, eat, and connect.

Travel has always been a part of my life; to date, I've been to 79 countries. My desire to travel began with my family's relocation to Tokyo for my father's job as a civil servant when I was 12, and I'm still always dreaming of my next destination.

During a house-sitting stint in Tokyo, I got into trading. I was bartending nights, and during the day I'd read about trading; I was self-taught. At one point, I cold-called everyone I could think of, and one call really paid off. I started working at Merrill Lynch for free a couple days a week until they hired me into the global rotation program. I was one of 13 people who could rotate anywhere around the world. I worked at Merrill Lynch for 12 years. My last day was in 2008, just before the financial crisis was about to start. I spent a while backpacking in South America, and when I came back to Toronto for a wedding, I met Sam. That was it: I settled down in Toronto, and then made up some excuse about having weevils in my apartment and moved in with Sam.

Sam: My parents divorced when I was six. I was lucky to have aunts, uncles, and grandparents who created a community around me, and I grew up with many places I called home. I think that's why community is so important to me—the importance of serving community is something Chris and I share. It's one of our core values both in business and in life.

Like Chris, my life was also uprooted at 12, when I moved from Guatemala to Toronto. One of our beers is actually named after my dad; during one of his visits, he brought us coffee beans from his property in Lake Atitlán and Chris brewed what is now known as Grandpa Miguel's Coffee Stout. The image on the can is from a photo of my dad's face on his boat (his favourite place). Chris Del Degan hand-sketched it and it's perfect.

I had a great career in marketing at TELUS. I was led by inspiring mentors and leaders who believed in me and invested in my development; while working there, I earned my Executive MBA from Rotman. Chris and I met during that time, and after about six months of coffee dates, we were smitten, and I knew he was the one.

We got married in the County in 2010, in Waupoos. We'd been visiting the County often, as Chris's parents live in Picton, and it felt really right to gather here with all our friends and family from all over the world. We originally bought this property as a cottage, and at one point, we had all these other opportunities in front of us: moving to

Japan, Argentina, London. But we felt that this was a good place to raise our kids, that we'd be happiest here. We moved here full-time in 2013, and Parsons opened in 2016.

Chris: I bought a Sabco system; the Sabco isn't dirt cheap, but it's not a massive investment either. The deal was that if it turned out that I had a knack for brewing, we'd figure it out. Otherwise, we'd just sell the system, or maybe use it to brew once a year for Christmas or something. One night, we had a bunch of people over, and we were like, okay, well, maybe this is the way to go. We ordered the rest of the equipment we needed and started to get the space ready to operate as a commercial brewery.

But then we had a turning point after we'd built the original building and the rest was still under construction. We had our bottle shop, but we had no hydro, no electricity, no water. A diesel generator at the back powered the lights and the kegerator. It was so cold. We didn't get hydro until January. We were still vacillating: okay, we could move the brewery in here and make this a commercial brewery space and just sell beer to go and do tastings. Or we could go about bringing a full restaurant experience and beer garden and it's so expensive that you never sleep again.

Sam: When the business started to come together, what excited me was the hospitality piece. Having grown up in a large family, I had a vision of welcoming guests to our large communal tables. I liked the idea of creating a beautiful space and meaningful experiences. I often lean on my experience in training and development as well as in marketing and communications when leading our team at Parsons. I had incredible mentors growing up, and it's a privilege that as a business owner I get to be someone's mentor for a short period of time. I take that to heart. I also want to create a sustainable business that supports our family, supports local employment, and gives back to local entities—like the Prince Edward Learning Centre—that help champion solutions for some of the challenges faced by the most vulnerable members in our community.

Chris: I did a tally, and we've had 300 people work for us. That's 300 people who have contributed to the fabric that makes up Parsons Brewing. We've hired full-time, year-round staff and a ton of seasonal workers. Some are high school kids and this is their first foray into working, and some are in university or college and are trying to find themselves in between finding a career. They come here for the summer and they leave a little bit too early, because we'd like them to stay all the way to Labour Day, but they never do. But they often come back to work or to visit; they're like a large extended family.

Sam: This all started so organically. Chris is good at whatever he sets his mind to, whether it's banking or architecture. I saw the passion he had for brewing and I saw how happy it made him. And whether this is our forever path or not, right now it's ticking all the boxes. We're tired, we're exhausted, we're proud. Working together and raising a family and living together isn't always easy. It's amazing to have built something from nothing together as a couple. There was nothing here. There was a cornfield. And we built it—the design, the hop yard, the vineyard, these harvest tables—we built the community brewery of our dreams.

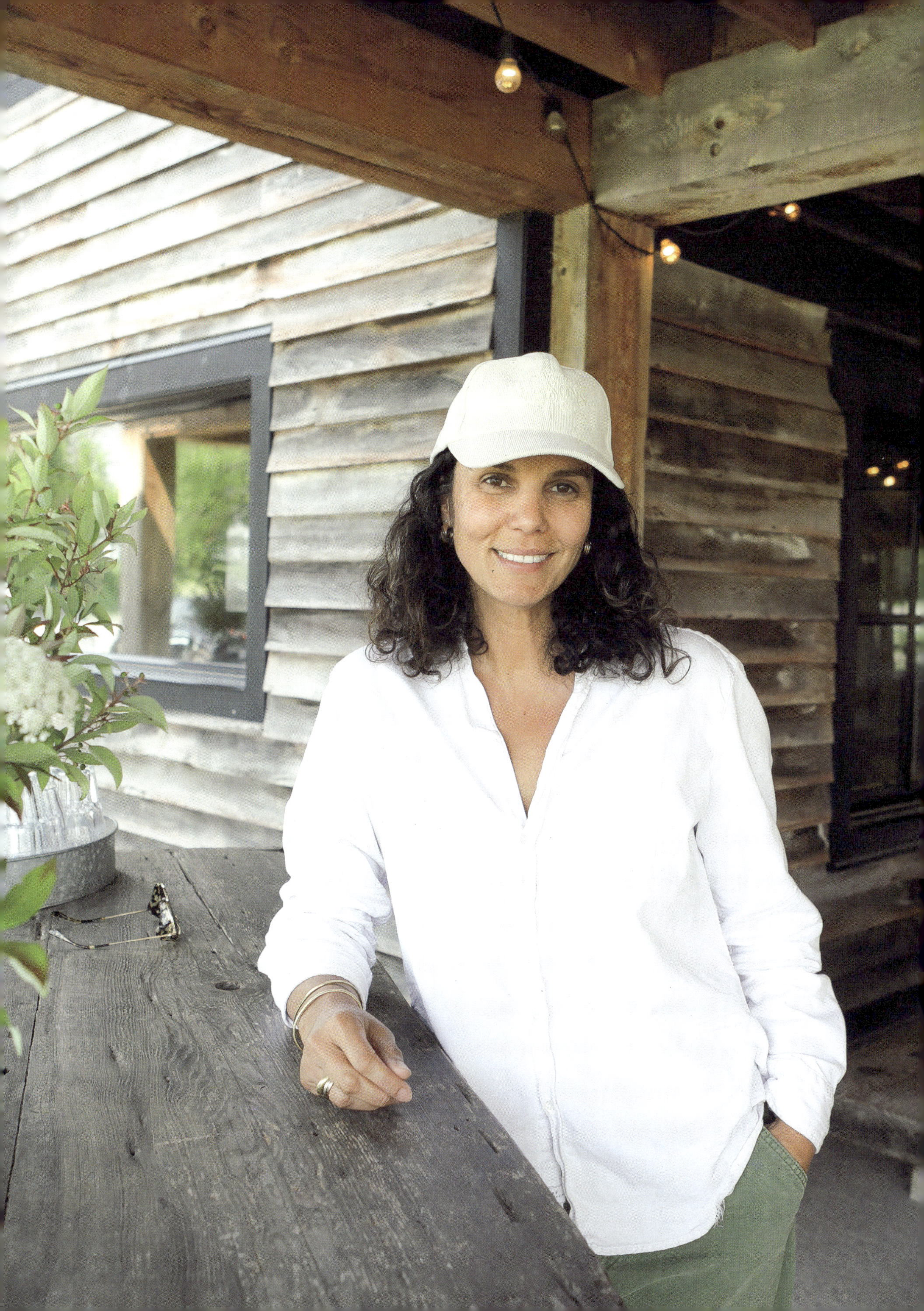

DRAUGHT MENU

...NER ABV 5%
↳ ...pilsner Malt
...y Finish

...E ABV 4.8%
↳ ...zu + lime zest,
...days

...LE ABV 5.7%
↳ ...IPA in a can

...TE ALE ABV 6.6%
↳ ...in a rich nutty

...ES ABV 5.1%
↳ ...cal hoppy goodness
...llow finish

STOUTS

STALWART BASTION OATMEAL STOUT ABV 6.1%
↳ oats balanced w/ spicy bitterness and notes of chocolatey rye

GRANDPA MIGUEL'S COFFEE ABV 5.9%
↳ Guatemalan coffee w/ citrus + herbal cremas

RUM BRÛLÉE ABV 7.5%
↳ rum spice w/ caramel creme burlee chocolate

SEASONALS

FARMERS TAN HARVEST ALE 5.3%
↳ lemon forward and piney

BROWN IS THE NEW BLACK ABV 5.4%
↳ ...black lager...
...flavours...

"RICK" BROWN ALE ABV 5.4%
↳ a nutty brown ale with a smooth hoppy and toasty finish

THE GUV'NOR ESB ABV 5.6%
↳ a deep chestnut brown ale with chocolate, malt, toffee, and raisin notes

THE "IT" NEIPA ABV 7.7%
↳ bathing in the hoppiness beyond with a dark wholesome thickness

NOICE IPA ABV 6.1%
↳ tropical fruit flavours with a mellow piney finish

BELGIAN TRIPEL 8.4%
↳ so soft yeasty with a sweet dry finish & notes of apricot fig and mineral

MARYSBURGH VORTEX IPA ABV 5.75%
↳ hopsters hop bombs with many amazing tropical flavours

CIDER

County A...
OR
Stock...
Seven...

Featured
Flig...

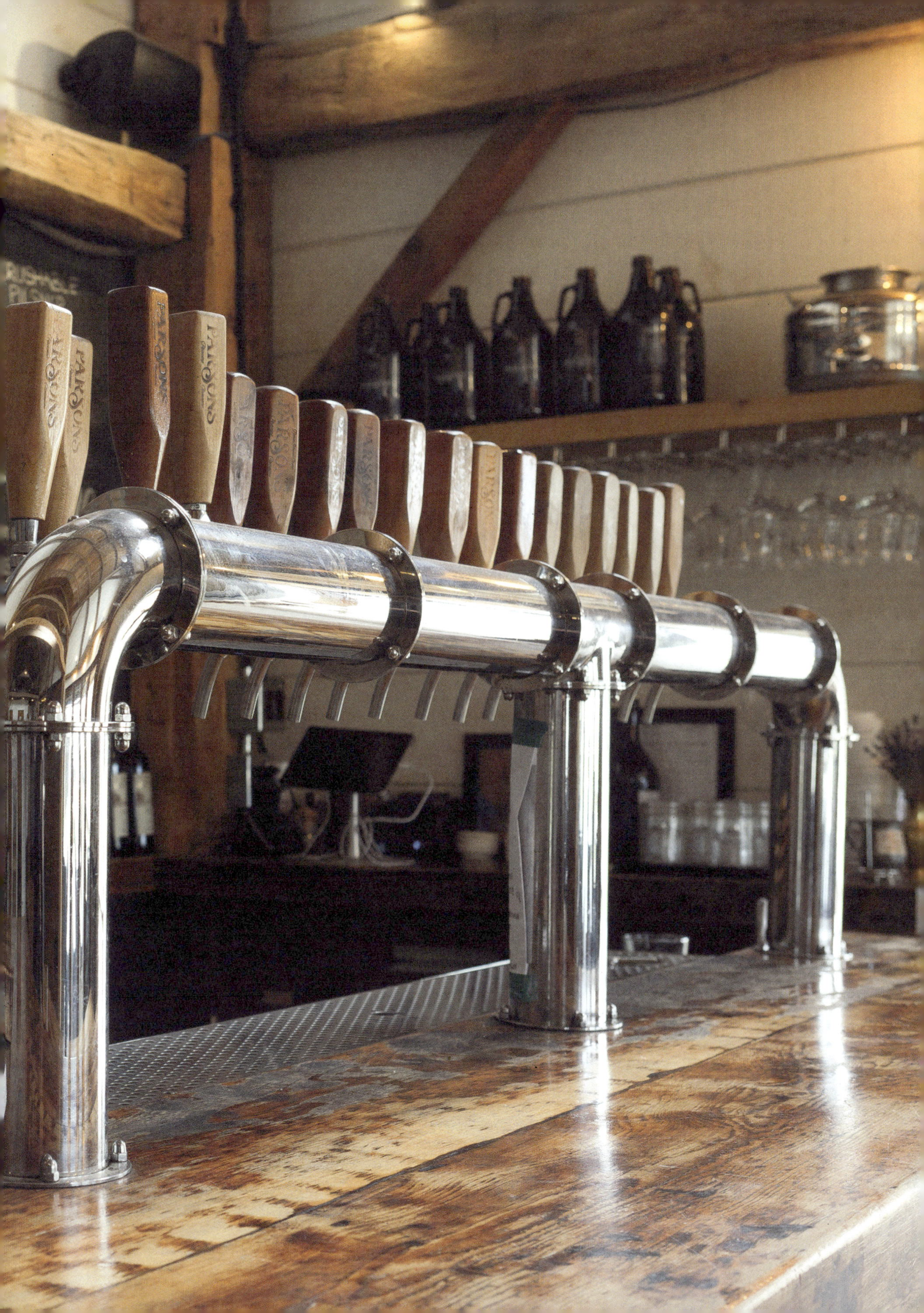

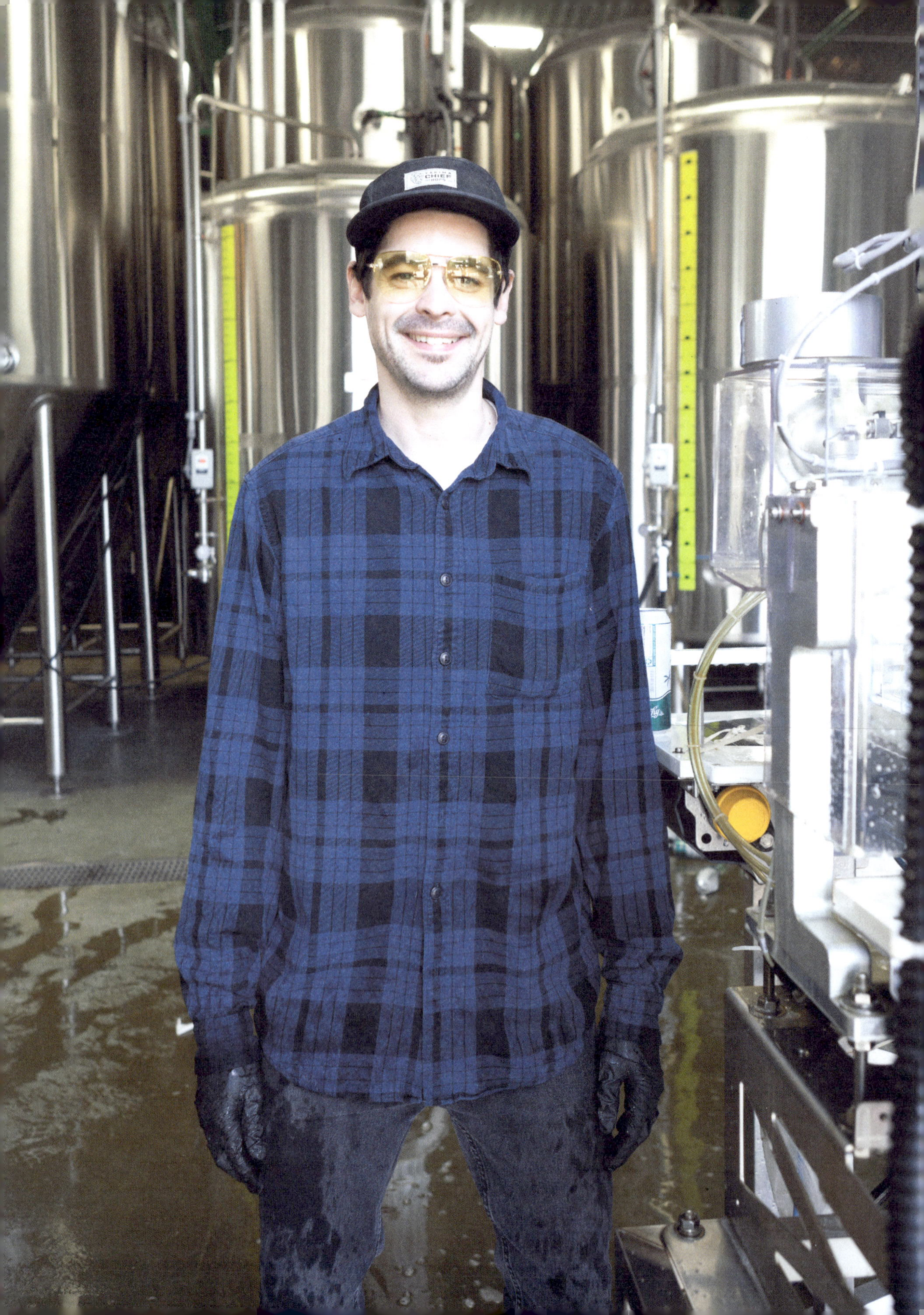
CHIEF

Prince Eddy's Brewing Co., Picton

Prince Eddy's is a surf-inspired brewery that produces pure and premium craft beers.

JONATHAN MINAKER

My mom and dad both grew up in the area; my dad in Picton and my mom in Napanee. My family started a vineyard and winery on the Adolphustown side of the ferry in 2002 and my brother, sister, and I worked there seasonally; I helped plant the vines and mostly did vineyard maintenance work and harvest until I had to go back to school in Ottawa. It was a bit of a struggle to get on the map, because we were out of the way of typical County tourism. Working in the family business kick-started my interest in fermentation and alcohol production. We sold the vineyard and winery in 2012. It still goes by the name 33 Vines; there's a red caboose in the centre of the property.

These days, I enjoy drinking European beers as well as local craft. I remember back in 2012, when the craft beer section first appeared in the LCBO, I was keen to try all the new offerings. Muskoka Brewery's Detour was one of the first hoppy beers I really enjoyed—it was a really solid session IPA. Now every city, every small town, has their own heady topper level of beer, but when Detour first came out, it was life-changing. It really did send me down a different path.

My friend Lucas and I both got really into craft beer. He got a job at Ottawa's Bicycle Craft Brewery, and when Bicycle was finally big enough to take on another employee, they hired me. My first day there was on my birthday in 2015. I started as a weekend growler filler and taproom worker. Eventually, they took me on full-time and I began canning beer and doing the local deliveries. I learned by working around knowledgeable peers, and after a while, I was trusted to sparge, do transfers, and clean fermenters. As everybody above me moved on, I climbed the ladder and became the brewer.

When Prince Eddy's opened up, I made myself familiar there; I knew Aaron McKinney, Prince Eddy's owner, from the Westlake Wakeboard School. When the assistant brewer position came up, he asked me if I was interested in interviewing for it. I took the job and moved here full-time in 2018 with my partner. It was nice to move from a smaller brewery to a bigger one, and I was excited to work under Eric Hornauer, who was the head brewer at the time. He had previously worked for Phillips and Railway City, and he was savvy about how to run a larger-scale microbrewery. He's a great cellarman; he's really good at cleaning, he's good at brewing. He's good at everything. He's a tough teacher, though—he encourages you to do everything yourself.

I've been here for five years and I've been head brewer for three and a half. There were only four fermenters and one bright tank when I started here, and we've since added five fermenters, two bright tanks, and a canning line. I have this mental snapshot of what's in every tank, when it was brewed, where it's at, and when it's got to go.

The first beer I brewed on my own with this system was a blueberry wheat. I remember being so proud to have done it; I think I'd been here two weeks. I love working with farmhouse yeasts and barrel-aged saisons. I like making imperial stouts and juicy New England IPAs, but those don't typically sell very well around here. I'm into far-out pairings, like adding vanilla in IPAs—I love vanilla in most beers—but I also love a simple lager. We haven't brewed many Belgian-style beers or traditional-style European lagers, so we might produce some of those in the future. I want to try everything. Nowadays, I'm more focused on making good flavourful classic styles; we did a Cali common back in spring 2023 that I was pretty happy with.

 I love working with everybody. The most fun part about working in this industry in the County is that we're always running errands to each others' breweries and then finding a reason to stand around in the back, chit-chat, and have a beer or two. We all get along pretty well. I think the growth of the craft beer scene here attracts tourists and I think it helps to keep everybody afloat—the more the merrier. At the same time, it's kind of difficult becoming an older brewery here. We want people to keep coming back, so we have to find a balance of staying new and relevant but also keeping our core brands consistent for our loyal customers.

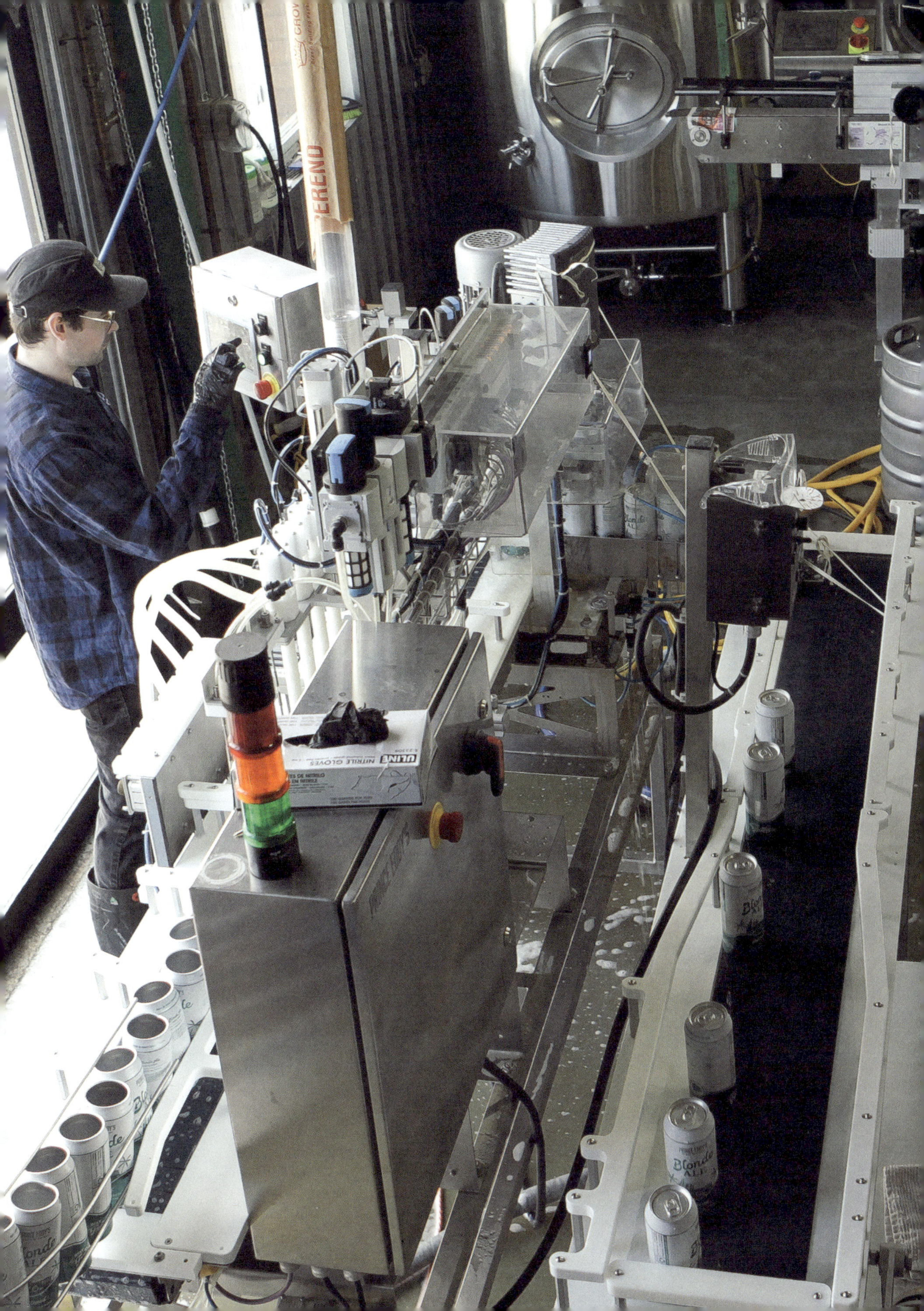
ULINE NITRILE GLOVES

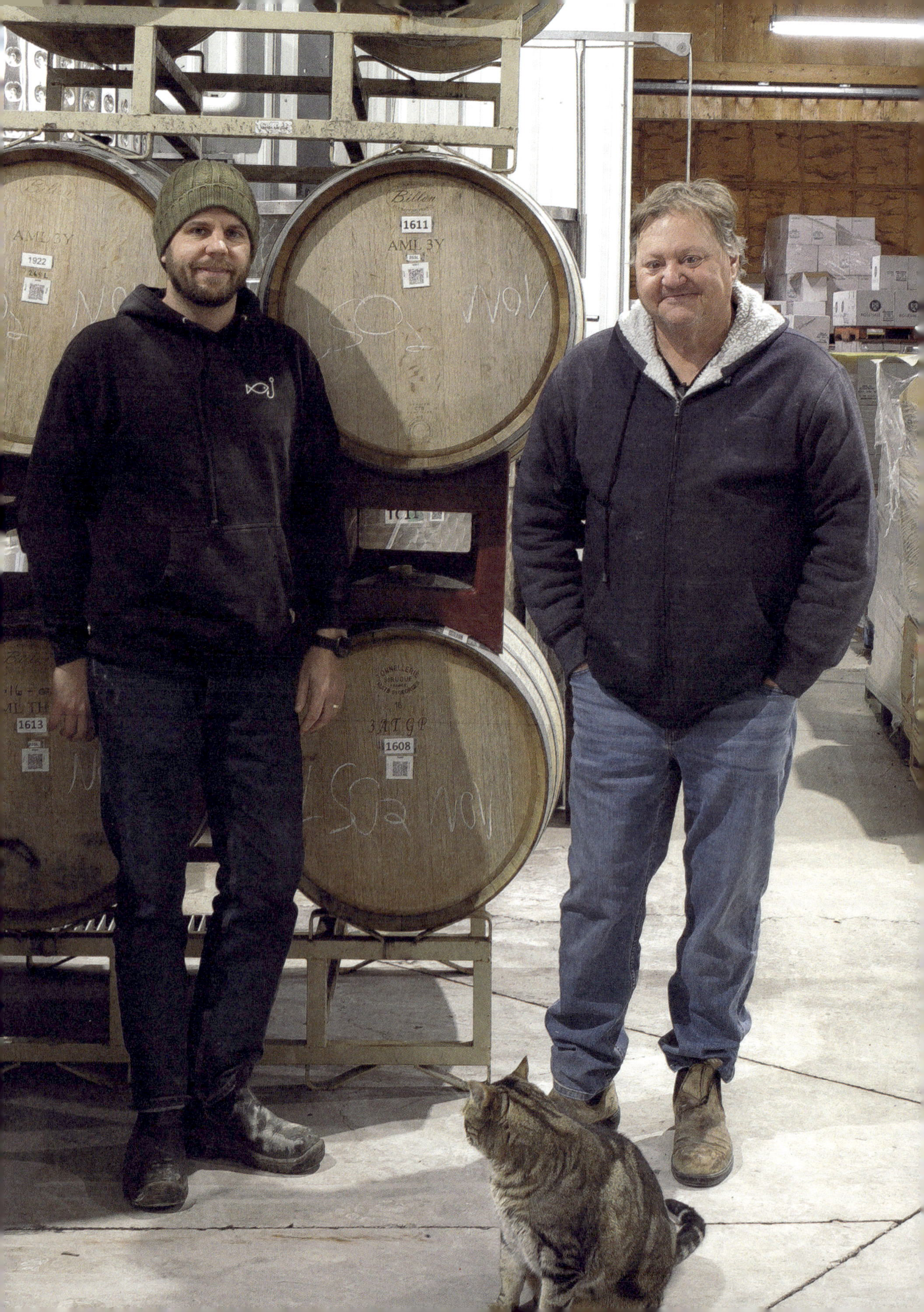
1611
AML 3Y
1922
1613
1608

Rosehall Run Vineyards, Hillier

One of the County's first wineries, Rosehall Run's wines are balanced, elegant, and a reflection of terroir.

LEE BAKER, DAN SULLIVAN

Dan: Some people are lucky and they know what they want to do, but I wasn't one of them. I took a year off between high school and university. I had a fairly good lab technician background, so I went back to doing that kind of work, and I was hired by a company and put on the road to run troubleshooting for process chemistry and stuff like that. Lynn and I bought out her father in the family business—a window and door company—and we became partners with her brother. We sold that in 2005 to help finance this place and went into winemaking full-time.

I blame my now-business partner, my brother-in-law, Cam, for pouring me a Pommard. I tasted it and it was like the light went on. And I went, oh, now I really get it. I started buying a lot of books, self-studying, buying different wines and tasting them with groups of people here and there. There wasn't really a formalized pathway to learning wine so much in Canada back in those days. I bought a press from a friend of the guy who introduced me to home winemaking, and I used that as my first press in my garage in Scarborough. Seven friends and I all threw in 200 bucks. I bought a lot of grapes and got lucky, made a couple of decent wines. That was 1995.

In late 1996, I discovered the Pickering Wine Guild and got to know people like Dave Gillingham, Richard Karlo. Battista came in as I was going pro. Lorne Weyers ended up as my assistant winemaker out here for a few years. I discovered there were all kinds of other clubs across Ontario for amateur winemakers. There was also a competitive aspect of putting your wines into competition and getting them scored. That was kind of fun; I actually think that was one of the most informative and best wine experiences I had in my life.

We bought our property in the fall of 2000. I think the biggest first wave of investment came in the year we purchased the land. Huff bought their property, put vines into the ground. The Grange restored their property. Black Prince started that year. Steve Singer, who used to be the owner of Fieldstone Vineyards. There was a whole bunch of people in 2001, and some of them aren't around anymore.

I remember Gunther Funk, the founder, along with his wife, Mary, of Funk Vineyard in Niagara, taking me out into the middle of his five acres, looking me in the eye, and saying, "Dan, look around you." I looked around. Out in the middle of the vineyard, all you can see is vines. And then he asked, "Can you handle this?" I was about to put in my entire north block as it exists today, but this gave me pause. I said, "I know what you're telling me. Start small." So the first year I planted one acre and was actually able to manage it. And then the following year we planted the rest of it and it got out in front of me a little bit—I had weeds that were higher than the plants. Finally wrestled it under control and planted a small planting with the University of Guelph rootstock trial in the back, but it was only an extra acre. So the third year, I was able to get more reliable help in and got it a little bit more managed, under control. And then the following year after that, that's when I started bringing in my farmhands with an agricultural worker plan. And that's when Jose started working with me. That was in 2004, I believe.

Jose's my lead hand in the field. He manages the rest of the guys who work with him. I'll do a strategy of rotation of what we might be looking at as far as spring, making the final call on the timing of doing things like leaf-pulling. But he's usually coming to me and saying, "Listen, I'm seeing this." And so there's a lot of very proactive scouting going on.

The legacy of those first places like Huff, The Grange—we were like a little place way down at the end of the road that nobody really knew about. It was a real cast of characters back in the day. So here we are 20-something years into the industry in the County, it's really happened so fast. I think we're at this interesting crossroads. Some of the original people in the industry are retiring and looking to get out.

Lee: A friend was managing a retail store at a place called Stone Church that doesn't exist anymore down in St. Catharines and she said, "Why don't you come work with me for a season?" I started selling wine and it was really slow, and there was a bunch of wine books around so I started reading. The guys in the back let me climb into tanks and use a pressure washer and I thought it was the best thing ever. I love the pressure washer. I love forklifts. I worked the harvest and there was such camaraderie. I thought it was the coolest thing ever.

I was able to work my way into the Brock University program, which was a challenge because I didn't have the prerequisites. As long as I maintained a certain average, they'd consider me to get into the Cool Climate Oenology and Viticulture Institute. It's one of those programs where you start off with 25 kids and then you go right into chemistry, biology, statistics, calculus, and physics. After the first year there's 12 students left, and by the end there were only 4 of us graduating. I graduated second in my class. My mom was blown away.

I landed a job at a place called LaStella and Le Vieux Pin, two sister wineries in BC. I spent four vintages out in BC and then we made the choice to come back to Ontario. I saw the writing on the wall; forest fires weren't great, the cost of living was super high, the wages weren't super high, and we felt isolated without any family nearby. I landed two positions: one was assistant winemaker at a bigger place down in Niagara and the other one was a full-time winemaking and vineyard management job at Keint-he Winery. I was separated from the vineyard my entire time in BC, and I missed walking vineyards and driving tractors. So we moved to the County.

It takes a special type of person to want to grow grapes here. This whole burying and un-burying or blanketing of vines is unique. We all have this common goal of making wine but also making it as best as possible and getting everybody else to make it as best as possible.

To tell you the truth, when Dan reached out and offered me a job, I was amazed. I'd been in the County for seven years, grinding it out, and for one of the founders, for somebody as respected as Dan, to trust me with his wine, is huge. The validation of being good enough to be the guy at Rosehall—I guess I did something right.

ROSEHALL RUN
ROSEHALL RUN
CHARDONNAY MUSQUÉ
ESTATE GROWN & BOTTLED
2022
VQA PRINCE EDWARD COUNTY VQA
BRONZE
ROSEHALL RUN
2022
BRONZE
ROSEHALL RUN
ROSEHALL RUN
RIESLING
2022
GOLD

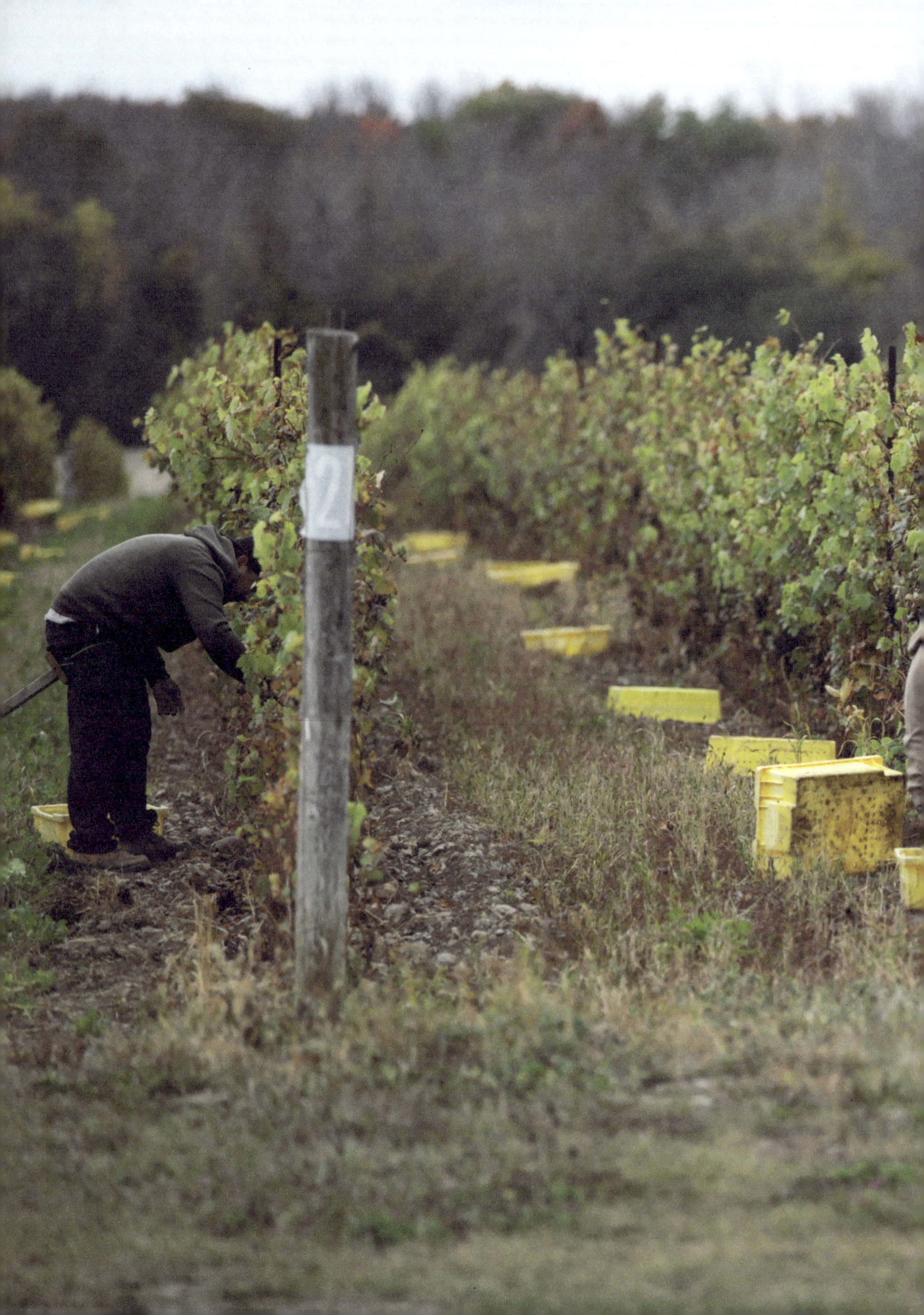
2

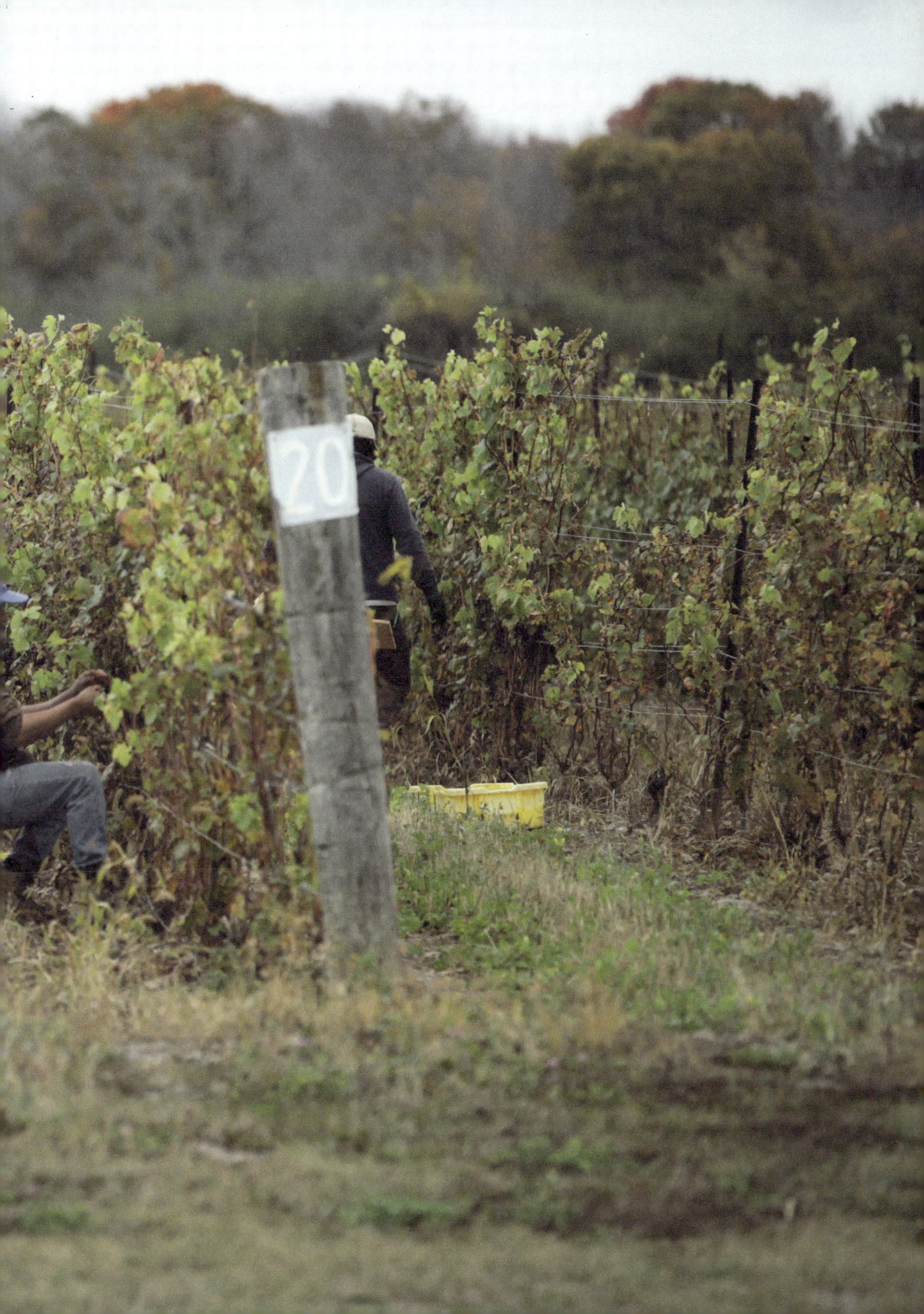
20

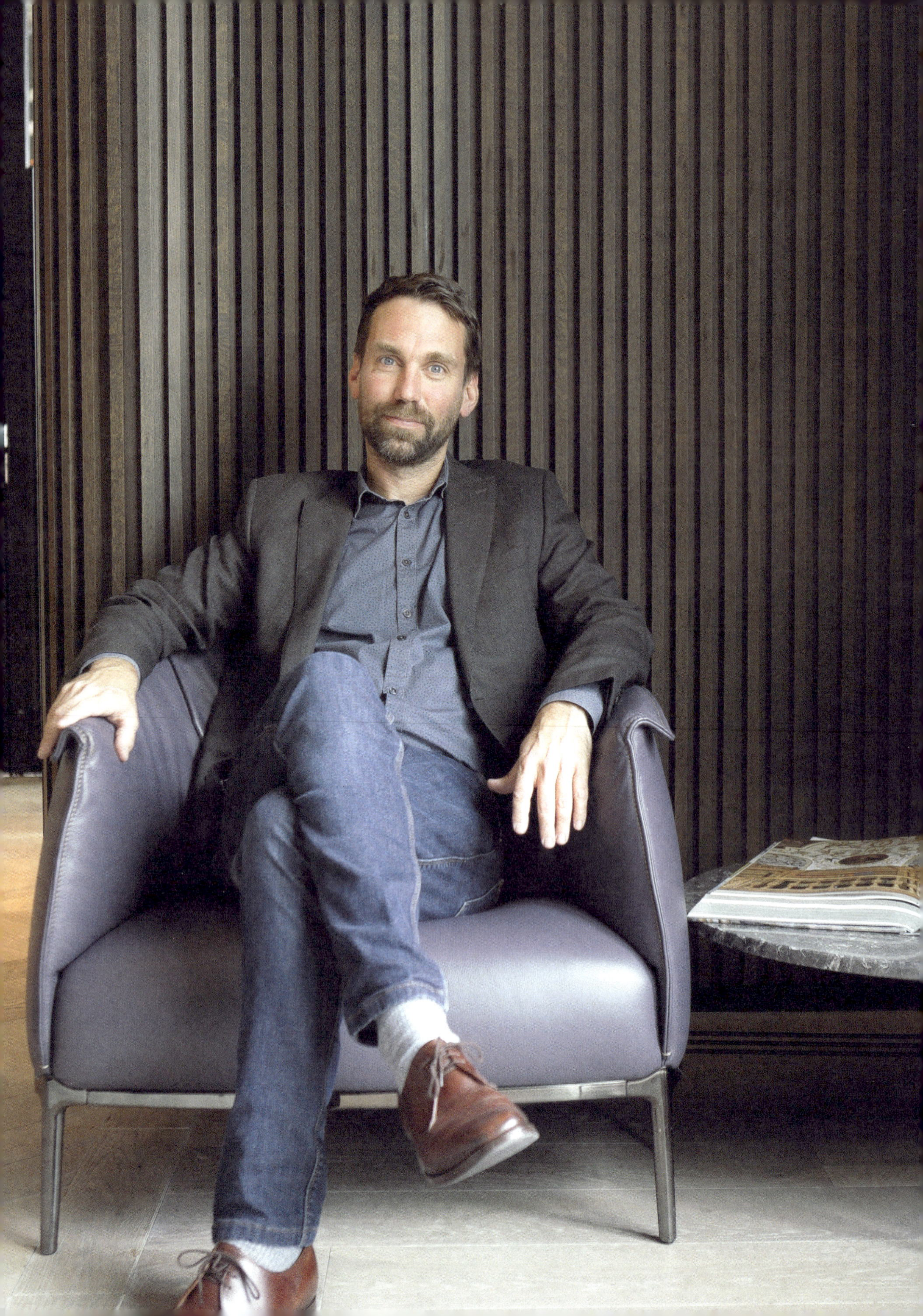

The Royal Hotel, Picton

The Royal is a gorgeously restored 1879 hotel on Main Street in Picton.

PAUL HARDY

I love theatre, reading plays, reading Shakespeare—I've always wanted to know who's who, who's influenced who—and that established how I operate in the wine world. What I didn't love was the idea of graduating from university and being in debt. Waitering seemed like a really good way to make money while I focused on theatre. I started out at Jack Astor's at Sherway Gardens in Toronto. I remember distinctly that, at 19, I hit on the idea to try to sell my tables bottles of wine—I liked wine, so I thought it would be easy for me to sell it. A bottle of Wolf Blass Yellow Label that cost $70 was way more expensive than the giant beers everyone else was slinging and would net me more tips.

After that, I landed at Le Sélect Bistro on Queen Street (Royal Hotel chef Albert Ponzo's alma mater). While there, I met Jean-Jacques Quinsac and Frédéric Geisweiller and Shamez Amlani, who are big influences on how I think about service and wine. Shamez now owns La Palette; his knowledge of wine in particular made me excited about the idea of being a part of the gregarious restaurant world. I also spent a bunch of years working with Av Atikin at the Rosedale Diner. Av's love and passion for wine education added a new layer to my skill set, and he introduced me to Jennifer Huether, the first female master sommelier in Canada. I also spent a lot of my early career working for Elie Benchitrit at Provence Delices, who was the maître d' and sommelier, and an owner. I was learning from people who had run restaurants for 15, 20 years already. I wasn't working with the new kids; I was working with stodgy people who were stuck in their ways, but running restaurants was in their blood.

But I still was really focused on being an actor and a theatre director and staying involved in that world. I loved mise en scène. I loved creating worlds that people can disappear into. In my later 20s, though, I found myself less inspired by some of the work I was doing. And then when the financial crisis happened, it completely bottomed out our world in a really heavy way. I was working in a pub that I loved, the Brass Taps on College Street. I remember walking up the street one day to do laundry and looking in a window beside the laundromat that had a For Lease sign on it. I thought, maybe we should do something crazy and open up our own little bistro, serve nice coffee in the daytime and nice wine at night, snacks and charcuterie and whatever. Maybe that'd pay our rent so we could keep doing theatre. My partner, Heather, and I renovated the whole place with help from our friends—and help from Visa. Zocalo Bistro opened in 2010. Two months later, Steven Davey from *NOW Magazine* called us and said we had a five-star review coming. Our little sandwich slash wine shop became a five-star restaurant overnight.

We put every dollar back into the business. Heather did a bunch of theatre stuff. I did a bunch of theatre. It was working like we'd wanted it to. And then, after a while, the business started to become pretty daunting. We explored the idea of selling, and we were quickly romanced by a real estate agent who put a number in front of us that we thought was phantasmagorical in exchange for a liquor license and a lease. But he was 100% right and we sold the restaurant.

After about eight months of bouncing around and trying to figure out what to do next, I decided I wanted to get serious about wine. I told Heather, "I'm gonna go to school for wine. It's gonna be fine. It's only a couple thousand dollars. It's fine, there'll be lots of wine around."

I went back to work for Shamez Amlani again at La Palette on Queen Street, and I got better at working a bar, better at cocktailing, and better at wine. I deepened my knowledge and my service style. At the end of that summer, I found out that my friend Alessandro Pietropaolo, who runs Bar Isabel, was looking for a waiter. At the time, Bar Isabel was a hard place to get a job at because everybody stayed there forever. The money was great. It was a super-fun place to work. Al had worked for Niall McCotter, and they had a kind of mentor–protege relationship. So when I went to work for Al, I gained everything Niall had shared with him as well. Nate Morrell, who is a huge inspiration for me as a sommelier, was their head sommelier. I went through my CAPS program with the Canadian Association of Professional Sommeliers during my time there.

In the early Covid-19 pandemic days, Heather and I moved to Gananoque. I didn't know what was going to happen in my career. One thing I'd never done was a harvest, so I went to Trail Estate and worked as a cellarhand in the fall of 2020. I learned so much more than I thought I would from that experience, and I really fell in love with the County and the romance of the wine culture here. So naturally, when I heard Niall McCotter was going to be a part of the new Royal Hotel project in Picton, I thought it sound like another great opportunity. I figured I would throw my hat in the ring—I didn't know when I'd ever get another chance to be a part of a project like that one, to help build something from the ground up. I knew what I learned along the way would become a lifelong piece of me. And it really has.

In putting together The Royal's wine program, we leaned into Pinot Noir and Chardonnay as Prince Edward County's flagship grapes. We asked ourselves how we should explore Pinot and Chardonnay around the world in addition to Prince Edward County's, and how to best compare and contrast wines on the list to give people the opportunity to try things from here and things from elsewhere.

I think that when hospitality is done correctly, it can be as meaningful as any moment in theatre or music. It can really elevate a person's day, and feeling cared for can also elevate any experience. For me, contributing to those sublime moments is really what all of this is about.

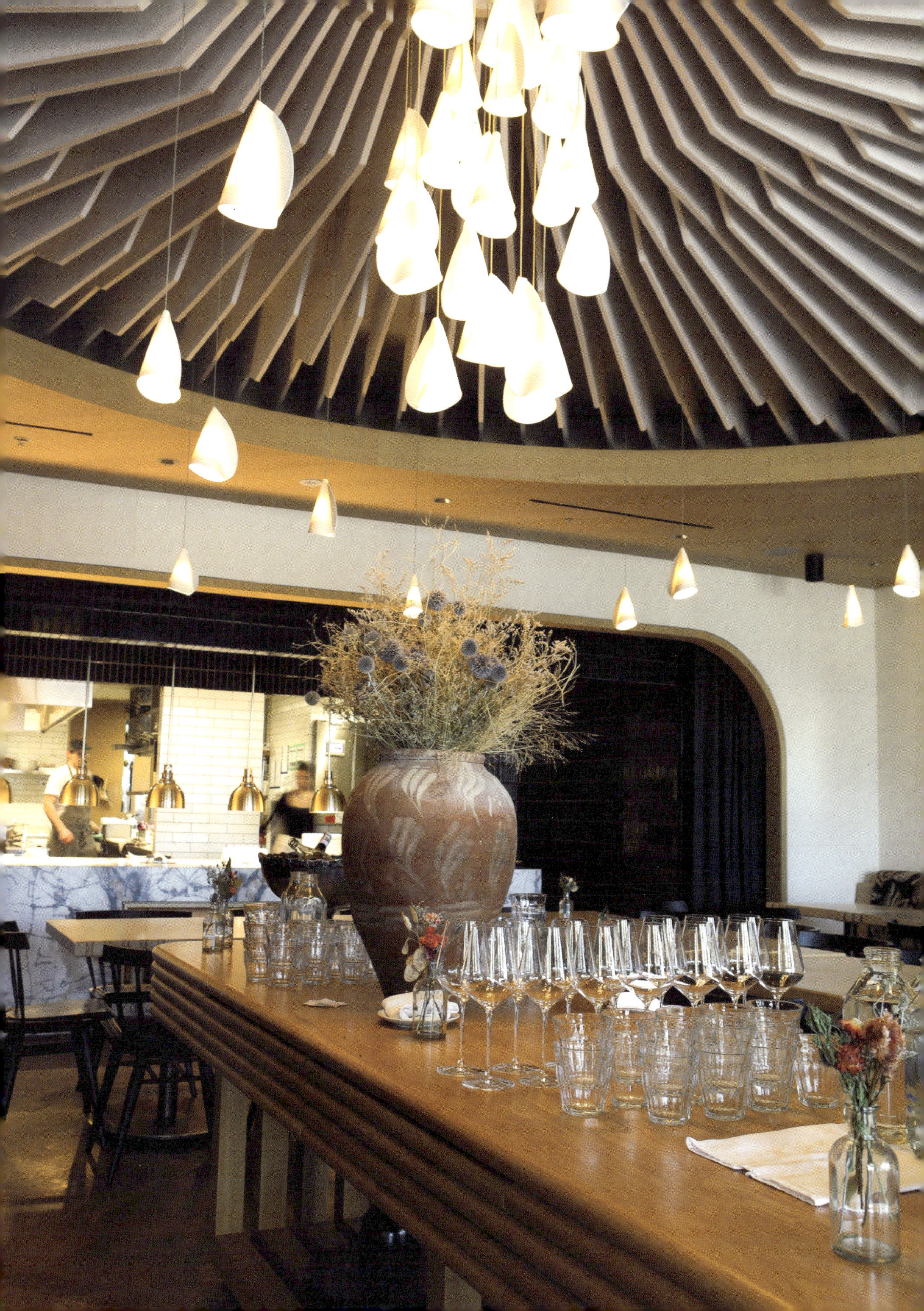

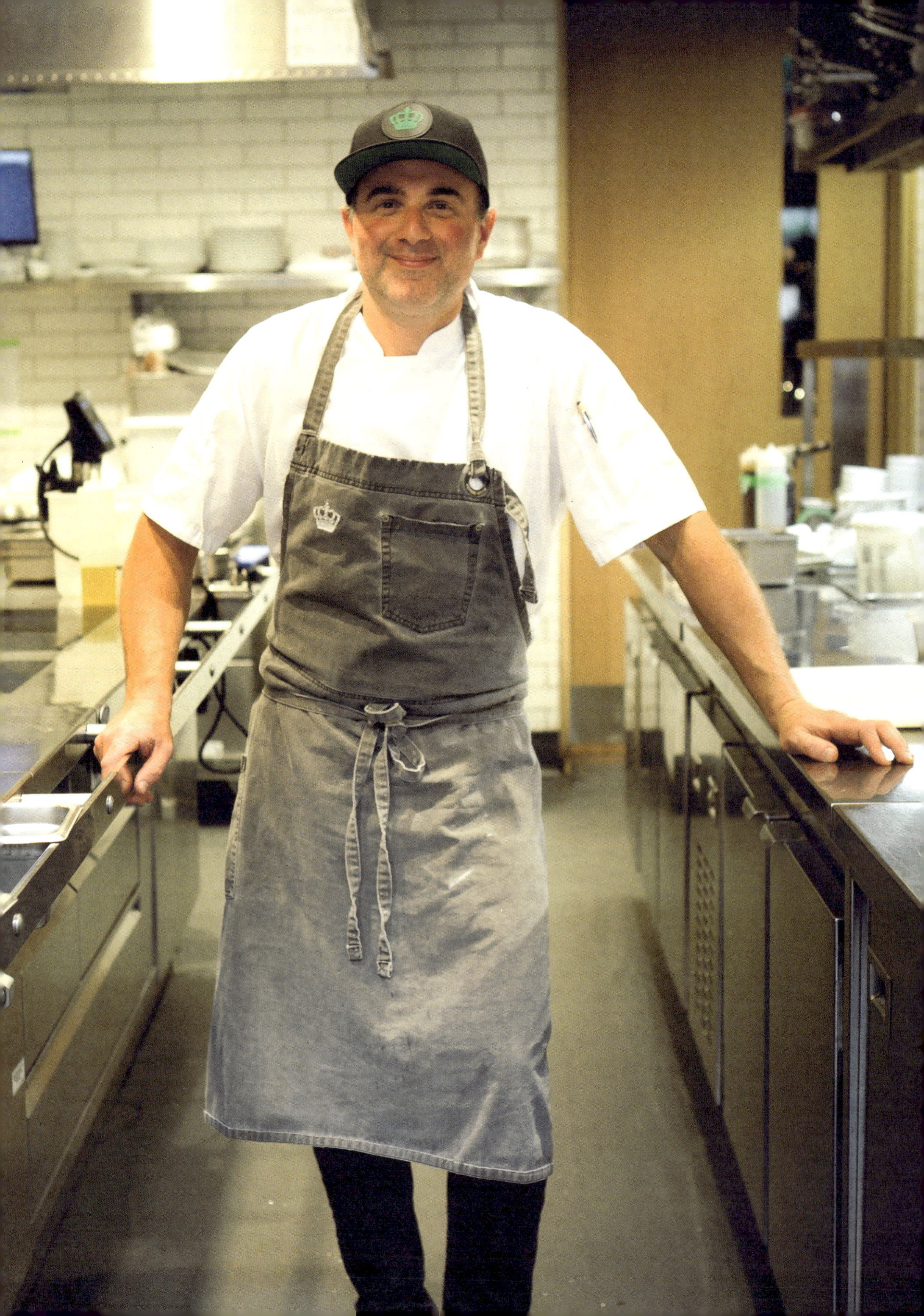

The Royal Hotel's Braised Pickerel Cheeks

ALBERT PONZO, EXECUTIVE CHEF

We are spoiled by the quality of pickerel in Prince Edward County. We get ours from our friend Peter Williams of Bay Williams Fisheries. Pickerel cheeks are a great part of the fish that hold texture well to a quick braise and have lots of deep flavour. The cheeks are braised in a flavourful fish stock until they are tender and succulent. The result is a dish that is comforting, elegant, and the perfect way to showcase their deliciousness.

Prep time: 10 minutes
Cooking time: 30 minutes
Servings: 4

Ingredients

1 lb trimmed pickerel cheeks (or skinless, boneless pickerel fillets cut into 1" x 1" squares)
to taste salt and freshly ground pepper
¼ cup all-purpose flour
2–3 tbsp sunflower oil
1 cup cleaned black trumpet mushrooms (or other seasonal mushroom like sliced morels)
½ cup shallot, finely chopped
½ cup carrot, finely diced
½ cup celery, finely diced
2 cloves garlic, finely minced
¼ cup dry white wine
1 cup fish stock (or chicken or vegetable stock)
2 tbsp cold butter
¼ cup Parmesan cheese, grated
2 tbsp fresh parsley, chopped
1 tbsp lemon juice
2 cups polenta croutons, fried until crispy (or crispy roasted potatoes squares)
extra virgin olive oil and lemon wedges, to garnish

Method

Pickerel
Season pickerel cheeks with salt and pepper; dredge lightly in flour, shaking off any excess. Heat sunflower oil in a large, preheated skillet over medium-high heat; sear pickerel cheeks for about 1–2 minutes per side until golden and crisp. Transfer to a plate and keep warm.

Sauce
In the same skillet, add black trumpet mushrooms and sauté for about one minute. Add shallot, carrot, celery, and garlic; cook over medium heat, stirring occasionally, for about 4 minutes, until softened and shallot is translucent.

Add wine and bring to a boil, scraping up any browned bits from bottom of pan. Reduce heat to medium; simmer until wine reduces by half, about 7–10 minutes. Add stock and simmer, cooking for about 4–5 minutes, until slightly thickened.

Assembly
Return pickerel cheeks to the skillet, spooning sauce over them. Simmer gently until heated through, about 5 minutes. If using pickerel fillets, reduce cooking time to about 2–3 minutes, until fish becomes flaky but still holds together.

Stir in butter and Parmesan; cook until emulsified and smooth, stirring constantly for about 1 minute. Stir in parsley and lemon juice; season with salt and pepper to taste.

Place pickerel cheeks and sauce into warm bowls, with crispy polenta croutons or roasted potato cubes placed around the edges. Garnish with drizzles of olive oil and lemon wedges; serve immediately. Enjoy!

Chef's Notes
Use your favourite recipe for making polenta (a creamy cornmeal mixture enhanced with butter and Parmesan). When prepared ahead and chilled, slice it into crouton-shaped squares and fry in a little sunflower oil until crispy.

Drink Pairings
Rich and succulent offerings on the opposite side of the spectrum: The Grange of Prince Edward County Chardonnay 2020, Prince Eddy's Yonder Oatmeal Stout.

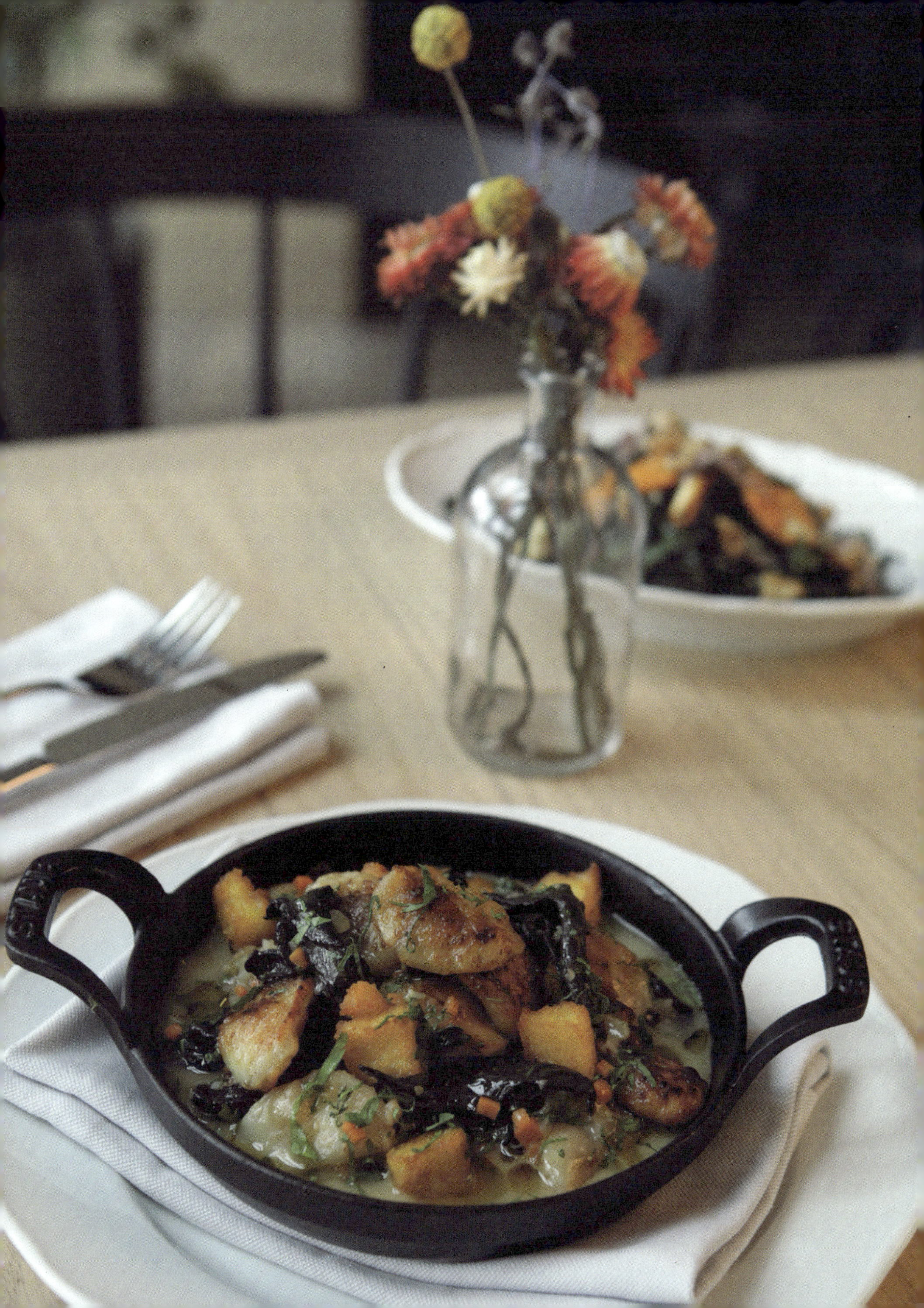

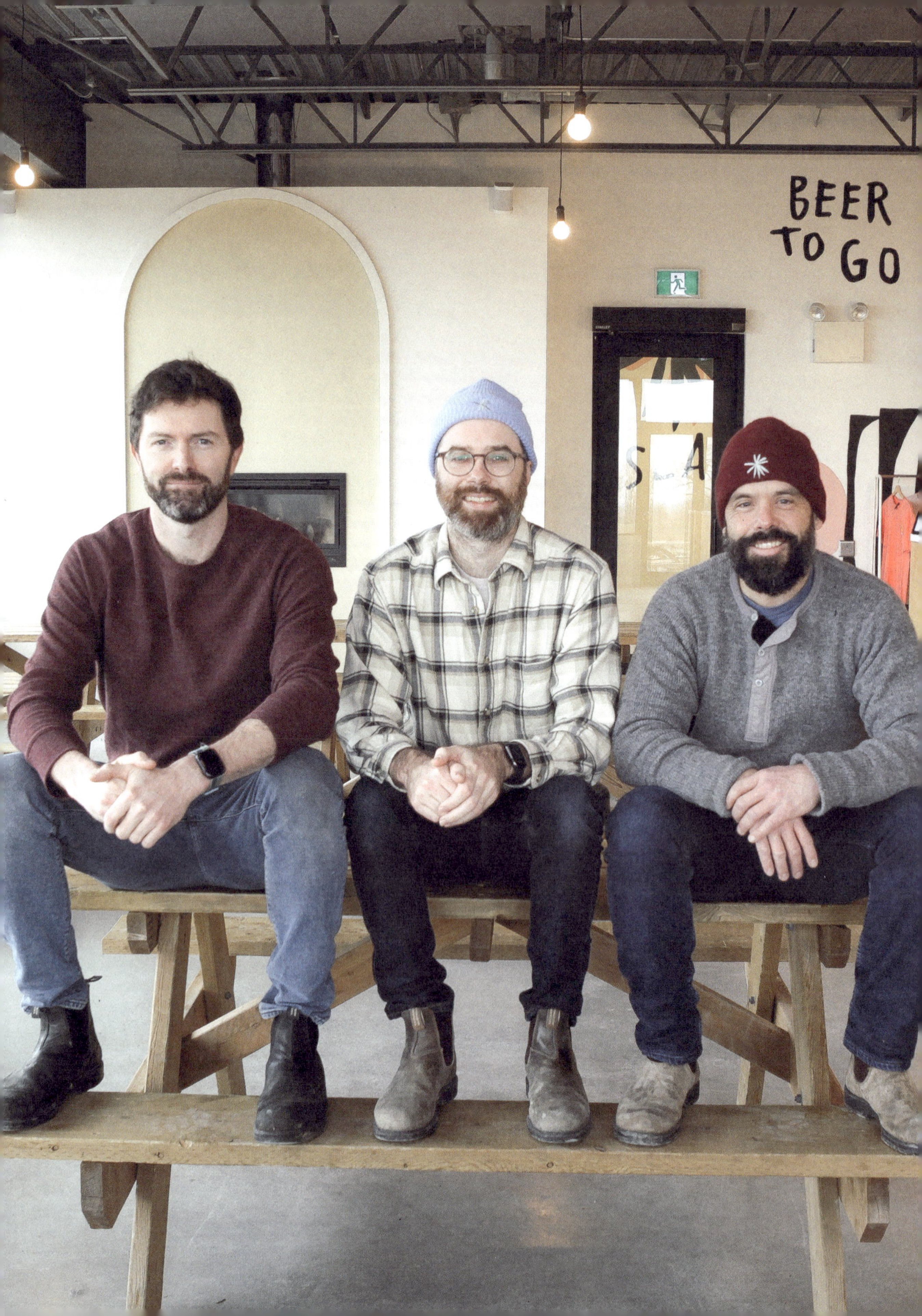
BEER
TO GO

Slake Brewing, Picton

A small brewery built on a limestone hill, Slake has some of the best views of Prince Edward County.

NICK BOBAS, GREG LANDUCCI, ERIC PORTELANCE

Greg: We built here for the view. I was always marching family and friends who came to visit up to the top of the hill for sunsets because there aren't a lot of spots in Prince Edward County where you can walk up a hill and have a view. So after years of parading people up here, I decided that if we ever built anything, this is where it had to be. Obviously we needed a purpose-built, real production facility that was a beer factory first. We didn't want to throw a bunch of tanks in a barn and bitch about it. The modern bent came from working with Scott Bailey of Branch Architecture.

I moved out here 12 years ago after visiting on a cycling tour; we bought the farm and got pigs. I started getting grain from Barley Days, and that's how I got into craft beer—to feed my pigs. I met Alex Nichols, who was the brewer there at the time, and they were looking for a sales rep slash delivery driver for Toronto. That was basically the beginning. My partner and Eric's partner are family, and we met at family functions. I was working at Barley Days and he was doing Eric things, and then he started working on a business plan to start up a little brewery in Toronto.

Eric: I started home brewing around the time Bellwoods Brewery opened in 2012. There was a craft boom in Toronto beer. I had severance from a tech job, and Callum Hay and I started talking about opening a brewery. I brought Greg into the conversation, and we started Halo in 2016. The first idea for Slake came when we were at Halo. Greg, many years prior, had thought about setting up a brewery here somewhere on the farm. So he'd had planning conversations with the County about whether a brewery might be possible on his property with its zoning. At the time, it was really complicated because the zoning bylaw had no definition of a brewery or a farm brewery. It was basically relegated to an industrial zone, and so Greg got the sense that a brewery would be treated the same as a farm winery, which was allowed with his zoning. And that's how everybody's treated now, thankfully.

Greg and I left Halo at the same time, and we spent the next year not really knowing if we wanted to open another brewery. Somewhere in there, Nick and I met at Indie Ale House. Nick owned a house in Bloomfield that he was operating as a rental property, but he wanted to move his family out here and potentially open a barrel-aged brewery. I think we all wanted to make a living out here and brewing was the thing that would allow that.

Nick: I was doing all the barrel-aged brewing for Indie Ale House in Toronto. I think we all had enough experience at other places—we'd learned a lot and could use our knowledge in a new project, not only for brewing beer, but also for the construction, equipment, staffing, cash flow, all that stuff. Slake opened in October 2020. It should have been May but we had some real delays. There was the Covid-19 pandemic, plus some real construction and equipment deficiencies. Unfortunately, we missed that summer, which was super busy. So we had a longer start-up period, and then we had a great fall after opening in October. November was beautiful and people could be outside. We kept campfires going, and then we plunged into six months of lockdowns, with all bars and restaurants closed.

We want to be fairly adaptable, to produce what people actually want to drink. We've killed some of our children because nobody wants to drink them. If you make a brand and it's not working, you obviously have to pivot. We're using 100% Barn Owl local malt, which is grown outside of Belleville. And that has a really, really huge impact on how we brew. We're buying anywhere from 800 to 1,500 kilos a week, which is a big portion of their production. I see Devin Huffman, Barn Owl's owner, every week, and he tells me about the lots and the varietals and the protein content, and how that could change what I do. My mash temperature changes depending on enzymes, the lengths of my rest change to make sure that the residual sugar at the end changes depending on the barley. Devin came by a couple months ago to tell us that he'd gotten a smaller kernel than what we've been running with. And that sounds like nothing, but it actually has the potential to make a massive change. So that's had a pretty big impact on our beer style as a whole.

I think we try and go for balanced, generally lower ABV beers—we mostly make lagers and pale ales. Unfortunately for IPAs, they have to be at least 6% to do what they do. Part of our conversation was recognizing that people would have to drive here, hopefully with designated drivers, because there aren't many taxi services in the County. We want people to have a good time, but we are sort of in the middle of nowhere—how could we honestly serve double IPAs and then send people away in their cars? So all of that shaped our focus on balance and producing summery, approachable beers. We didn't make anything over 5.4% until one of the lockdowns. We went, all right, screw it. We're going to make an IPA. And we made it at like 6%. It was a lower ABV IPA.

Eric: We know what the popular styles are. Anyone can go on Untappd and find out very easily what will get high ratings. So we aren't driven by that. We know how to make those beers and play for ratings, but most people who come here are average people who like good beer and appreciate quality. We're making beers that are inherently pretty expensive. We're using niche yeasts that cost a lot of money, local malt, and large amounts of very expensive hops from the other side of the world. There's only so much you can do—they're going to be expensive. Plus, we're in the middle of nowhere, we use single-phase power, propane, truck in all our water, truck out all our waste. And all that keeps getting more expensive.

Greg: During the pandemic, there were moments when you couldn't be inside, couldn't see your friends. But there were also great moments when you could come and have a beer here outside by one of the firepits with your friends and family and feel a bit normal. I thought that was awesome. It doesn't get old when people walk in and say, "Wow." They walk past the bar, they totally ignore the staff, and go right to the window. The view doesn't get old for us either. Sometimes I stare longingly out at the lake. It's not a bad place to work.

SLAKE
NICE
BY SLAKE
PILSNER
CHOCOLATE VANILLA DREAMS
BY SLAKE
LONG
BY SLAKE
DREAMS
WOOHOO

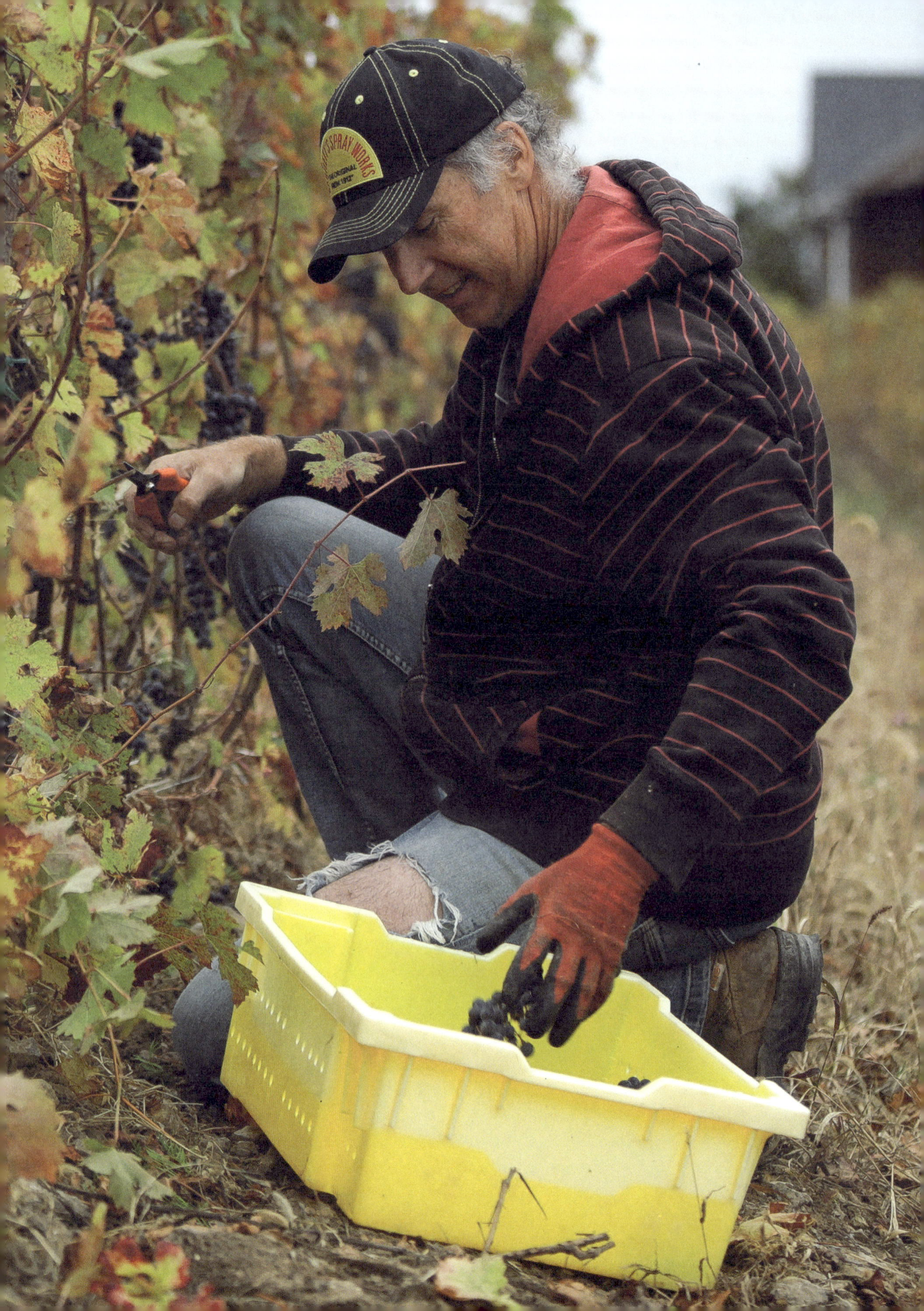
SPRAY WORKS

Stanners Vineyard, Hillier

Stanners is an artisanal winery and vineyard dedicated to producing premium Pinot Noir.

COLIN STANNERS

I did a PhD in physical chemistry, then my wife and I moved to California and lived in the Bay Area for 16 years. I started pursuing a post-doc at UC Berkeley and the Lawrence Berkeley lab. I ended up getting a job at a start-up company, and I realized that I didn't want to end up doing that for the rest of my life. That's when we became interested in wine. I've always loved wine, but back then I was surrounded by it. We were going out to different wineries, and then I started making wine at home. Eventually, I bought some small stainless steel tanks.

It was good because people had small vineyards that were too little for the major wineries to bother with, but they were still professionally managed. Their grapes were available to amateur winemakers and they would often advertise on different winemaking sites, I guess that's how I found them. There was a guy who ran a winery close to us in the Santa Cruz mountains. He held a several-day winemaking course, so I took that. It was just a few of us. I also took a correspondence course from UC Davis; it was all email and VHS tapes. At the end of that, after picking grapes and making a few vintages, I thought it was a good idea to start up a winery. My parents had found Prince Edward County; they'd done a cycling trip here and noticed that it was a good area for wine. We visited and ended up tasting some of the early wines. This was around 2003. And then we bought this property with my parents. In 2005, we planted grapes in what we call the Narrow Rows. My parents looked after them for a year, and then we moved here in 2006.

There were maybe 10 or so wineries around at the time we started. It was tough at the beginning. A lot of people had different ideas about what direction we should go in, but there was also strong advocacy from people here to make us a designated viticultural area. That happened pretty soon after we moved here—that was in 2007. Wine critics were interested in the County, which meant we received a lot of press right from the beginning. But there was still a group of people who thought that because we're a cold-climate area, we should be growing hybrid varieties to suit our climate. And there was another group that believed the soil was perfect for Pinot Noir and Chardonnay, and we decided to go in that direction. And other people didn't even want to be a designated viticulture area because that meant some hybrid varieties wouldn't be recognized by the VQA, and under the laws of the VQA, they wouldn't be able to put Prince Edward County on their labels once we became a DVA. The VQA ensures that wine is actually coming from the region you say it's from, so if your wine isn't approved by the VQA, you're not allowed to put Prince Edward County on the label. There was a lot of debate at the beginning about our direction as a region.

We went in the Pinot Noir and Chardonnay direction because I liked those wines, and I knew that if we could make good ones, we'd at least be able to sell them. At the time, I wasn't that thrilled with the taste of wine from hybrid varieties. We planted in stages because we didn't really know much about how to manage grapevines. We found out very soon here that it's a whole lot more work than you might think. We planted an acre at first, then we planted maybe another two acres. So we planted from 2005 to 2009. That was more manageable for us.

When we started, Mary, my wife, was doing a fine arts program at Queen's. She went back to school as a mature student. I was working in the vineyard alongside my parents, and then once we opened and Mary was done school, it felt like a natural path for us to work together. I was in the vineyard and making the wine, so I was doing all the technical stuff while Mary took on the tastings and the marketing. My mom still does the finances.

I'm okay with repetitive work—I go in knowing, okay, this is a one-month job. We tried to get our kids to help out, and it went in stages. At first they thought it was cool, and then they didn't like to actually work at it because it's so repetitive. There's like 17,000 plants out there, so you're doing the same thing, the same job, for a week to a month. They didn't have the attention span or the meditative ability to sit there with a plant for hours because they were so young. But they liked being outdoors and could happily focus on frogs. Now, we have three people who work in the vineyard, plus my brother who works part-time in the vineyard and in the winery. And then during the peak season, we have about three people who work in the tasting room.

I do drink my own wine. It's amazing how good the wine is from this area. I have everything written down. Every time I do something, I write it down in a book, and I keep a spreadsheet as well. It helps if I write it down; if it works out, I can remember what happened. It's like, what the hell did I do? Oh yeah, there it is.

Because we're a cool area, the wines have higher acidity and a lighter body. I think consumer acceptance has grown a lot; we used to have all kinds of people come with the idea that a red wine is supposed to be this ridiculously thick, black-looking wine in the glass, which is very low in acid. There's a misconception that the only good wine comes from a really hot climate, and that's not the case. They're just completely different things. It's not that one's better than the other. This is the wine that comes from here. So changing consumer perception is the challenge.

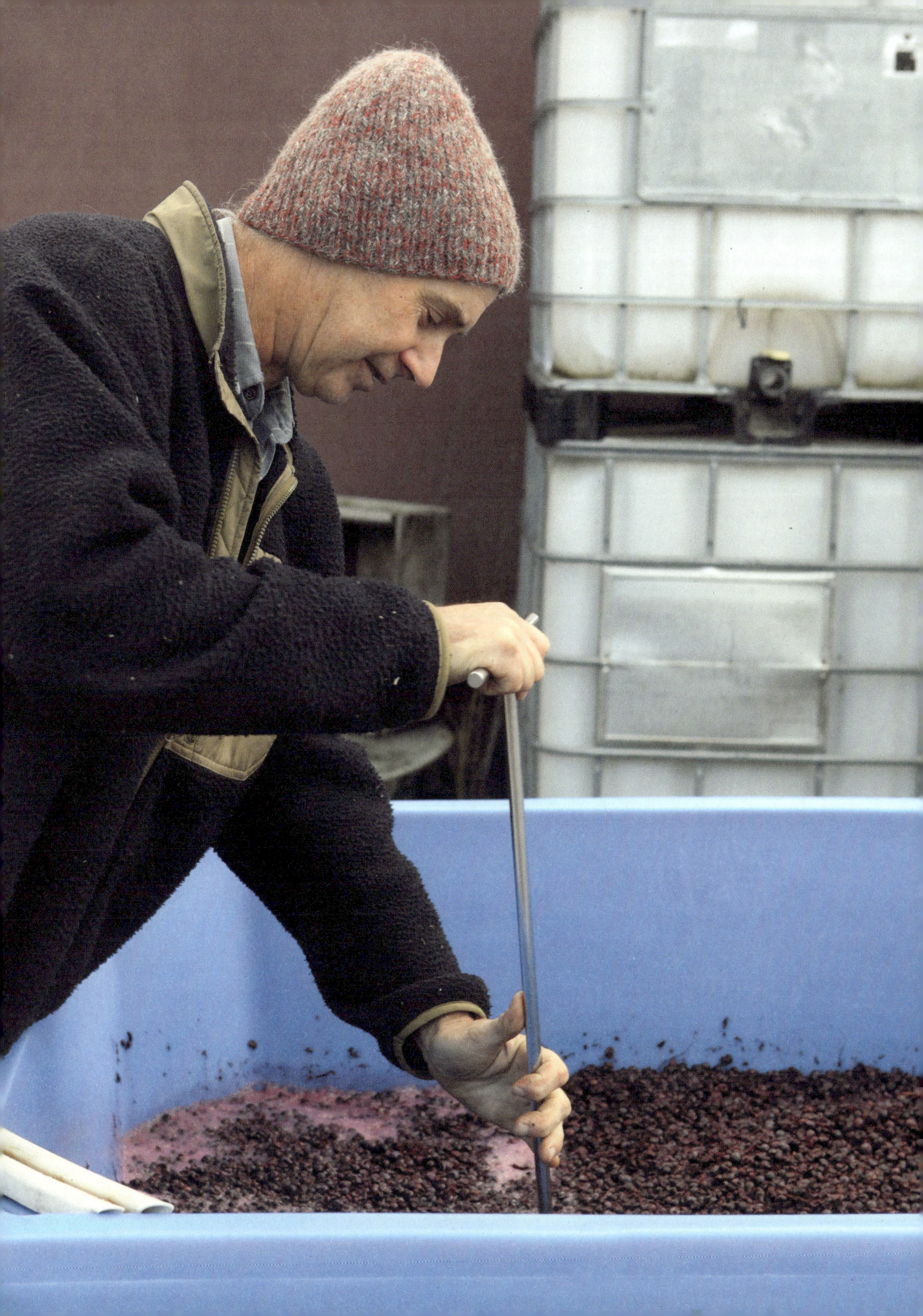

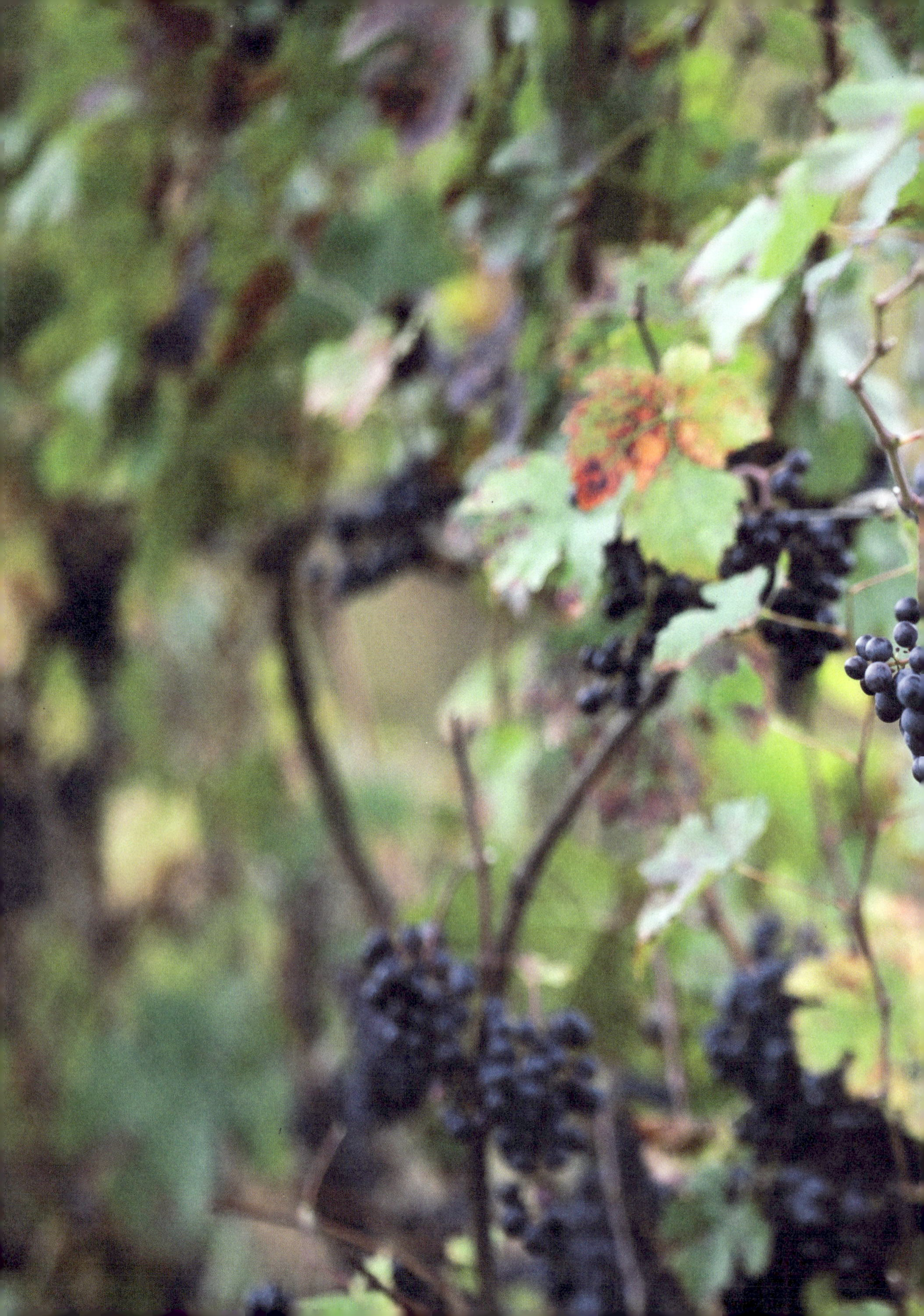

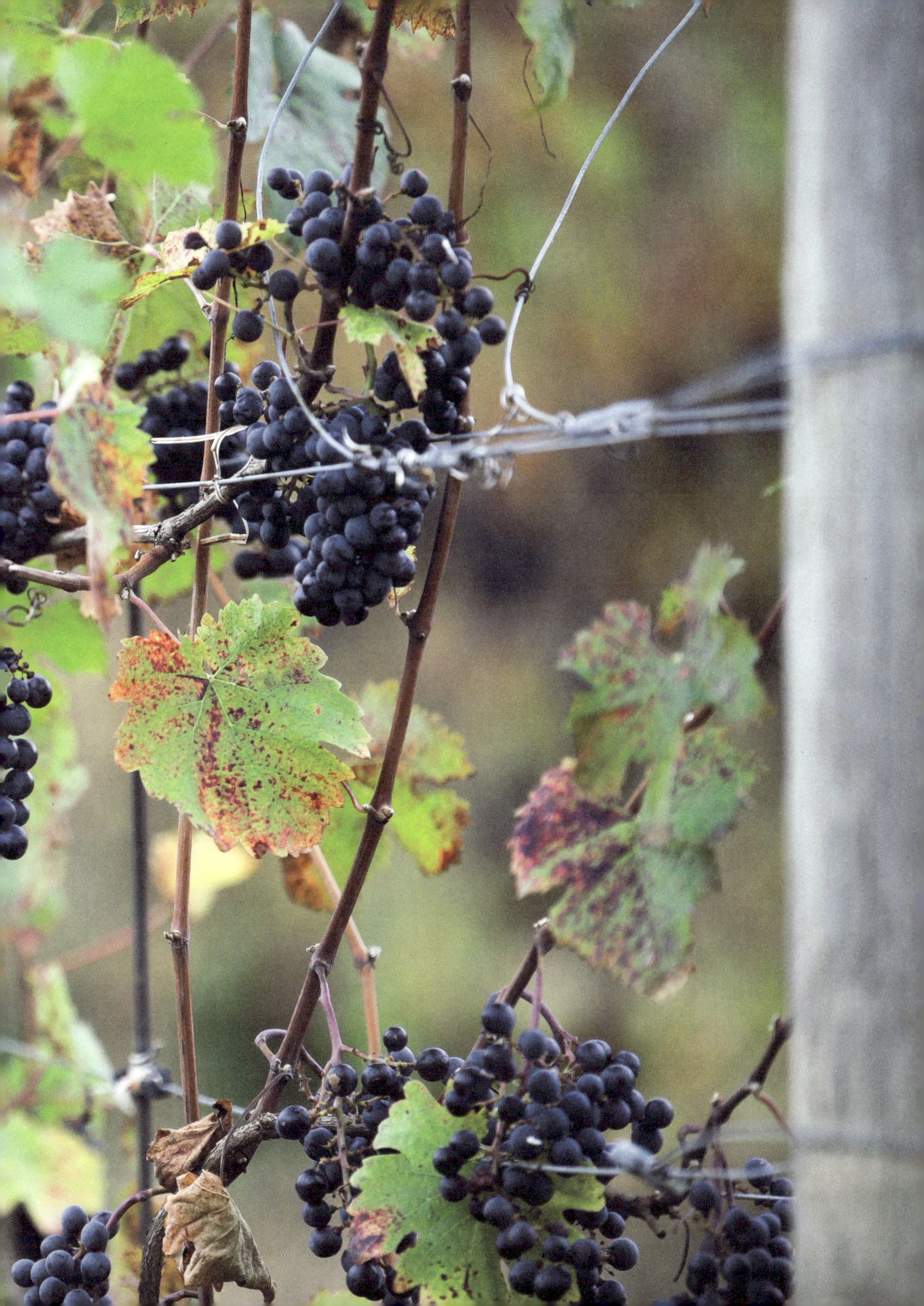

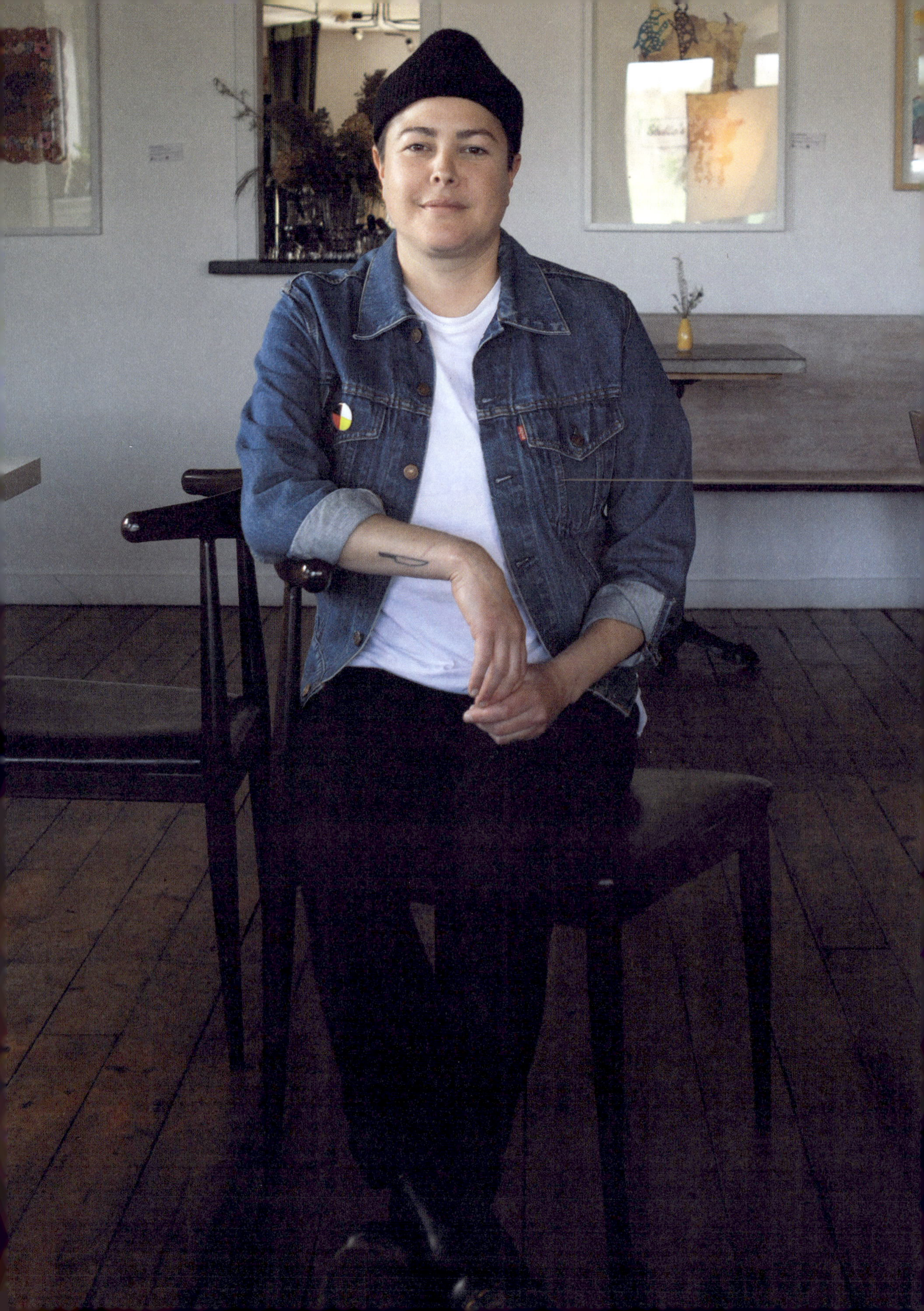

Stella's Eatery's Wine-Braised Rabbit Stew with Fried Bannock

Based in Waupoos and named after Leah's great-grandmother, Stella's Eatery features local, fresh, foraged, seasonal food and Indigenous-inspired cooking.

LEAH MARSHALL HANNON, OWNER AND CHEF

Although we don't use her cast iron Dutch oven at the restaurant often, I have special memories of my grandmother using it at her Pickerel River homestead to make bannock. Our rabbit for this stew is sourced directly from Shades of Gray Rabbitry, a woman-owned First Nations business located in the nearby Trent Hills area. It's a delicious, lean ingredient that's worth exploring and perfect for a slow braise.

Prep time: 35 minutes
Cooking time: 25 minutes (+ 1½ hours for braising rabbit in oven + 15 minutes to fry bannock)
Servings: 6–8

Ingredients

Rabbit
1 3–4 lb rabbit, cut into pieces
1 tbsp salt
½ cup organic all-purpose flour
1 cup thick-cut smoked bacon, diced
2 tbsp butter or bacon fat
1½ cups onion, finely diced
1 head garlic, cloves peeled and crushed
1 cup large celery, diced
1 cup large carrot, diced
1 cup leek, sliced
1½ tbsp ground sumac
1½ tbsp paprika or ground mild chili powder
3 bay leaves
1 cup red wine
4 cups chicken or rabbit stock
2 cups crushed tomatoes
1½ tbsp maple syrup or honey
1 tbsp Cressy Grainy Mustard (or other grainy mustard)
2 diced large potatoes
3 sprigs fresh thyme
fresh herbs (like Italian parsley, thyme, or celery leaves), to garnish

Bannock
3 cups organic all-purpose flour
2 tbsp baking powder
1 tbsp salt
1 tbsp sugar
¼ cup lard or butter
2 cups warm water
1 cup vegetable oil, for frying

Method

Rabbit
Season rabbit pieces with salt; coat evenly with flour.

In a large heavy saucepan with a lid, cook bacon over medium heat until crisp. Remove bacon from pan and set aside. Sear rabbit pieces in hot bacon fat over medium heat for about 5 minutes per side until golden brown, cooking in several batches without overcrowding, if necessary. Remove rabbit from pan; set aside.

Add butter to the same pan the rabbit was cooked in, together with any remaining bacon fat, over medium heat. When hot, add onion, garlic, celery, carrot, and leek, stirring for 3–5 minutes or until softened. Reduce heat to low; add sumac, paprika, and bay leaves, stirring for 2 minutes. Add red wine to deglaze pan, scraping up any browned bits from the bottom.

Add stock, tomatoes, maple syrup, mustard, potatoes, and thyme; bring to a boil. Return bacon, rabbit, and any accumulated juices to the pan; return to a boil. Check for seasoning, adding more salt to taste.

Immerse rabbit in sauce, cover with lid, and bake in a preheated 300°F oven for about 1½ hours or until rabbit is tender.

Bannock
In a large bowl, mix flour, baking powder, salt, and sugar until evenly combined. Melt butter and add to warm water.

Place dry ingredients in a stand mixer fitted with a paddle attachment (or use your hands and a mixing bowl). Slowly add butter mixture until lightly incorporated, mixing for about 2 minutes, being careful not to overwork.

Rest dough for at least 15 minutes, covered with a damp cloth.

Lightly flour a clean surface, and using a rolling pin or your hands, roll dough into 6½" thick rounds.

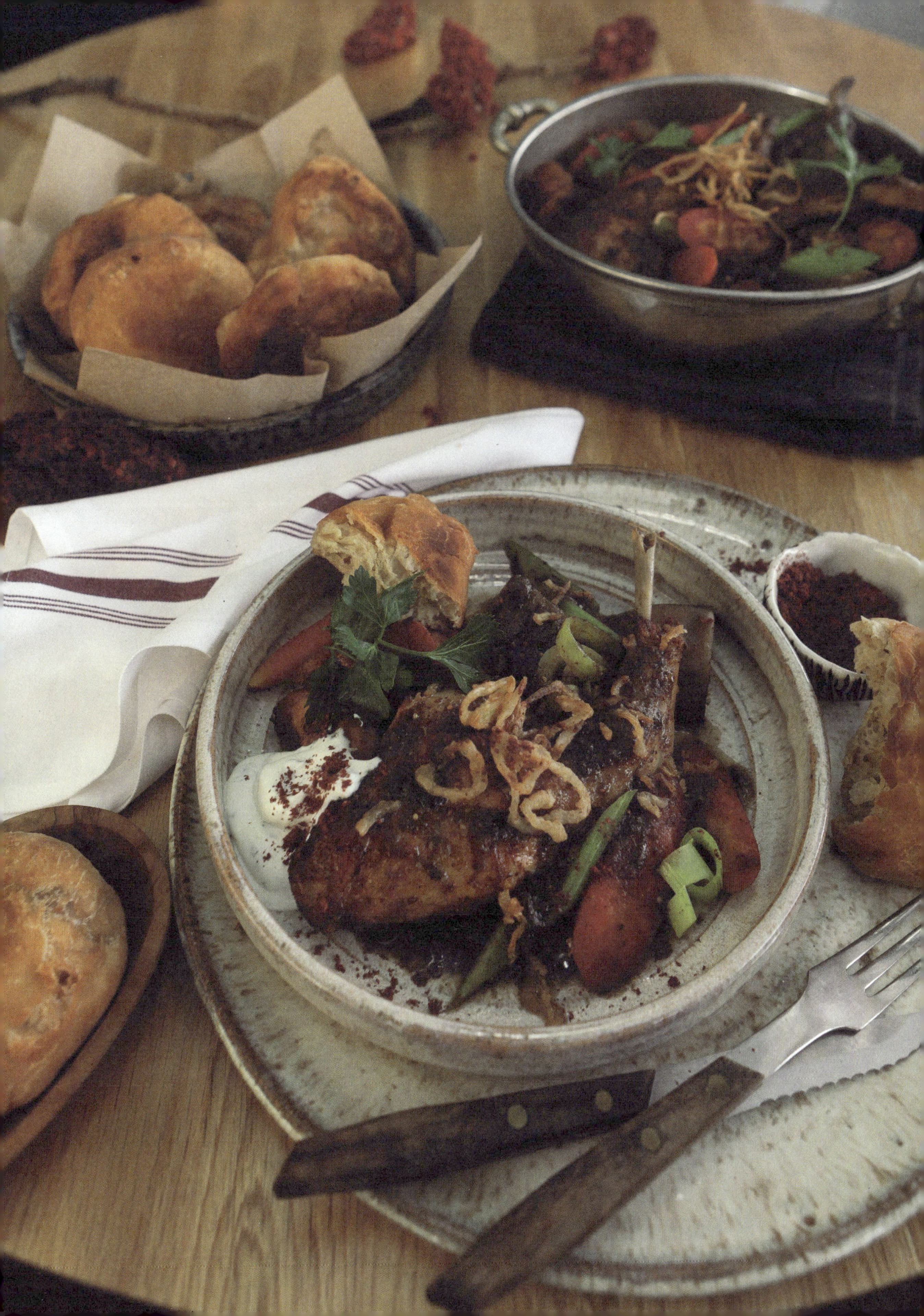

Heat 1 cup vegetable oil (or enough to be 1" deep) in a medium-sized frying pan over medium heat. Without overcrowding the pan, fry the bannock for about 2 minutes on each side until golden brown and cooked through. Set bannock on a warm plate covered with a tea towel until ready to serve.

Assembly
Serve rabbit pieces and sauce in warm bowls, with a dollop of high-fat sour cream or labneh, chopped fresh herbs of your liking, a dusting of sumac, and warm fried bannock.

Chef's Notes
Ask your butcher to cut the rabbit into pieces, or you can do it yourself.

You can reserve certain parts for making stock, like the belly flap, neck, and rib sections.

Want to know if your oil is hot enough for frying bannock? Add a small cube of bread to the hot oil. When it browns in about 1 minute without burning, it's ready (or use a thermometer; your oil is ready for frying at 350°F).

Drink Pairings
This opulent offering is a perfect foil for this complex and earthy dish: Lighthall Pinot Noir Single Vineyard 2021.

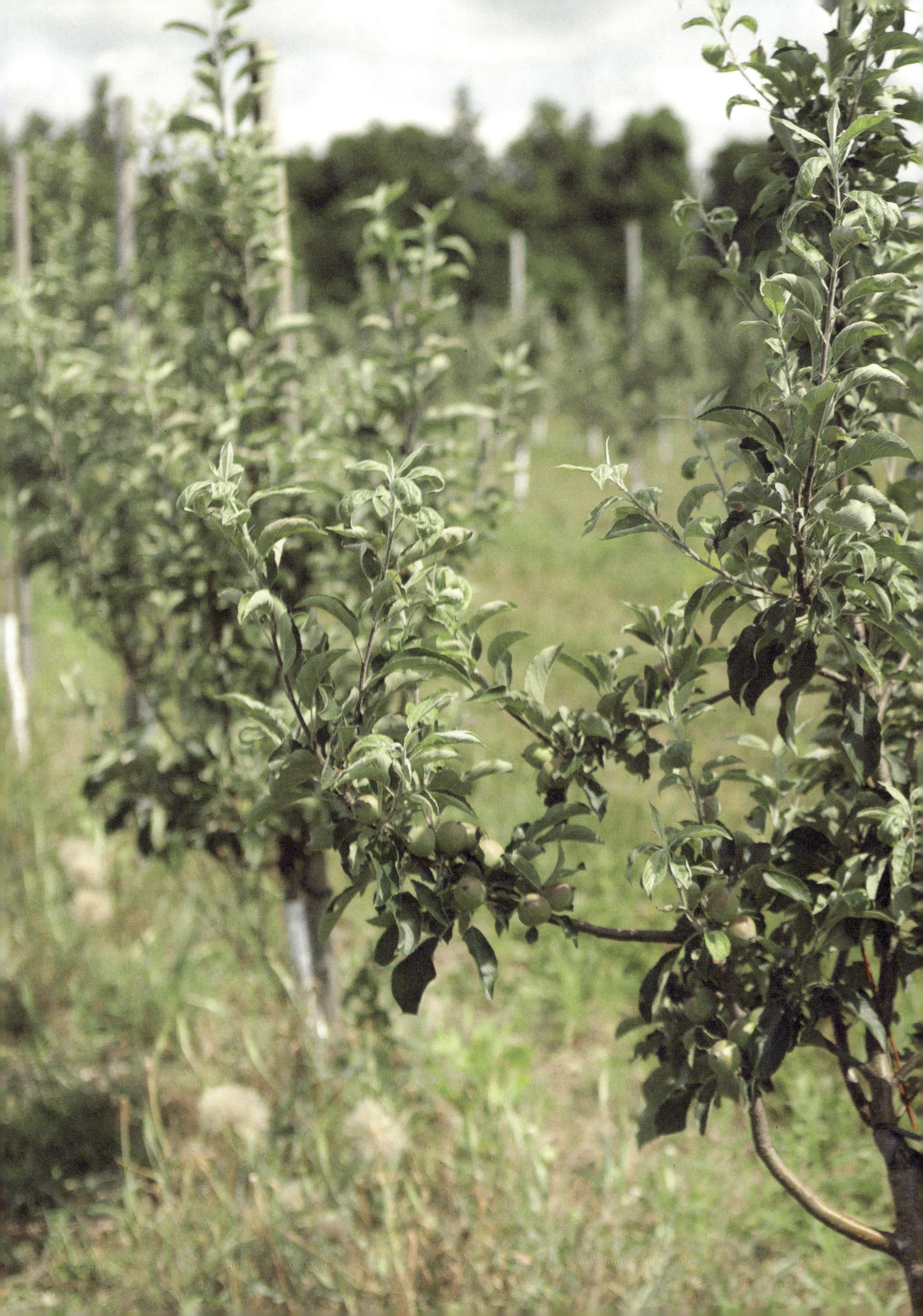

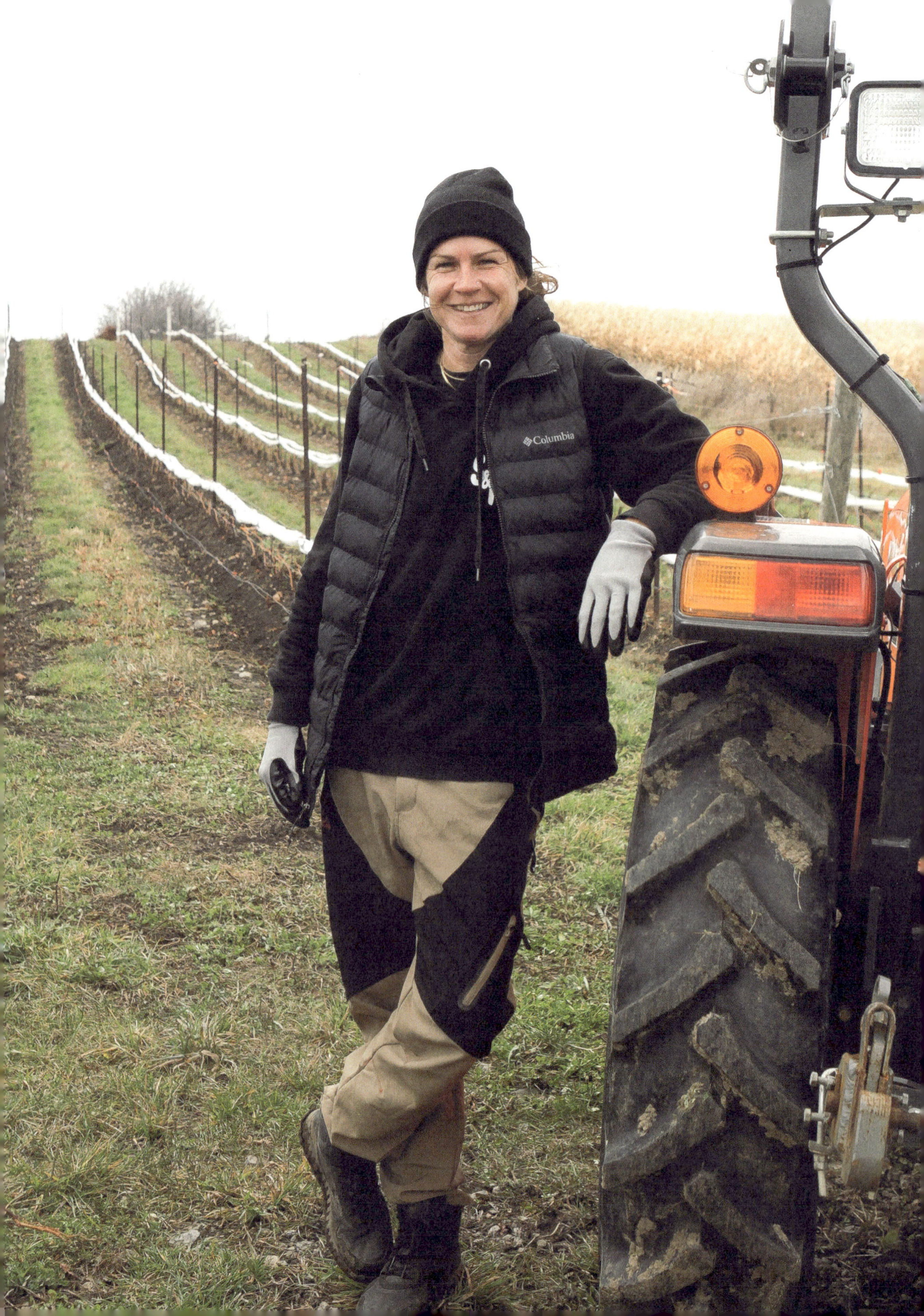
Columbia

Stock & Row Cider, Bloomfield

Stock & Row follows the classic traditions of cidermaking while adding their own twists to certain flavours.

ZOE MARSHALL NARES

In Grade 12, I did a six-month co-op at my local fire department. I had so much fun that I applied and was accepted to Texas A&M's specialty firefighting program. It was a pretty amazing experience—they had acres and acres of buildings, airplanes, tankers, just an incredible number of things for us to train on. I became a certified firefighter but realized that I wasn't yet mature enough to be a firefighter at 20. So I moved back to Canada and had to decide where to plant my feet for a few months. I flipped a coin between Vancouver, where my sister lived, or Montreal, where my brother lived. That coin toss landed me in Montreal.

I thought I would be visiting my brother for a couple of months—turns out I stayed in Montreal for a decade. At that time, Old Montreal only had a couple of year-round restaurants. The loft I rented was above one of the first gay clubs in Montreal. When that commercial space became available for lease, my brother took the opportunity and opened a fine dining restaurant called Garde Manger. I spent the majority of my time in the Old Port working there as a server, bartender, and sommelier. My life centred on learning fine dining and experiencing some of the best foods and wines available.

After 10 amazing years, I took an opportunity that brought me back home to Ontario, and that marked the beginning of my life in cider. I began working for one of the largest cider companies in Ontario, and that's where my now-business partner Justin and I met and where our friendship began. I ended up leaving that job, but my passion for cider was ignited. I enrolled in an advanced cidermaking course in Oregon, which afforded me the privilege of learning cidermaking from Peter Mitchell. I came home with a detemination to make great low-sugar and low-alcohol cider. Shout-out to my best friend Jordy who opened his basement to me and my ideas—he gave me the space and support to create over 60 different kinds of cider over a span of a couple of years.

Family friends of mine own and operate an apple orchard just outside of Toronto. They taught me how to plant, grow, care for, and maintain an orchard, all skills I would need in the coming years. In 2017, we purchased an old dairy farm on Gilead Road, which we slowly transformed into the Stock & Row tasting room. And in 2020, we hand-planted a 5-acre cider apple orchard and a 3-acre vineyard. The overall growth in wineries, cideries, and breweries in the County was a huge motivator for us to take on almost 10 acres of fruit farming.

Justin and I are the two managing partners of Stock & Row. Justin lives in Toronto, and because of his connections in the bar and restaurant industry, we were able to tackle the Toronto market early on, before our brick-and-mortar location was open to the public. In March 2020, the world as we knew it changed when the Covid-19 pandemic began.

Those clients and connections became our focus as all bars and restaurants were forced to shut down. After the first Ontario-wide lockdown, we decided to donate 100% of profits from our home delivery sales back to bar and restaurant staff who couldn't work. Four years earlier, that would have been both Justin and I. That decision ended up growing our brand unexpectedly. When we were able to start selling again, we hit the ground running. It felt like the goodwill we shared came back to us.

I love our farm on Gilead Road and I love working on it daily. I like hands-on work, like being able to plant something and then see it grow. I also really love production and using real ingredients to showcase amazing Ontario fruit. I use 100% Ontario apples and natural ingredients for all of my cider recipes. Our flagship cider, Slow & Low, was selfishly made for my taste—it's dry, crisp, and clean. Our second cider was inspired by Justin and his forward-thinking creativity. Cold Tea is an apple-based cider infused with cold-steeped, loose-leaf black raspberry tea. This cider was made to compete with the exploding seltzer market, which started to take shelf space away from local craft producers. Essentially, Justin's idea was to make a cider seltzer a staple of our portfolio. It's become a fan favourite. I created our third release for both Justin and I and our common love of margaritas and sour beers. Lime Crush is an apple-based cider blended with key lime purée to create a mouth-watering and refreshing drink that makes any day feel like summer.

Our tasting room is run by my partner, Taylor. We met on a dating app when we were both living just outside Toronto. She bought a house in the County before I even knew if I would be here permanently. I was lucky enough that she felt drawn to working for Stock & Row. Not only does she run the tasting room, but she also keeps the paperwork organized. And if I'm lucky, she makes it out to do farm work with me. Our work-life balance isn't always great, but I'm grateful to have somebody I love and trust in the trenches with me. We work 12-hour days but I'm okay with that because I love what I'm doing—it doesn't feel like work.

My brother and I have started a small side project with the vineyard we planted on our property. Stoss Lee wines are also produced by Stock & Row. Cidermaking is pretty similar to winemaking, especially the fermentation process. I'm becoming a better cidermaker because of what I'm doing in wine. I've been going to California for the last four years as an intern to hone my skills with Justin Willett, a well-known winemaker from Santa Barbara. His brands include Tyler Wines and Lieu Dit; he's a master in cool-climate Chardonnay and Pinot Noir, which aligns with the most popular grapes grown in Prince Edward County. We've planted both on our Gilead Road farm and we plan to release our first vintage in 2024.

Taylor and I have a lot of plans to travel. I love experiencing different places, cultures, foods, and libations. Doing this inspires me to explore new flavours and create new recipes. I'm grateful to be in this industry, and to be able to take time to reflect on how lucky Stock & Row is to be continuing to grow. I'm naturally competitve, which I feel has helped me get to this point, but what encourages me is wanting to be better for my friends, for my family, for myself, and for the company. That's what I look forward to every day.

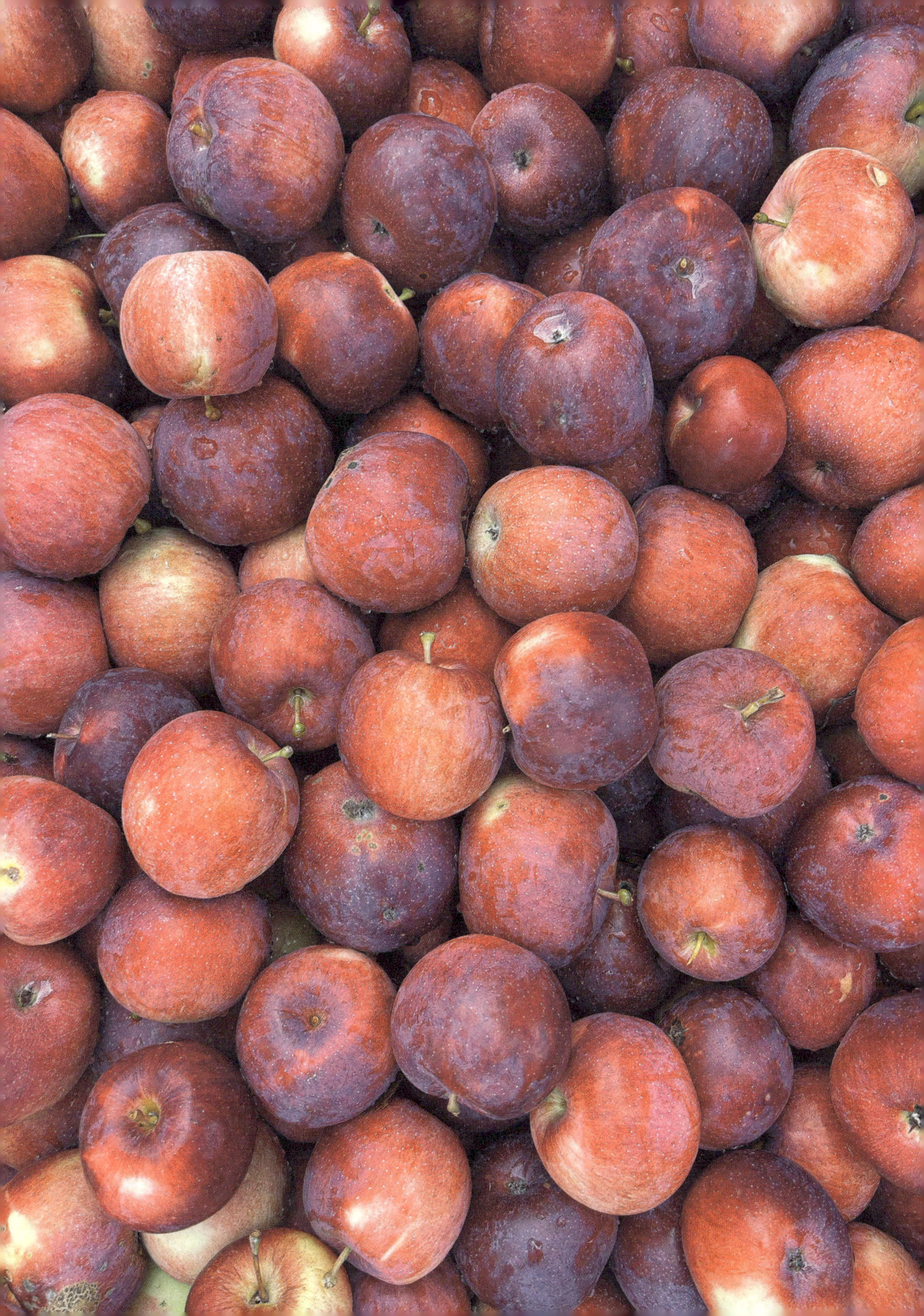

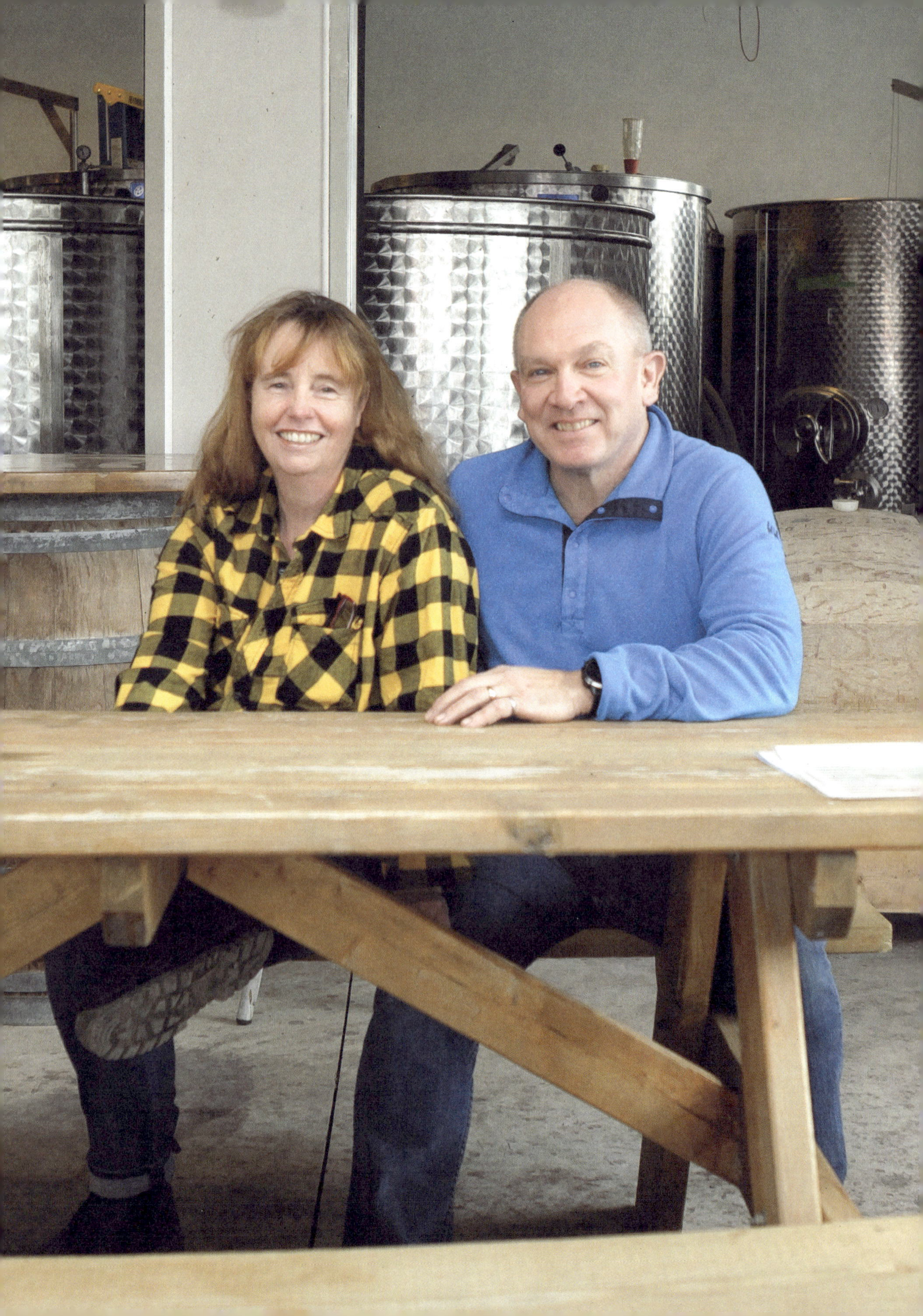

Sugarbush Vineyards, Hillier

As a small family-owned vineyard, Sugarbush produces 100% estate vinifera wines with love and care.

ROB PECK, SALLY PECK

Sally: A friend set Rob and I up, and we got married in Calgary. We went on a wine tour in the Okanagan in 1997, and at the end of the day we sat in our car, saying, "Wouldn't it be fun to have a winery?" If we'd gone wine touring and visited some of the really big wineries like Inniskillin or Jackson-Triggs or even Southbrook, I don't know if we'd have thought it was possible. But we saw all these really small businesses, tiny little wine-tasting areas, and realized that it was possible for regular folks to start a vineyard and winery. A couple of years later, in 2000, we were visiting Rob's parents at Easter, and Rob's mom told us that people had planted grapes in the County. Back in Calgary, I started researching grape-growing in Prince Edward County. We came back in the summertime and drove around looking at land. There were no wineries open in 2000, but Rob's mom and dad had gone to a couple of the Prince Edward County Winegrowers Association meetings for us, and somehow we found out about Mike Peddlesden. We visited him while he was outside working at his vineyard, and he told us about a nice piece of land on Wilson Road. We looked it up but it wasn't for sale, so we left a letter in the owner's mailbox asking if they would like to sell us part of their farm. We didn't hear back for a couple of months, so we sent another letter, and then I think I finally phoned. The answer was yes: they had received our letter and were interested in selling. The original farm was 100 acres, but we asked if they could sever it because we figured we only needed 50 acres. We ended up buying the land at the end of 2000.

Rob: We probably should have bought all 100 acres, in hindsight. In the 1960s, this land was originally cherry trees, and when I was a kid in the '70s, it was still a cherry orchard. I was born here; I'm one of the few winery owners who are from the County, like Lanny Huff. I grew up on a small farm on Rednersville Road, along the Bay of Quinte. This area was the beach—Sandbanks, North Beach—and that was it. There was no other tourism draw. The County was economically depressed. Supermarkets were no longer buying from fruit farmers and the local farms; instead, they were buying through global chains. And that decimated the small farms here. When that happened, my parents decided that farming just didn't make sense anymore and they shut down their farm.

We planted our first vines in the spring of 2002. We came in from Calgary to plant and planned to stay for three weeks. We thought that was plenty of time because the guy who plants the grapes was very loosey-goosey about a date, but we were able to pin him down to early June. So we showed up at the beginning of June and it was too wet. We'd taken three weeks off work, and here we were, just waiting. We found out where he was planting another vineyard, so we drove over there and caught him on his lunch break. We asked him if we could be next. In return, he asked about our spacing; our plan was for nine feet by five feet. He said, "Well, that's what my tractor's at right now. So I'll come over and see you guys tomorrow." And then it rained again. We were literally here for three weeks and we planted on the last day of our trip, which was a Sunday. And then we got up on Monday and drove back to Calgary for work. I was so stressed. That was my first experience of farming. We continued to live in Calgary for the next two years, which meant we spent all our holiday time back here. We would fly in for a weekend to work, or sometimes for a two- or three-week spell and just work the whole time.

Sally: 2006 was the first commercial harvest. So our wines didn't come out until 2007. We didn't have a very big harvest that first year. We decided to make a blend, a white blend and a red blend. And we called them red and not red. People thought that was funny.

Rob: According to John Cleese, there's only two kinds of wine. Red and not red. So that's what we named them.

Sally: Later on, we made an almost red, a rosé, which we still have. It's popular. When we started, we planted 5 acres. The second year, we went up to 8 acres. Then we sat tight with 8 acres for a while. Then we decided we needed to increase production and in 2012 we planted a few more acres. Now we're sitting at just over 13 acres, which is where we plan to stay.

Rob: My mom and dad basically ran the farm for us those first couple of years. When the vines were really tiny, the work was basically weeding and spraying. Dad did all the spraying on the tractors and my mom, a couple of aunts, and uncles were out here all the time weeding. We moved here full-time in 2004.

Sally: I just really like it when people come in and tell us that this is their favourite spot. In the summer, we have a nice big outdoor seating area with lots of picnic tables. Large groups can spread out, or there are comfy cabanas for smaller groups and couples; generally, there is tons of space for folks visiting with children or dogs. People really seem to enjoy the space and the wine-tasting experience here. We hear that over and over again, so I feel like we've kind of hit our stride.

Rob: I kept working a corporate job for a long time so we didn't have to take on debt. So now, we figure our latest addition is our last big expenditure. We still might spend money on tanks and stuff like that, but now that we've had the last big infrastructure expense, I retired last year from engineering and now work on the farm full-time. We started this business and kept it small so we could make all the decisions, be involved in day-to-day operations, and pay ourselves a reasonable amount to live on. We don't have to be rich or anything, just comfortable. Now, everyone's idea of comfortable is different, but we were hoping to get a couple of engineering salaries. That was the goal and we're pretty much there. It only took 15 years longer than we thought to get here.

VQA
20TH ANNIVERSARY
Sugarbush
VINEYARDS
RESERVE
2021
CHARDONNAY
VQA PRINCE EDWARD COUNTY VQA
ESTATE GROWN & BOTTLED

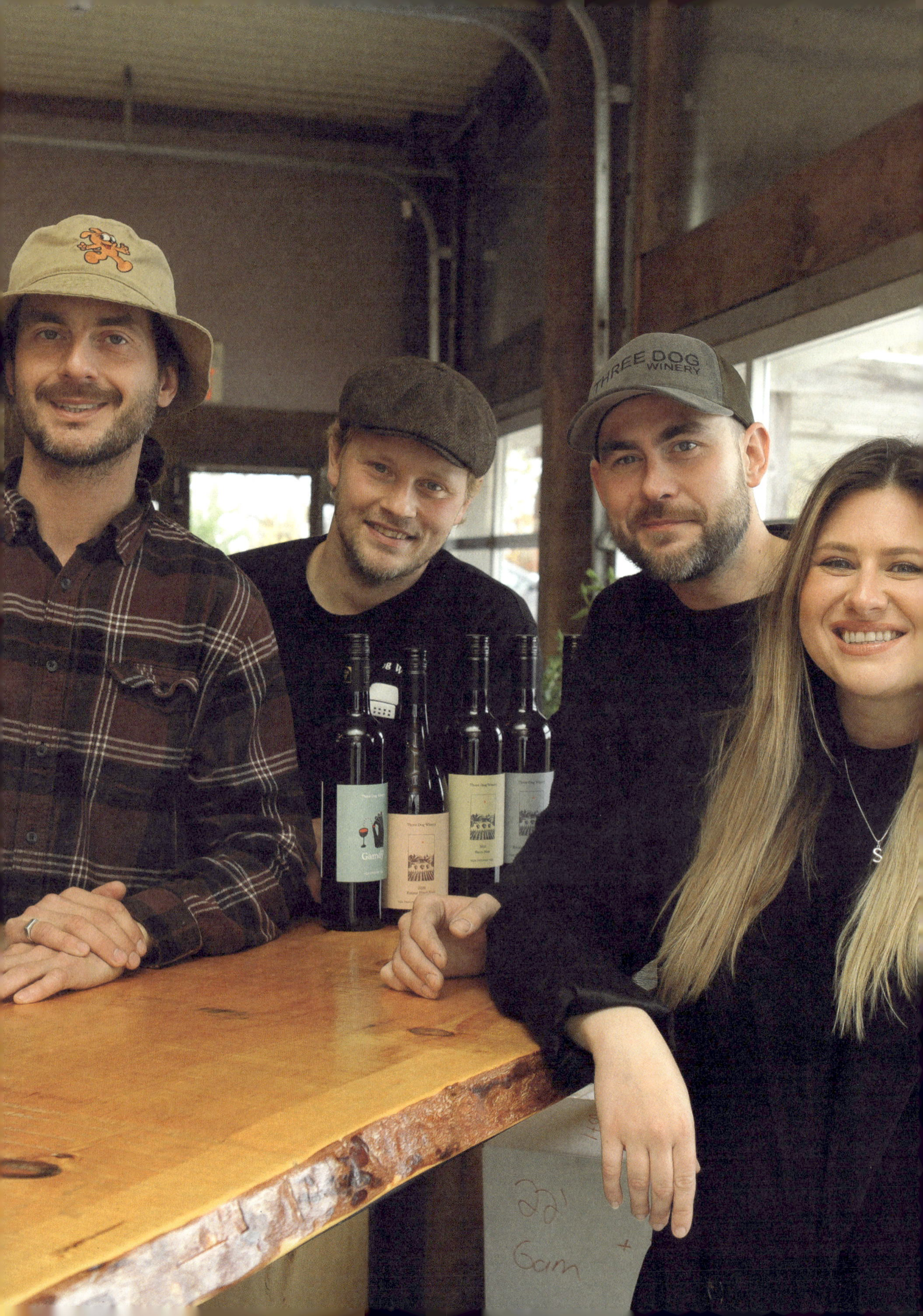
THREE DOG
WINERY

Three Dog Winery, Demorestville

Three Dog is an award-winning, family-owned winery that's off the beaten path.

SARAH COFFIN, ANDREW RYTWINSKI

Sarah: Three Dog is me, Andrew, Adam, and Kyle, Andrew's childhood best friend. Plus Anne and Cecil, my in-laws, and Red Dog.

It can be hard to come in, buy a business, and make it your own. Three Dog's founders, John and Sacha Squair, were a pretty big force in the County. But our dreams and hopes are similar. That's why Three Dog appealed to us—we love the laid-back atmosphere they cultivated here because that's who we all are to our core. We're serious when it comes to the business, but we also really like to have fun and we really want other people to have fun too. And that part of the transition has been easy. I love the clientele we've inherited.

We spent a month here working with John and Sacha, trying to learn everything before they left. As we drove in to stay the night for one of the first times, we passed the blue sign on the 401 that reads *Three Dog Winery*. I'll never forget that moment. Everything had been moving so fast, and the realization just hit me: We'd bought a business that was advertised on the 401.

I'm a makeup artist and there are so many parallels with wine—it's all about human interaction and experience. I've spent my entire life working in retail or customer service, so this felt like a natural shift. The amount of organization it takes to put something out, all the moving parts when it comes to bottling, label design, managing a rebrand—making sure all the labels are done and up to code with the LCBO and that you have the right caps—it's a huge operation.

I always think about people who run businesses alone, solo entrepreneurs, because when shit hits the fan, at least here we're all in the same boat. We have equal investment and therefore we take equal loads when things are hard or bad. It's a family affair. Adam lived in a trailer in the parking lot for the first year. My in-laws lived in a trailer here. And Kyle, Andrew, and I lived over in the house when we first moved here. But then the boys got shacked up and now everybody's off the property. It's just Andrew and I.

Andrew's a perfectionist so his wines are so good. He did such an amazing job on his first vintage of wines. He even made a great Vidal; it's a hybrid grape, which Andrew hadn't worked with in Niagara. And he ended up winning like five medals in his first vintage across three different competitions.

Andrew: I always liked wine, so I applied to Niagara College, Brock, Okanagan College, and UC Davis for a bunch of different programs. I ended up picking Niagara College, and I moved down there and had the best two years of my life. It was awesome. I really enjoyed Niagara College. The program was very fun and very hands-on. I was worried because I thought I was kind of old to go back to school; I was 28 at the time. But I was in the younger half of the class, as almost everyone there was looking for a second career of some sort. My background in chemistry came in handy.

I spent four months on a summer placement in the vineyard at Malivoire, and I did harvest there afterwards. As soon as harvest ended, I went back to school for another few months and finished in the summer. And then I got a full-time job at Megalomaniac in the cellar and went right into wine production. It was just me and the winemaker in the cellar and we were doing some pretty big volumes. In 2018, I was recruited to The Foreign Affair Winery. I ended up working there for a little over two years. Malivoire, Megalomaniac, and Foreign Affair, and their three winemakers, all have very different styles in terms of winemaking and in the types of wines they make. Foreign Affair is huge, New World, high-alcohol big reds. Malivoire is a lot more restrained, Old World, very authentic, terroir-driven Pinot Noir, Chardonnay-type wines. And then Megalomaniac is a lot more commercial, a lot more big, big, big batch stuff, a lot more LCBO wines with that lower price point and easy-drinking style. The focus is a lot more on stability, safety, reproducibility. So it was really cool learning three different winemaking techniques and styles.

We looked at this place a couple times. It was just way too big in terms of scope and the fact that it was already a fully functioning business with a brand and a following. A hundred acres, the price, everything was way bigger than we wanted. And so we said thanks but no thanks. We didn't want to fall in love with the place. And then our agent told us to talk to the bank; because it was already a business, they'd be more excited about it. With a start-up winery, you don't get income right away. The previous owners here reached out to us as well and said they were motivated to sell. They wanted to go. So we spent a few months working out details to figure out something that made sense for everyone, and we took over on April 20, 2022.

Big things are coming down the pipeline. We've got the south-facing slope that's about 12-ish acres, the whole slope. It was mostly planted, except for the far side. We've spent the better part of 16 months clearing it out. Soil's been turned. Vines have been ordered. So we'll have a 3-acre block of Chardonnay planted next year. I cannot be more excited about that. And then an acre of Gamay coming in here to replace the Geisenheim. To have close to 12 acres of vinifera on a south-facing slope—I can't say it without smiling. It's cool in the vineyard because we have Pinot Noir, Pinot Gris, and Cab Franc left on the slope right now. And the Franc's the youngest by far. I think it's 2003 for the Pinot, 2017–2019 for the Franc. And the Franc is by far the healthiest and most vigorous. It just hasn't seen as many winters here. The Pinot Noir and the Pinot Gris are really struggling. But then to have this block of Franc that is just gorgeous and clean and healthy and green and nice fruit—and to see that we can do it—everything's going to be fine. So the big goal is getting that vineyard healthy, being a little more self-reliant on it for fruit. The other big thing is the production area. We're going to build a big warehouse and expand our production area and get three-phase power and better equipment to expand our on-site production. The goal is to have a full production facility and a warehouse and a lot more stuff on-site. We're making incremental changes and getting better every day.

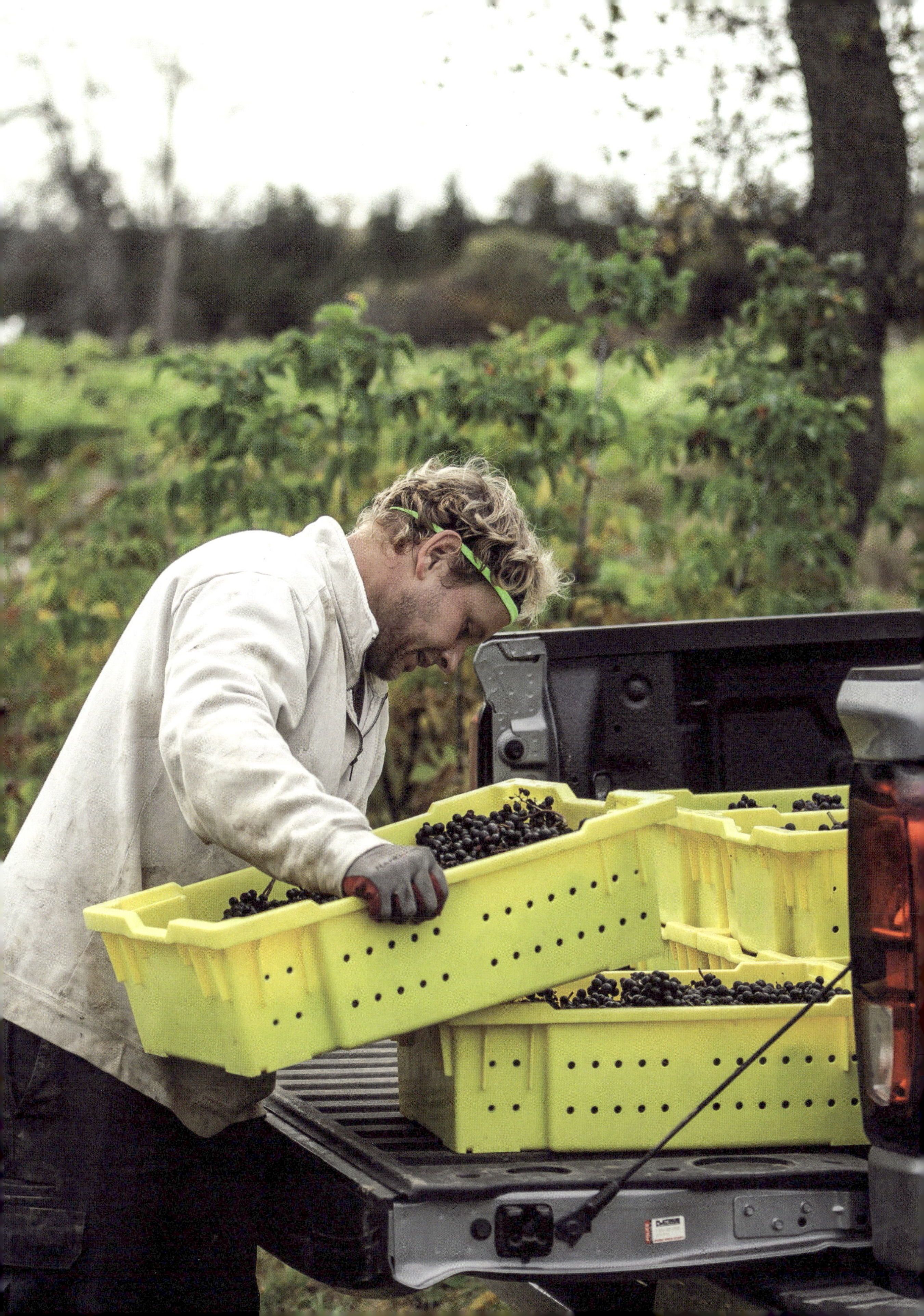

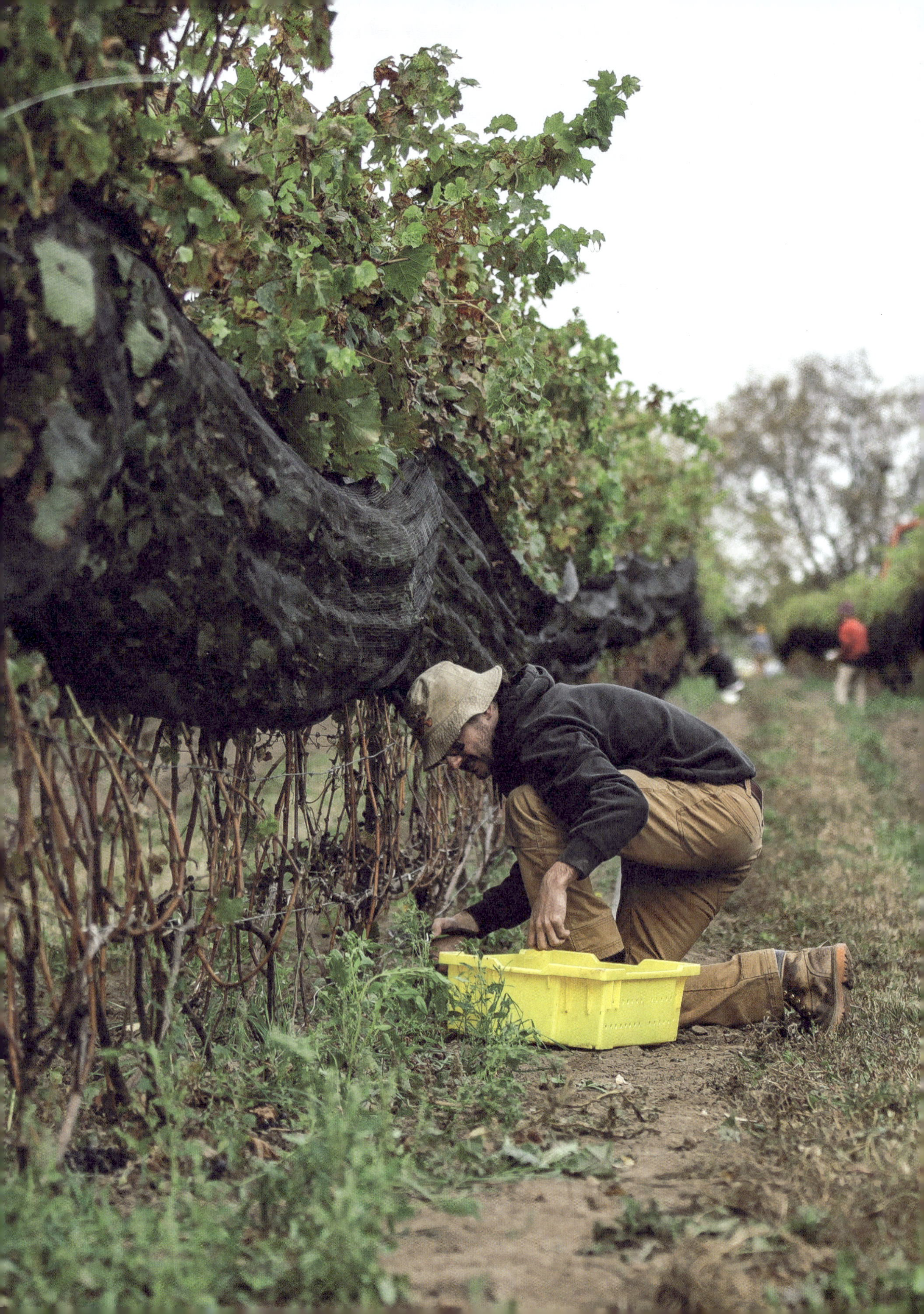

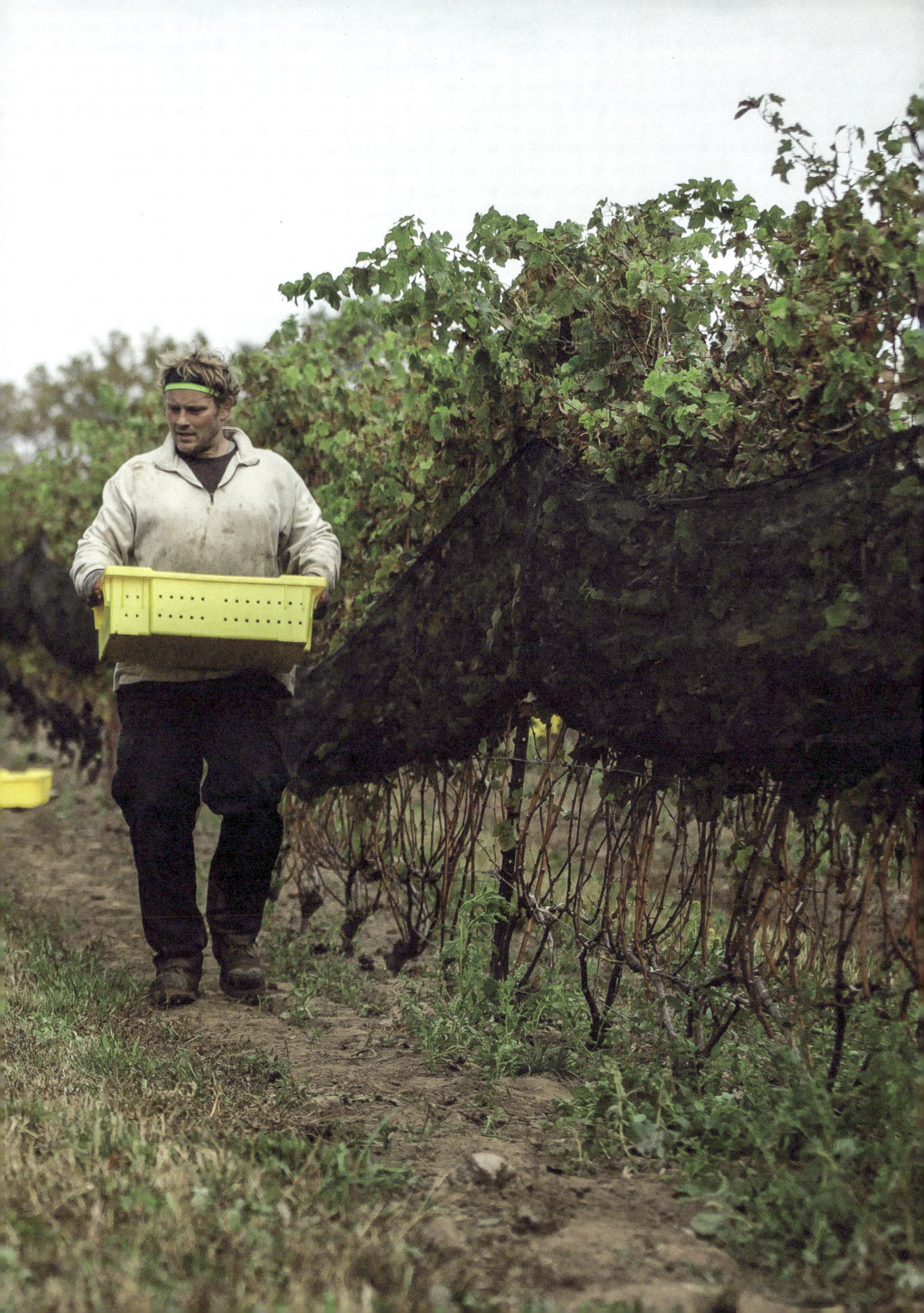

12 X 750 ml

Trail Estate Winery, Hillier

A minimalist craft winery focusing on low-intervention wines, Trail Estate makes vintages that are classical, funky, and fun.

MACKENZIE BRISBOIS, BROOKE TAYLOR

Mackenzie: I grew up in Carrying Place and then went to school in Trenton. I attended the University of Guelph, where I took biology and English. I really loved reading and tearing books apart and critical analysis. My degree is quite broad, which makes it a really good degree for winemaking. At that time, I thought I was going to be a teacher. And then, in my fourth year, I signed up for a hospitality course that held a wine appreciation class on Friday afternoons. That was pretty much where things started.

During university, I started working at one of the first wineries in the County—Carmela Estates. It's changed names and owners over the years; it was Peddlesden, and then it was Carmela, and now it's Casa-Dea. I was doing retail. They had a restaurant and a banquet hall, so lots of weddings, and all of those spaces were pretty separate from production. At that time, the winemaker there was Norman Hardie, I think Mike Traynor was in the vineyard, and Kimball Lacey was in the cellar. It was quite the lineup; each has since gone on to start their own winery.

I travelled for a year before going back to school at Niagara College, where I enrolled in the Winery and Viticulture Technician program. I worked part of my placement at a small and lovely winery in Niagara, but I didn't really get a lot of experience there. So partway through that harvest, I went to work at Norman Hardie here in the County, and then I worked there for five years once I graduated. While I was there, I also worked two harvests abroad in South Africa and New Zealand. I worked at Bouchard Finlayson—we would crush on the roof, and they had these huge container tanks inside the building. We were tipping bins from the roof into the destemmer, in this beautiful valley that looked down to the ocean. It was incredible. South Africa is gorgeous. But the New Zealand harvest at Central Otago Wine Company is where I learned the most. They're so fast-paced and you're just crushing it—literally.

This is my ninth vintage at Trail Estate. We've slowly moved away from conventional to more organic methods, using biodynamic and regenerative agricultural practices. Brooke, my assistant winemaker, has a background in sustainability and has been instrumental in introducing compost teas that include horsetail and stinging nettle. We harvest the plants from our garden, compost them, and spray our vines to give our plants nutrients and build up resistance naturally. It's a closed loop. We've been planting permanent cover crops since 2018; the blend includes clover and forage radish, which beat out the weeds. We re-evaluate and regroup every winter to see what worked well. Our soil looks a lot better, with way more organic material and lots of worms. It's satisfying to see. It's important for us to take the time to figure out what works for our site; I don't think you can take one philosophy and apply it indiscriminately. We've had some real challenges with the weather. One year, we applied mostly organic sprays and then at one point went with something non-organic—but it saved the vineyard. We've made a lot of changes over the years to get things in a good place environmentally, to be sustainable.

My sister and brother both have PhDs and are involved in environmental work, and they often share information with me. In grape-growing, we're pretty careful with what we use, but the realities of being a commercial grower are pretty harsh, and we're also surrounded by cash crops. I want better choices for plants and for people and animals. A lot of growers in the County are environmentally conscious, and a lot of the original growers were focused on organics. Part of what we're trying to do now is close the loop a little bit more by making compost teas, and then compost from grape skins and stems themselves. We put them in a row once they're pressed and then cover it all with straw. We incorporate nitrogen and turn it, and it turns into compost. That kind of thing.

In 2023, we had a really challenging year with all that rain throughout the summer, but the weather dried out in September, which helped a lot and turned it into a really great vintage. I've done a good job of getting the Pinot in balance and working with the different clones. I find we have a really leather-driven site and sometimes the structure is not super tannic. So we hand-destemmed some of the Pinot, we did some whole cluster, and some carbonic. It's like a jigsaw puzzle. I feel like we've actually got all the pieces together—it's tasting like it, anyway.

Brooke: I went into winemaking because it's so multi-faceted. I thought it would be beneficial to focus on one aspect of agriculture and then apply literally everything I've learned. I look at the vineyard like a giant garden. I love wine. I'm from Niagara, so I've been serving tables since I was 16 years old. The whole time I've been working in agriculture, I've also been serving in restaurants. Winemaking seemed like the perfect fit.

After university, I worked for a non-profit called Bowery Project; we built urban farms out of milk crates around Toronto on vacant condo spaces or other urban places waiting for building permits. Once the land development started, we would move the farm. We also ran workshops, and all the produce we grew went to local charities or organizations. I did that for two summers. And then I moved to an off-grid community and got a sustainable agriculture certificate on a permaculture farm in Panama.

I came to the County because I thought there was more opportunity here, and I was right—there's no way I'd be driving a tractor and also working in the cellar and in the vineyard back in Niagara. Making natural wine is really important to me, and seeing natural fermentation happen is really amazing. Being able to work within the vineyard from the beginning of the season through to harvest and then producing a product from that fruit is pretty amazing. At lots of other cellars, you only see the crush or get to pick once a year. Following the fruit from growth throughout fermentation is really cool.

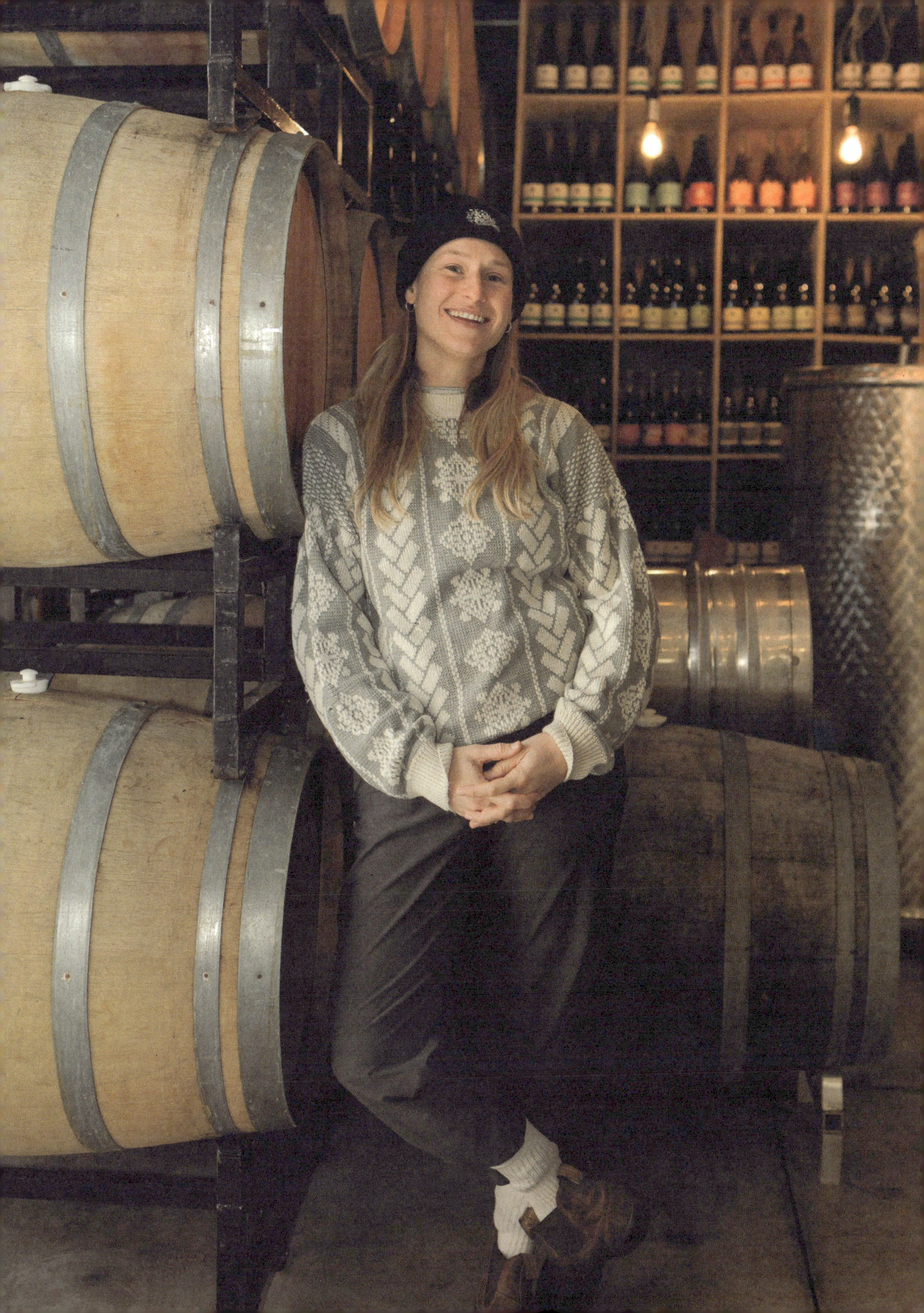

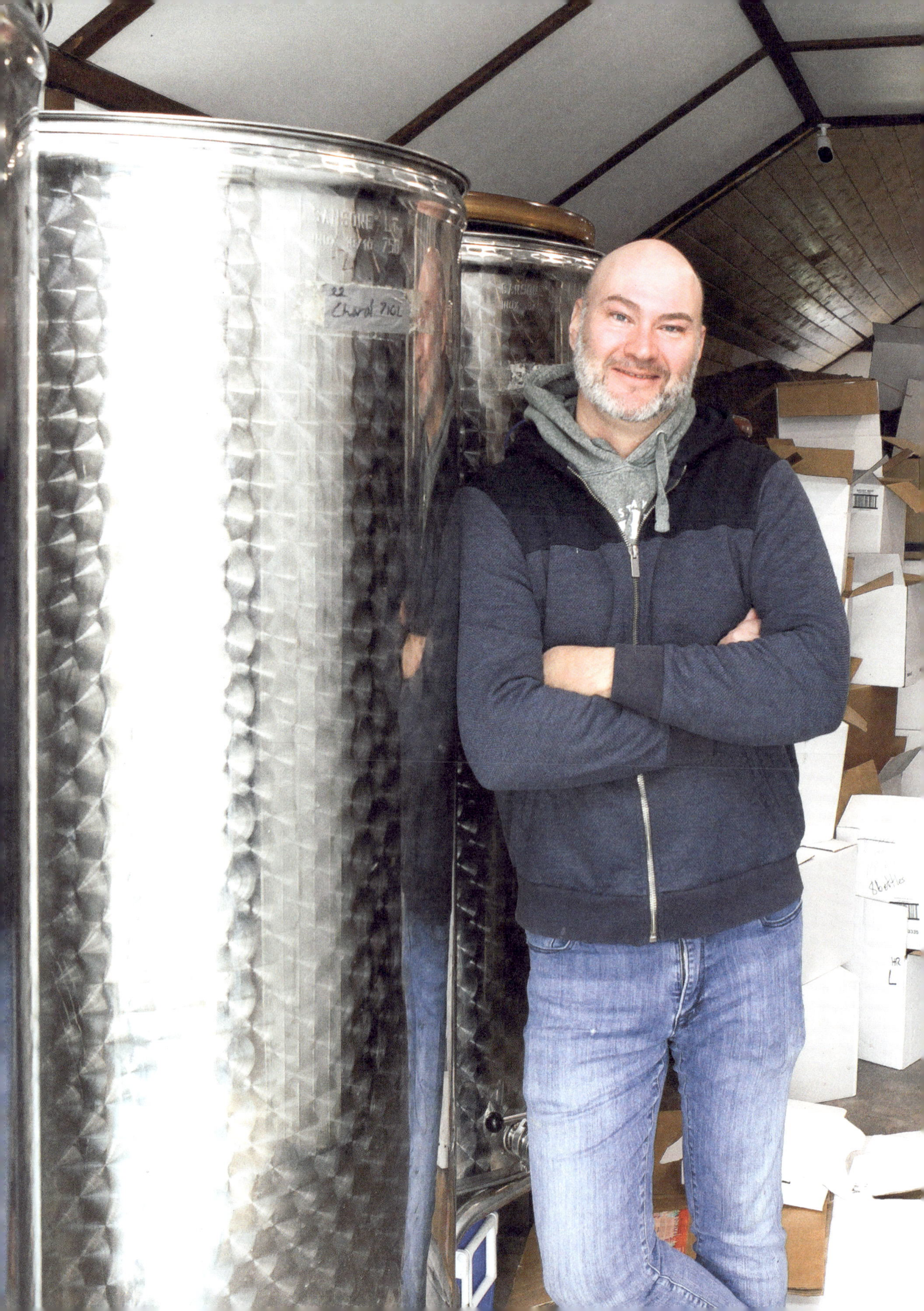

Traynor Family Vineyard, Hillier

Traynor has been cultivating grapes and creating exceptional sustainable wines since 2009.

MIKE TRAYNOR

Growing up in Peterborough, my family had apple and pear orchards and market gardens and ducks and chickens and things like that. I'd always enjoyed that lifestyle, and grapevines are very much the same jam, so it was a natural fit for me to jump from one fruit crop to another. I did my sommelier training while I was at Algonquin College. I started working in a wine shop in Ottawa, and I got more and more into wine; I was just really curious about everything to do with wine.

I moved to the County in 2000 and the first winery opened in 2001. I was on a newsletter group and I put a message out that I was new to the area and keen to work or volunteer in a vineyard. A winery in Stouffville, Willow Springs, messaged me and asked if I wanted to help out. I wanted to work in the County, but no one had responded, so I messaged my uncle in Stouffville to see if I could stay with him. I spent my weekends working in their vineyard, and then about a month later, a week before harvest was going to start, the owner and the winemaker got in a fight and the winemaker left. I'm not sure what the story was, but they said, "We're stuck and you're going to school for this, and you seem pretty keen, so do you want to be our winemaker?" I was 21 and had no idea what I was doing, but I said sure. YOLO. So I took on that job on the weekends and I went to Loyalist College for the viticultural winemaking program during the week.

My first in-County job was at Huff Estates—I was their first hire. I started with Lanny and I helped plant all the vineyards. That first year, it was me and one other guy, and then, after the season was done, Lanny hired me as the operations manager. I was going to school, I was Lanny Huff's operations manager, and I was doing the winemaking in Stouffville. It was busy—there was no time to get in trouble.

I left Willow Springs in 2005. In 2006, I started as the general manager at a new winery in Warkworth called Oak Heights, so my work in the County came to an end. It's a beautiful little spot; we had a restaurant at the vineyard and built that up, and then the 2008 financial crash happened and there was no money left. I was looking at unemployment, and the dream had always been to have my own place, so I bought our current property in November 2008. I planted in 2009, and then built the building—it was just me and my Mastercard.

The property is 10 acres, and we had 6,000 vines. In 2023, we pulled out one of the original plantings to replant, and we're going to replant the rest of the property. We'll end up with about 9,000 vines. Our focus here now is hybrids, for sustainability. We're a no-spray program; the only thing we'll spray is called Nurture Growth, and it's a completely organic biodynamic system that we're using. We're really focused on varieties that are long-term sustainable for us.

Back in 1998, I planted 350 vines in my parents' backyard so I could learn, and that was my first trial with hybrids. After school, I'd planned on moving back to Peterborough and taking what I'd learned and applying it there, but the County got its hooks into me. At Willow Springs, we were north of Markham, and the 14-acre vineyard had Chardonnay and Pinot Noir. After a couple of years, we realized it wasn't working, so we pulled the vines out and replanted hybrids to make it more practical, more sustainable. I know a lot of places here stick to Pinot Noir and Chardonnay and fully traditional methods, but there are other places in the County working with hybrids too. Harwood has St. Laurent. Sherry at Karlo has some Frontenac and Marquette. It's interesting to see who's taking it on.

Our style has changed quite a bit since the beginning. I think this is my 27th year in the wine industry, and sometimes you want to try something new. We're bursting at the seams. My dream was to sell 1,000 cases a year and that's what this was built around. I think we're at 9,000 cases this year and we haven't grown the facilities at all. I feel that it's one of those things we need to invest in now. I didn't have any money when I started, so the only thing I could spend money on was my inventory, because I needed the inventory to pay for everything else.

I love my team. One of my favourite things about what we're doing is the people we work with, the other winery people I see almost daily—the sense of camaraderie we have. We work hard together. We definitely enjoy wine together. I think that's the most satisfying part.

I think my love for wine is now a more mature kind of love—it's not that rampant teenage hormone kind of love. I'm middle-aged and this is my life and I wouldn't have it any other way. You accept the good and the bad.

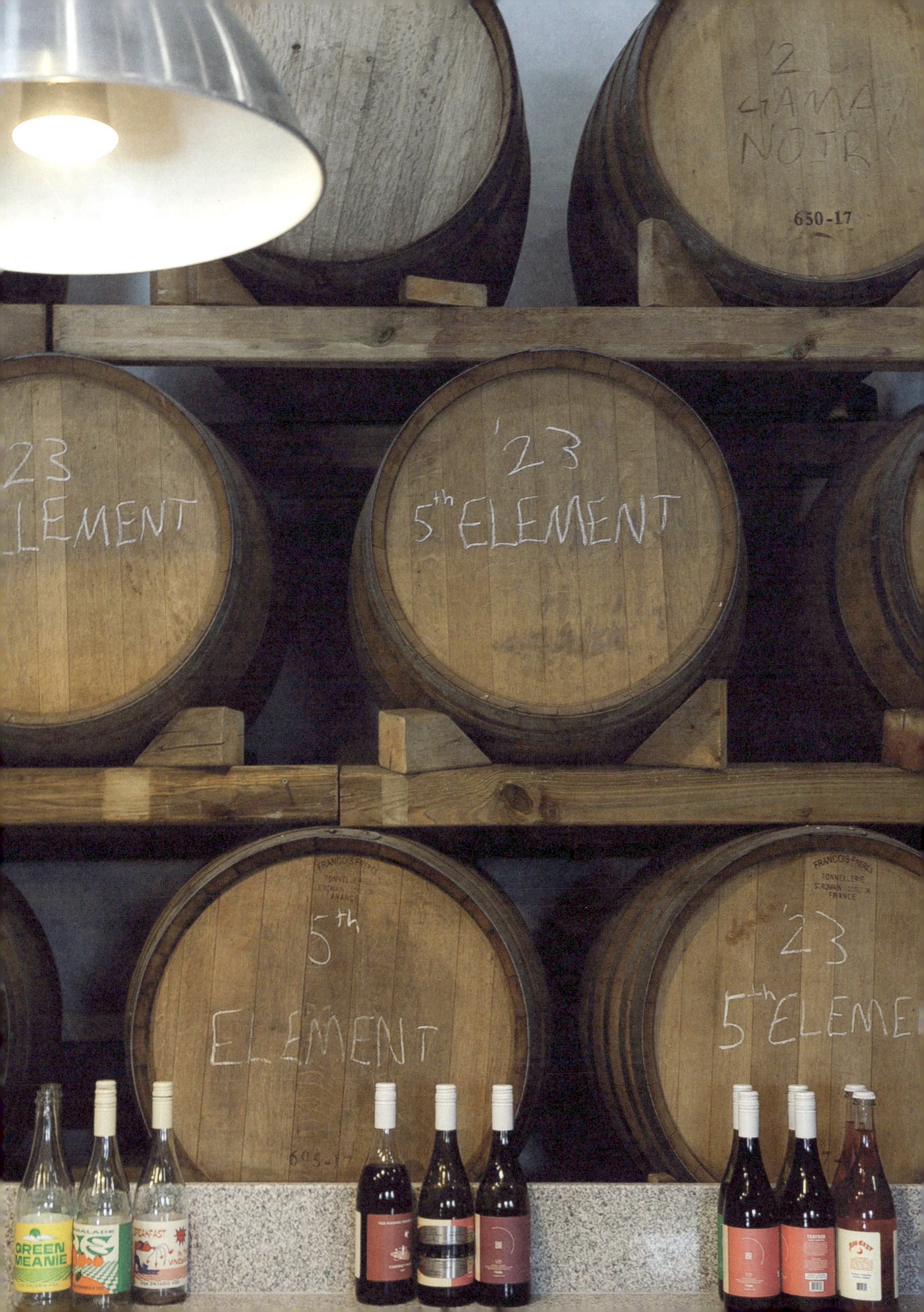
650-17
'23
5th ELEMENT
5th
ELEMENT
GREEN MEANIE

OPHELIA
BACO BACO
OPHELIA
BACO BACO
GREEN MEANIE
VQA ONTARIO VQA
FUMÉ BLANC
VQA NIAGARA PENINSULA VQA
FUMÉ BLANC
VQA NIAGARA PENINSULA VQA
FUMÉ BLANC

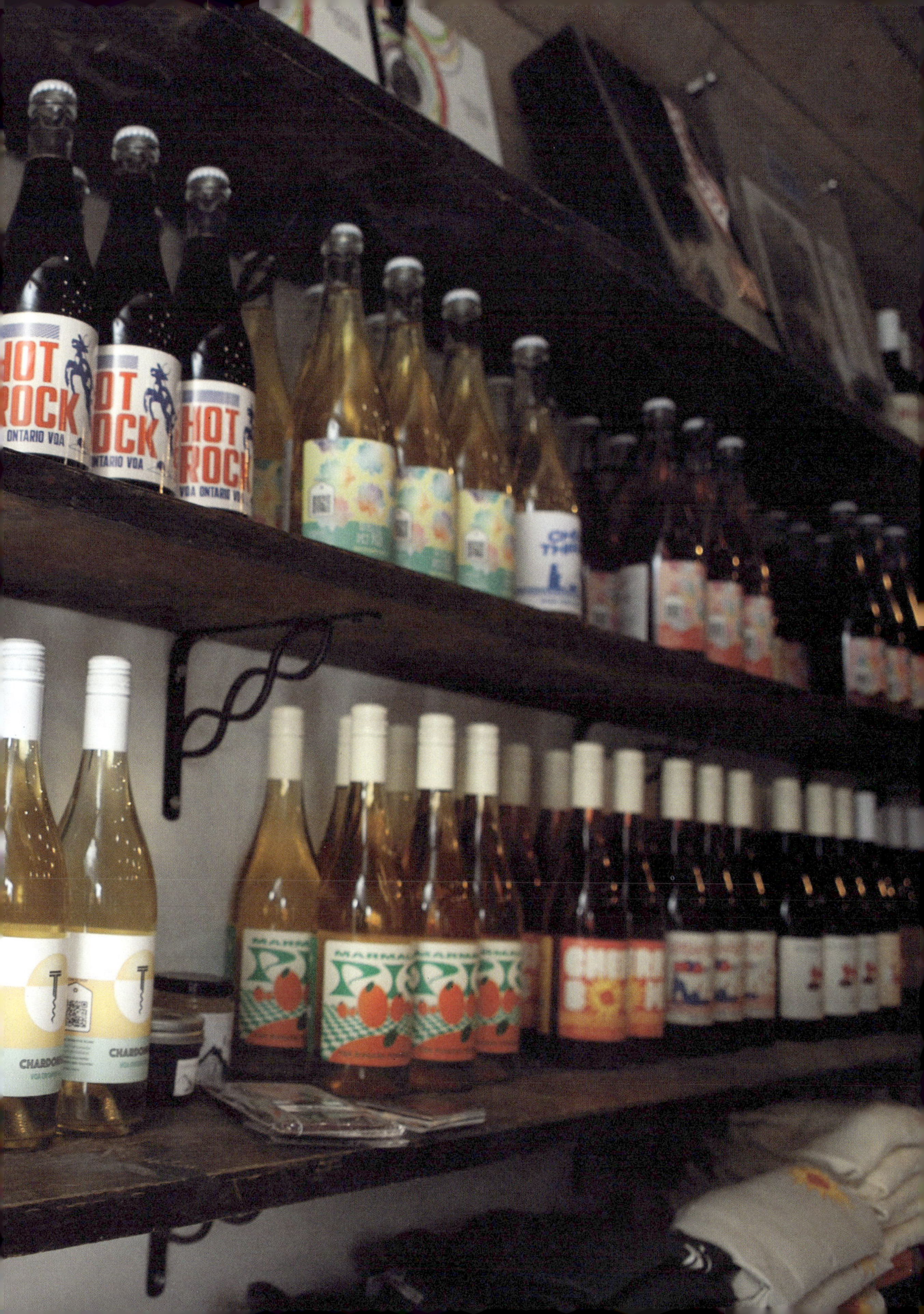
HOT ROCK
ONTARIO VQA

CHOCOLATE BARS
$4.50 EACH OR 3 FOR $12

CHOCOLATE BARS
$4.50 EACH OR 3 FOR $12

VIDAL LATE HARVES

Waupoos Estates Winery, Waupoos

Located on a stunning 100-acre waterfront property, Waupoos Estates Winery was the first winery in Prince Edward County.

AMY BALDWIN

I remember my mom and I were at the library going through all the college courses; this was before they were all online. I was 19 at the time, and wine wasn't really on my radar, but reading the course listing, I thought it sounded cool. There was science, nature, and the creative process, which I really enjoyed. So I thought, oh, what the heck? I'll give it a shot. Worst-case scenario, I'll learn about wine. And then to my surprise, I fell in love with it—the whole process of every year being about regrowth, every year being different. So I really enjoyed the process of learning. I attended Niagara College for their winery and viticulture program and their post-grad wine business management program.

This opportunity at Waupoos came up immediately post-college, which was terrifying. But I believe in taking opportunities. I did my co-op in retail, to see another side of a large business, at Reif Estate Winery in Niagara. Waupoos has had a long-standing business relationship with Reif; the founder of Waupoos, Ed Neuser, has a German background, and it was similar at Reif. They connected over that; Ed reached out initially for advice on planting in Ontario. Over the years, they continued a relationship, and that's how I ended up here. When Waupoos was in the market for a new winemaker, they reached out to Reif first. I started as head winemaker at Waupoos just after I turned 23.

It was a huge change to go from Niagara to the County. It was November and so snowy. Everything shut down at four o'clock. Where's the mall? What am I doing? It was an adjustment at first, but I've adapted really well to the lifestyle.

I met Kyle, my husband, here. Kyle's the general manager, so he looks after all the day-to-day business operations, as well as the animal side of the farm-to-table equation. He also spearheads our maple syrup production and looks after the property. Waupoos was the first in Prince Edward County to start planting a commercial vineyard. We've got history in the County; this was originally an apple orchard when it was purchased. Kyle's been here for about 30 years now, and when he started here as a teenager, one of the first things he did was help rip out all the apple trees and plant the vines. They're planted by hand. Ed would be up at the top of the hill, telling him to move something over just a little bit. It was a lot. We started planting in 1993 here, so they're pretty mature now. It's cool to see how they've grown.

We did have Pinot Noir at one time and it didn't work here. So we ripped that out, planted something else. There have been a lot of learning curves along the way, but the philosophy of keeping it an experimental vineyard, to see what's going to grow well here, has always been consistent. We have 17 different grape varieties almost equally split between white and red and vinifera and hybrid. So we've had a lot of fun playing with the varieties that do really well here. We've got some Syrah and some Cab Sauves, and then we've got Baco and De Chaunac, which are cold-hardy. Around our property, we have seven different vineyard plots, 20 acres of grapes.

My mentor is the winemaker at Reif, Rob DiDomenico; he's been there for a very long time. And the owner, Klaus Reif, too. Despite the grandeur of the winery, they were hands-on; I worked with Rob in production, and I feel really lucky that I can give him a call or send him an email when I run into issues. But it's a huge adjustment going from being part of a team, where you're someone who would receive instructions, to being the person making and delivering the instructions. It's a pretty small workforce here; our associate winemaker, Jessica McClure, has been at Waupoos for over a decade. We work together very well. Jess also wears many hats here, and aside from her many contributions to Waupoos, she has continued to build her wine knowledge; she's completed her WSET Level 3 and she's currently a WSET Diploma student.

I came from a place that does very traditional wines, and I've carried that over into my own philosophy. We have a cool climate, which means we're going to have higher acidity. I don't like to mess around too much with de-acidifying. My vision is to really showcase the styles of wine we can make in Prince Edward County.

I enjoy putting my wines in competitions; I like seeing a medal on them. It never gets old. I like knowing how my wine is perceived. In terms of years, 2019 stands out for me, because it was the first year I made four styles of wine from the same varietal in the same vintage. We made a Vidal table wine, a late harvest, a select late harvest, and ice wine. We made a progression pack of 200 millilitre bottles to show the difference in harvest time. I love educational stuff. That was also really cool because we don't always get the climate to make ice wine here. Being close to the lake has benefits and downfalls. It's so pretty, but it's tricky to have the grapes freeze on this side of the property.

I'm also the head cidermaker for Clafeld Cider and the 401 Cider Brewery. We got a pasteurizer this year, so we're dabbling in non-alcoholic apple cider. We've been pasteurizing and bagging and boxing—we have the fruit, so why not use it? It's in my personality to enjoy doing different things. I've always been good at wearing multiple hats; when it's quiet, I like to get stuff done, go out and prune, or go out and pick grapes. Sometimes it's cleaning the barn, tapping trees for syrup. We normally have about seven offshore workers who come in and help maintain the vineyards and the vines and the trees. Sometimes you just forget—I'm like, oh, I haven't pruned a vine in a while. You have to keep yourself sharp by going out and doing the work.

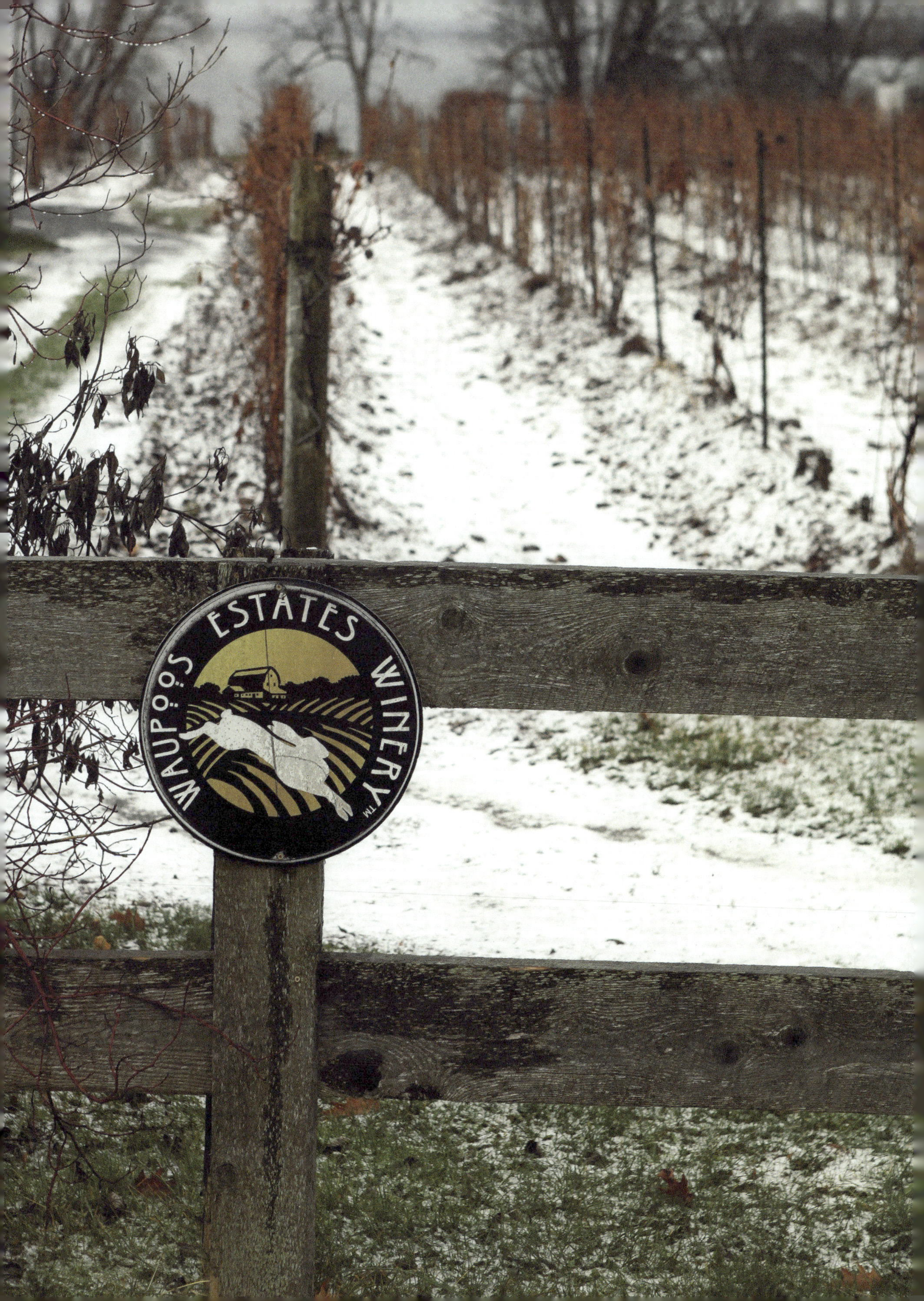
WAUPOOS ESTATES WINERY

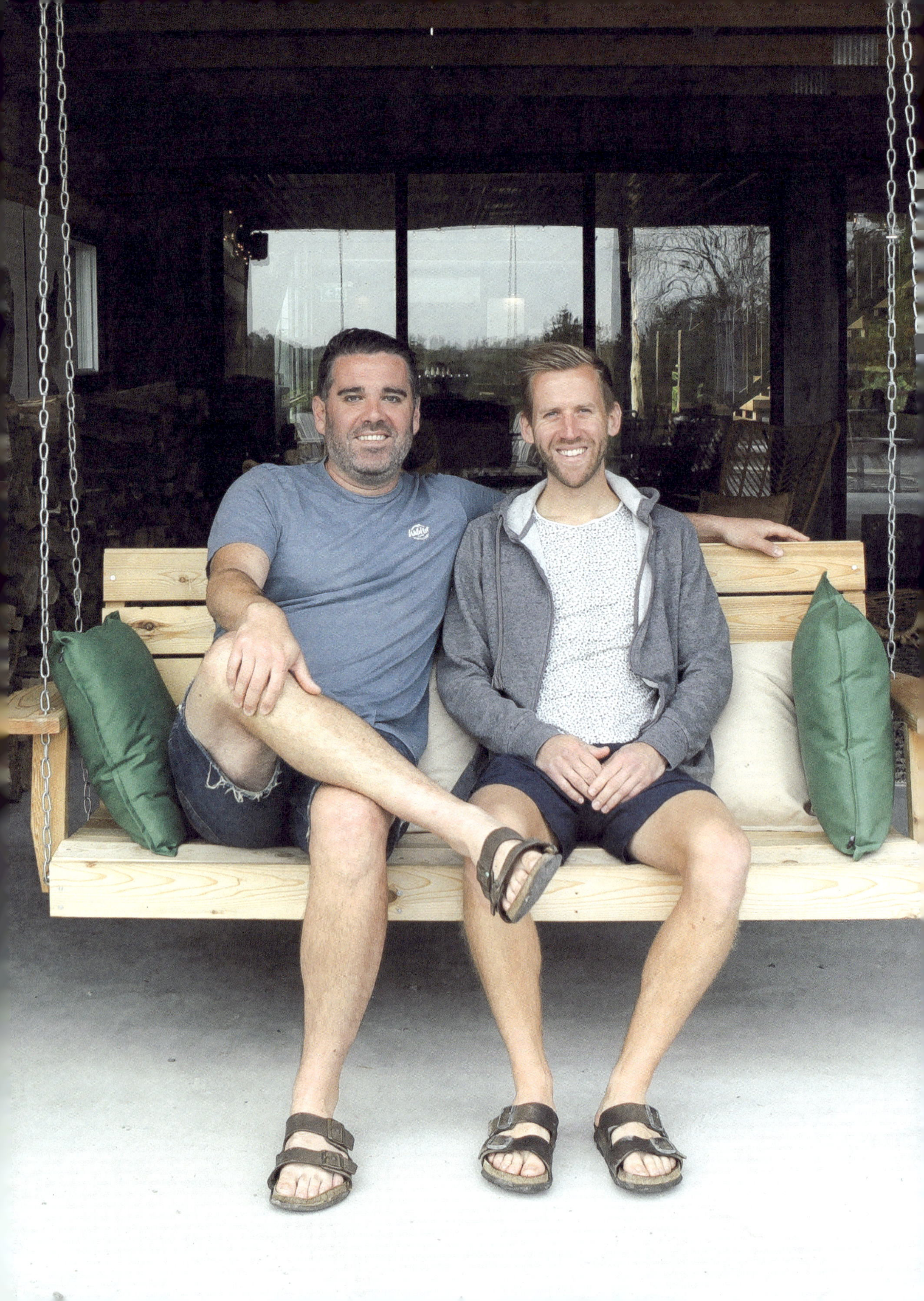

Wild Lot Farm Distillery, Demorestville

Set on 35 acres of farmland, Wild Lot is a century-old dairy barn and tractor shed turned distillery that highlights innovative spirits and crushable canned cocktails.

RYAN FOWLER, TAYLOR MCINDLESS

Ryan: We met in 2014 in Toronto, through an online dating app. We started coming to Prince Edward County fairly early in our relationship—we liked going to wineries and breweries and new restaurants. We came here at least once a year and fell in love with it. In 2018, we decided to invest in the County with the long-term plan of eventually moving here full-time and starting our own business. We bought a property just down the road from where the distillery is now. We had so many different ideas and iterations of what that business was going to be. When we were starting to fantasize about it, we knew we wanted to do something related to food and beverage—to build a brand and to be around people.

Taylor: There were many different versions of what we thought we would do. I think we started with alcoholic kombucha. Our condo at the time was filled with jars and scobies and different bad batches of juice. But we realized alcoholic kombucha is a bit too niche and we needed to think a bit broader. We thought: brewery. We love beer. And then we thought: maybe, oh, let's do a superfruit winery. I can just imagine a big cartoon grape. That never would have flown.

Ryan: In 2019, I was fired from my job. That was the moment we said, "Fuck it, let's figure this business out." Let's just start now. Life's too short and we don't want to be working in the corporate rat race any longer. So we were starting to plan and figure things out. And then fast-forward a few months to when Covid-19 hit. Taylor also lost his job. So we decamped from Toronto to our house in the County. What better moment to just dive in and start a business, right?

We decided to figure out how to be a distillery with a focus on ready-to-drink cocktails. We'd have food, and add retail and hospitality components. But after a lot of back and forth with the County and conservation authority, we determined that the zoning of our current property couldn't be changed to suit our needs. So we had to set out to find a new property to make it work. It took about a year to find the farm where our distillery is now located; we looked all over the place, like the garage in Bloomfield behind Darlings, from downtown Picton properties to farms to vacant land. We looked at old churches in Deseronto. We were all over the map.

Taylor: We both had to pick up new full-time jobs to finance the new business. I was working from home, testing recipes for HelloFresh before they went out to customers. Ryan was working for a big wine company at the time and would escape from his laptop to go for runs. His turnaround point was at the bend in the road, about five kilometres away. He would see the cows grazing in the pasture, the old barn with its tall silos, the rolling meadows, and it was so dreamy! And then one day, he raced home and barged through the front door: "It's for sale!"

Ryan: It was one of those properties that we'd fantasize about for the potential. It needed a lot of work; it was still a working farm when it came up for sale. This was ahead of the market booming and it was the dead of winter. It didn't show the best. Taylor was having a really hard time seeing the vision, so I had to put together a full-blown PowerPoint pitch deck and mood board showing what we could do to the space, how we could work the land.

Taylor: It was a massive farm with a house, a barn, a drive shed. It was overwhelming.

Ryan: So we came to view the property, and Taylor said no. I think we made three separate visits. We met with the farmers. They showed us how to work the well and the septic and all the infrastructure to make it feel less overwhelming. And finally, I don't know what clicked.

Taylor: I think you basically said, "We need to do this." We knew nothing about distilling, so when we decided that we were going to build a distillery, we reached out to Niagara College because they have a really great distilling program. We partnered with them to develop our recipes and our processes. They even helped design the space, including our floor drainage, the specs for our tanks, our water infrastructure, and all the things that take a lot of calculating and experience to figure out.

Ryan: It took a couple of years but it was a great process. We got to work with their professors and food scientists, and students had the opportunity to weigh in too. Ultimately, it was our decision on how we wanted to steer our initial product line, our flavours. But when they handed everything over to us, we recognized very early on that we knew how to start businesses and run businesses and start food programs and build and deliver customer service, but we didn't have the technical expertise to actually produce a safe product that wouldn't blind people. So we hired some help in the distillery.

We dabbled in different ideas, but we knew we wanted to be in the realm of the wild, to centre local ingredients whenever possible, and to explore wildly different flavour and ingredient combinations that haven't been seen before. We liked the visuals that the word "wild" inspires. It felt right to both of us. Because the spirit of the name Wild Lot quite literally describes the land that we were working on—it was an untamed piece of land. And we were setting out to tame that wild lot. It's also a nod to our journey, and the wild lot of the two of us diving into something we didn't know anything about and figuring it out.

Taylor: I think we got carried away with ambition. There are three buildings and 35 acres. We had 42 acres, but we severed off two lots to help fund the project, which in itself is a ton of work. We had to rezone the property. The rezoning took about 16 months, and they

wouldn't issue permits on the barn until it was done. While we waited for our rezoning and permits to be issued for the commercial buildings, we gutted the mid-1800s farmhouse on the property so we could live there. That was a nightmare!

Ryan: I think the two months leading up to opening were the epitome of stress, exhaustion, anxiety, and financial hardship. The most challenging emotions surfaced in that time. We were just going so fast, and once we declared an opening date, we had to stick to it. And it was so challenging to figure out how to set up production for the first time ever so we could have at least a couple of our own products ready for opening day.

It was pretty surreal when we made it to our grand opening. I think starting up is tough for any business owner because a lot of people have a really hard time seeing and understanding your vision. So that moment when your business finally becomes tangible, and people are actually there buying your products in your space, is beautiful. We did this. We actually pulled it off. And then the real work starts—it's a totally different kind of work once you're open. And that's what we're figuring out now.

Acknowledgements

Gratitude to: All of the contributors, who gave their time to be interviewed and generously shared their stories and workspaces and recipes. There would be no book without you. Thank you. ¶ Paul Hardy and Niall McCotter for selecting the perfect beverage pairings to complement the recipes here. ¶ Ruth Gangbar for making food-styling magic happen, and also for recipe editing. ¶ Greg Tabor for turning this into the perfect book-shaped package. ¶ Andrew Faulkner for admin support and typo-catching. ¶ Debby de Groot for getting the word out and helping to put this book into so many hands. ¶ Drew Wollenberg for constant troubleshooting of logistics and for 24 years of limitless support and love. ¶ John Nash, Cori Nash, Jean Faulkner, and Steve Leyland for invaluable contributions. ¶ David Sweet for being an early reader and all-around book champion. ¶ Andrew Scott for permission to include your epic painting (*MALAMUT*, 48" x 60", oil and varnish on canvas) on our front cover. It hangs over the Midtown bar if you want to check it out in person. ¶ Alternatives for Women for all the work you do to advocate on behalf of women and children and provide public education about domestic violence in Prince Edward County. If you, or someone you know, is experiencing abuse, contact their 24-7 crisis line: 613-476-2787.

Royalties from the sale of *County Social* will support Alternatives for Women.